BRIDGES OF TIME

SHELA PORTER

ISIS
LARGE PRINT
Oxford

First published in Great Britain 2007
by
Book Castle Publishing

Published in Large Print 2010 by ISIS Publishing Ltd.,
7 Centremead, Osney Mead, Oxford OX2 0ES
by arrangement with
Book Castle Publishing

British Library Cataloguing in Publication Data
Porter, Shela.
 Bridges of time. - - (Reminiscence)
 1. Porter, Shela.
 2. Women authors, English - - 20th century
 - - Biography.
 3. Authors, English - - 20th century - - Biography.
 4. Bedford (England) - - Biography.
 5. Large type books.
 I. Title II. Series
 823.9'14–dc22

ISBN 978–0–7531–9584–0 (hb)
ISBN 978–0–7531–9585–7 (pb)

Printed and bound in Great Britain by
T. J. International Ltd., Padstow, Cornwall

To my dear husband Bill for all his patience
and understanding.

CONTENTS

CHAPTER HEADINGS

PROLOGUE

March 2005
Mother's Day

Daffodils are blooming again in St. Mary's churchyard in Cardington. Beneath them rest Mum's ashes gently placed there just over three years ago. It is here in this quiet place that I make up my mind at last to write my own story.

A chill March wind stirs the yellow blooms and drops of rain splash on my new glasses as I think back to the bitter cold of the last day of 2001 when we said goodbye to our mum in the old church she loved so well.

"Nothing too sentimental, now, Shela."

The dear, remembered voice whispered in my head as my husband's reassuring hand covered my cold one and I waited for my brother, George, to finish his chosen passages from the Bible.

Behind me, the church was full. Around the coffin and along the path leading out to the gate were the flowers and wreaths from the large, extended family our mum left so peacefully just a week before Christmas.

I heard the quiet voice again as the vicar moved from the pulpit to stand at the head of the coffin to read the committal prayers and I realised with an equal mixture of shock and relief that he had forgotten my carefully prepared reading as part of the funeral service.

"Don't fret, Shela. Write something instead. Just get on with it."

That was always Mum's philosophy and those few words described exactly how she herself had coped with difficulties and heartaches for much of her long life.

"She would have seen the humour in that situation, Shela!" smiled George later as we all gathered in the village hall to talk about Mum and how much we were going to miss her.

So here I am, gazing at the daffodils we planted in her memory and listening again to that quiet, insistent voice telling me to "get on with it." She is with me still as I write these words just as she always was, from my earliest memories through my own tribulations and triumphs, failures and successes, and as I look back I know that she is still standing on the sidelines of the game of life, cheering me on.

PART ONE

1936–1945

CHAPTER
ONE

Early Schooldays at Goldington Road

"Shela will look through her little windows and I will look through mine."

The quiet voice of the reception class teacher came from behind the tall desk and stool where she sat high above the forty small children in her care on that warm, September morning in 1936. The pale, fair-haired child squinted up at Miss Nears and fidgeted nervously. The children laughed and pointed at her new, pink-rimmed spectacles. On her first day at school Shela was already curious about the big pile of books above her on the teacher's desk. She knew that they were full of things called letters and words that told stories, and she wanted more than anything to understand them and read those stories for herself.

Miss Nears was a comfortably round woman with short, grey hair, horn rimmed glasses and a voice that controlled and reassured at the same time. Already Shela saw that she was different from the other children, for she was the only girl in the class wearing glasses. One boy wore steel rimmed ones with heavy, bottle bottom lenses that made his eyes look enormous and she was sure that he was staring at her. She looked down at his feet and saw that he was not wearing socks and that his ankles and feet were dirty. He smelled.

"We'd better move you to the front, Shela," continued Miss Nears. "You will see the blackboard more easily from there." Then she added softly, "You move forward as well, Gerald."

Now the boy with the strange glasses was sitting next to her at the twin desk with its two inkwell holes through which she saw his dirty feet sticking out in front of them. She sat as far away from him as possible. She bit her nails again and quickly hid the spot of blood oozing from under the quick in the small square of Izal toilet paper, which served as her daily handkerchief. Gerald stared at her as she replaced it in the pocket of her navy blue school knickers and he grinned. She noticed that his front teeth were missing and the others were black around the edges.

On this first day at school she began to learn the alphabet and watched intently as Miss Nears held up cards showing the letters.

"Repeat after me, children. Daddy A, Baby A. Daddy B, Baby B. Daddy C, Baby C."

Chalk motes swirled in long shafts of sunlight as she moved to the blackboard supported on wooden pegs on the shiny easel next to the open fireplace behind her desk. For a long time the girl thought that all letters in the alphabet were daddies and babies, until she began to read and at last understood why they were different. So the first, puzzling morning passed quickly, as the small children sat at their desks on hard, wooden benches separated by narrow aisles but united by the frightening newness of this place called school.

Before playtime, Mr Setchell, the caretaker, arrived with two heavy crates of milk and everyone lined up to drink this stuff through straws poked through holes in the cardboard disk on the top of the little bottles. Shela's had a picture of a cow and as she poked out the hole she laughed when the straw went right through the hanging udders. She was not used to drinking milk except in cocoa or on porridge, which Gang-Gang made every day for breakfast. There was a thick layer of cream at the top of her bottle and she tried to avoid this as the level of milk went down as she drank. Cream made her feel sick. Gang-Gang was her grandmother Thomas who had always lived with the Winch family. Her mother told Shela that grandfather Thomas died just before her older brother John was born.

"It was either the workhouse or coming to live with us," she said one day as Gang-Gang set off to Woodward's, the Post-Office on the corner of Castle Road and Pembroke Street, to collect her weekly pension. Shela liked pension day, for Gang-Gang bought sherbet dips for all the children from Turvey's, the confectioner's further along the road. In the afternoon she walked into town to buy the week's bread flour from Mayes, the corn merchants in St. Paul's Square, for the big, family baking day on Thursday. When Shela came home from school on that day the house smelled of lovely fresh bread and scones and she had ginger parkin and drop-scones for tea. She had often heard her mother tell Gang-Gang that she should keep some of her pension money for herself, but there never seemed to be any change left out of ten shillings a week. She often wondered what a workhouse was and if other children's grandmothers had to go there if they had only ten shillings a week and couldn't live with their family.

Later, Mr Setchell came back into the schoolroom carrying a heavy, galvanised metal bucket filled with saw-dust which he shovelled on to a small pile of smelly, brown stuff on the floor beneath Gerald's side of the desk. Shela watched fearfully as he scooped it up again and then wiped the wet patch with a big, floppy mop.

"Go to the lavatory, Gerald," instructed Miss Nears quietly. "Mr Setchell will see to you there."

When the boy returned to the classroom he was crying and Shela noticed that he was wearing a different pair of faded, old short trousers and that his knees and feet had been washed.

At twelve o'clock, the journey home from Goldington Road Infants' School seemed to be much longer than the school-bound one she had taken earlier. Shela always waved goodbye to the children who lived in Laundry Square just across the road. The sun was shining and she was too warm in her winter school uniform of navy blue gym-slip, white blouse and a navy blue, maroon and yellow tie. She would have liked to walk along beneath the shady trees in Rothsay Gardens but iron railings kept out all but the key-holders who lived in that leafy square. She was thankful when at last she turned the corner into Rothsay Place past the big house with green tiles and two girls from the school turned in to Featherstone Buildings where they lived and she knew she was nearly home.

"It was good, Mum," Shela replied to her mother's anxious questions about her first morning at school, "but no-one's been given any books yet."

The little house at 14 Newnham Street smelled of washing on that Monday morning. The family tucked in to steak and kidney pudding and Mum and Gang-Gang put the last sheets through the heavy wooden rollers of the clothes mangle in the back kitchen. Then the baby cried in the big pram in the garden and Joycey, her older sister, went to her to pop the rubber dummy back into her tiny mouth. By the old, red-brick wall dividing the garden from the yard of "The Ship Inn" in St. Cuthbert's Street, a haze of purple Michaelmas daisies bloomed and in the small aviary near the bathroom window, her Dad's budgerigars and canaries sang in the autumn sunshine as Shela and Joycey left the house for afternoon school starting again at two o'clock.

On each desk now were two books and Shela opened hers in excited anticipation to find a full-page, colour picture of the fairy king and queen. She couldn't yet read their names but Miss Nears told her that they were Oberon and Titania and she remembered and savoured those strange names without realising that from her first, puzzling day at school the world of fairy, myths and spells was already working its magic on her imagination. Years later, she would still feel the excitement of that first book which she was allowed to take home for the rest of the week.

"Heads down, children. Close your books and rest."

Miss Nears' voice broke into Shela's absorbed fascination with her book. Then every child in that 1930s' classroom folded their arms on the desks and lay sleepy heads down to rest for the next twenty minutes. So the days of the autumn term passed quickly in ordered routine as they all learned to read from the blackboard and write on small slates with scratchy slate pencils. And now there was a coal fire burning in the big fireplace behind Miss Nears' desk and Mr Setchell came in every morning to bank it up with slack from the big heap near the lavatory block dividing the boys' playground from the girls' playground. Whenever she went to the lavatory, Shela looked carefully at the wall dividing the two blocks, for John, her older brother, delighted in telling her that some boys from his class had made a small hole through which they looked at the girls on the other side.

"If Miss Cutteridge finds out," warned Mum as she told Shela to take no notice of him, "she and Miss Knott will punish the lot of you!"

"Well," grinned John and his friend, Derek Pateman, who lived just over the road next to Whiffin's, the barber's shop, "'old ma cut-a-bum' and 'Miss Snot' have to catch us first!"

Shela never knew if her brother was caught, but for a long time she looked for that hole in the lavatory wall. Years later John told her that he made the story up.

One icy, winter day she found a big, blood marble near the field at the bottom of the playground and carried it around with her all day, hidden away in her knicker pocket, fearful that the boy who lost it would catch her on the way out of the school. She was in such a hurry to cross the playground that she slipped on the boys' big slide and reached home with a huge bruise on her forehead and broken glasses. But she treasured that blood marble and kept it safe for many years afterwards.

So quickly it seemed, it was nearly Christmas and Shela was to be a shepherd in the class nativity play. Mum made her costume out of an old, striped mattress cover and a checked tea-towel and she stood behind dirty Gerald, who was playing Joseph, and a girl called Pansy who was playing Mary, and her baby doll who was Jesus in the manger. Shela held a toy lamb and a long stick called a crook and, as she blinked out from behind her round spectacles at the smiling faces of the audience before her, she wondered why her stick had the same name as a character in John's Eagle comic. A baby wailed at the back of the hall and she saw Mum and Gang-Gang waving at her as little Mary settled to sleep again, wrapped in the Winch family baby shawl. Shela loved this place called school and wanted to stay in Miss Nears' class forever.

And then she was nearly six and could read the fairy stories in the big book and write words in the half-sized, pink exercise books with double spaced lines, and on Monday mornings she took in a story carefully written on Izal toilet paper for Miss Nears, who gave her a double star to stick on the big chart by the classroom door. The date was May 1937 and all the children in the Infants' School were to have a party to celebrate the Coronation of King George VI and Queen Elizabeth.

"Take a flag from the box, children," the teacher instructed the class. "Then file quietly out to your places in the hall."

Miss Nears shepherded everyone out of the classroom into the big hall filled with excited children, all waving tiny, cotton flags. Shela wondered how they knew whether they were the right way round. She had been told that this was the Union flag and she now knew that the big, red cross in the centre was for England.

"Rule Britannia, Britannia rule the waves," they sang as they all marched round the hall waving their flags. Shela looked longingly towards the three trestle tables spread out with lemonade, iced buns and bright orange jellies. She also looked at the big wall map of the world behind the assembly platform. She had been taught that all the pink bits belonged to England. There were a lot of them and she thought about all those children in all those pink countries waving their little flags just like her.

At teatime a few weeks later, a young singer crooned softly "Pennies From Heaven" from the big radiogram with a sunrise design on the front, as Dad took another Player's Navy Cut cigarette from the slim, silver cigarette case he kept in his breast pocket.

"He's married her, then."

"DUKE OF WINDSOR MARRIES WALLIS SIMPSON," Shela read slowly from the big, black headlines on the front page of the *Daily Express* and watched as Dad lit up his cigarette and Mum started to iron another striped shirt taken from the big clothes-basket on the floor behind her. She noticed that her mother's hair looked untidy and her face was pink. She also noticed that her tummy was very fat again.

"Who's Wallis Simpson?" she asked later, as Gang-Gang poured out her cocoa ready for bedtime.

"Never you mind, my girl," she replied shortly, and Shela wondered what this oddly named person had done to provoke such a sharp reply from her grandmother. She decided that Wallis was probably a witch and had cast a spell on the duke like those fairy stories in her book.

In December of that year of 1937, Shela's older brother John took her and Joycey to see "Snow-White and the Seven Dwarfs" showing at the Plaza cinema on the Embankment not far from the house in Newnham Street.

"Here you are then, John," said her mother, carefully counting out a half-crown and a sixpenny bit. "Three shillings should be enough," she added, before pulling Shela's scarf closer round her neck and tying up her woolly pixie hood even tighter against the cold outside. "You can go in the ninepennies," she continued, as she ushered all three children out of the door onto the front path.

Across the road, Shela's Godmother, Mrs Pateman or Pate-Pate as the Winch children called her, waved from her front window and John added up three times nine and told his sisters that they would have ninepence left over for ice-creams in the cinema.

"Take care of them now, John," called their mother as they turned the corner and walked past St. Cuthbert's Church where they had all been baptised in turn by the friendly vicar. Shela had been looking forward to this treat ever since she read about the big, new Disney full-length cartoon in Mum's *Film Star Annual* that Gang-Gang bought for her every August on her birthday. They were at the back of a long queue stretching right along the river as far as the Swan Hotel on the corner. It was very cold and she longed to get inside the warm cinema to see the magic on the big screen.

"Ninepenny seats full," announced a fat-bellied doorman dressed in a blue and gold uniform which was too tight for him. The daylight was fading as people turned away, and John walked to the back of the shorter, one-and-threepenny queue.

"There's enough money for Joycey and me," he stated in his big brother voice. "You go back home, Shela four-eyes. You can see it another day."

Four-eyes was his current, favourite name for her when he wanted to be bossy. Gang-Gang explained that it was because she had a squint in her left eye that her brother and his friends thought was funny. His other name for her was Dopey Daisy when she had her nose in a book.

"One-and-threepenny seats full," shouted the door-man with a huge grin on his face, and Shela wondered

14

how he could feel so cheerful when she was so disappointed and she watched, shivering in the cold wind blowing up off the river, as John moved to the back of the two-and-threepenny queue.

"Take her home, Joycey," he shouted as the queue began to file through the doors into the cinema. "There's only enough money for one to go in now."

Then he disappeared inside and Joycey put her arm round her little sister as they stood beside the dark river and watched the fat doorman close the doors against any latecomers and place a "House Full" notice at the top of the steps. The short journey home along Newnham Road led past the dark hump of Bedford Castle Mound and Shela looked up fearfully at that huge, tree-covered place where a mighty castle had, long ago, towered over the town. And she remembered that Gang-Gang once told her that sixty-four knights were hanged there, and she shivered as they began to run back towards St. Cuthbert's Church past the church hall and turned at last into Newnham Street where a pig's head leered at her from the window of Linger's the butchers. Wooding's the grocers was just closing and Miss Lane's the hairdressers was already dark and shut up for the night. Joycey opened the front gate and called to their mother through the front door letter-box and they were both crying — Shela with disappointment and Joycey with rage at the way John had behaved. They were in bed when he returned, but they heard him later crying in his little back bedroom. Her last thought before Shela turned over to sleep and cuddled up to Joycey was that she hoped his bum hurt.

Before she went to bed herself, Mum took the big, white chamber-pot round to each of the children and when it was Shela's turn she tried to tell her again what happened at the cinema.

"Never mind that now," Mum whispered, for there were three other children still asleep in that room. "Have you finished?" she continued, as Shela's bottom touched the pee already in the pot and she wiped it dry with her nightie. "Get back to sleep now, there's a good girl."

Before she slept, Shela wondered if John had peed in the pot or if he was made to go down to the cold bathroom next to the back door. She hoped he had, for she knew how cold the brick floor of the small bathroom could feel to bare feet on a winter's day. Her dreams that night were full of knights and fairy kings, and her brother was the bad baron who ended up in the dungeon of the castle. The following Saturday, John was made to hand over his weekly pocket money to his two sisters and was told that Mum would take them to see Snow White in the afternoon. Shela didn't hate him any more because she knew that he was planning to spend his money on a new aircraft kit from Golding's, the model shop in the High Street. Now he would have to wait until next week. She hoped he felt sorry. She found out just how sorry he was about a month later when he came to visit her in Victoria ward in Bedford General Hospital and waved to her through the window, because visiting children were not allowed onto the ward for fear of infection.

"You have a horrid abscess on your leg," explained Mum, as Shela clung to her hand and cried to go home with her. "Just a few days more." She tried to comfort her small daughter and then gave her a surprise present from her brother. It was the airplane kit he bought the week after the cinema trip, and he had made it up especially for her. That night, two nurses held Shela's hands and feet down as the abscess was hot poulticed, and she woke the other children on the ward as she shouted and struggled with them and the smell of antiseptic and pus from the burst abscess made her feel sick.

The next morning, she was allowed to sit at the low table in the middle of the ward and, as she ate her porridge, which was not as good as Gang-Gang's, looked around the high walls at the tiled nursery-rhyme pictures such as Jack and the Beanstalk, Little Red Riding Hood and Hansel and Gretel. Before she left hospital, just in time for Christmas, she wrote her own stories about those characters on the walls and later took them into school to show her teacher.

Christmas in the thirties meant waking early on Christmas morning to investigate the bulging stockings tied at the end of each child's bed. Always those old socks of Dad's were filled with toffees and oranges but everyone knew that downstairs were the real presents.

"Not to be opened until after breakfast," were Mum's strict instructions as the children bolted down the porridge made overnight by Gang-Gang and then waited impatiently for Dad to finish his bacon and eggs before they could escape into the front room to delve beneath the branches of the big Christmas tree for their own presents. Homemade paper chains hung wall to wall across the room, and a sprig of mistletoe perched on the ceiling light shade as everyone tore off the brightly coloured paper wrappers to see if their Christmas requests to Father Christmas had been answered. There were six other children in the family besides Shela, and each one received a "big" present and several smaller ones. The latter were usually homemade aprons or socks, gloves, scarves and woolly hats made by Mum and Gang-Gang throughout the autumn.

Shela always asked Father Christmas for books, and, each year, to her great delight, he never failed to leave her two and sometimes three. She never asked for dolls or fairy dressing-up frocks or nurses uniforms like her sisters but was content to lose herself in the magic of reading as the others played with train sets or jigsaw puzzles and skipping ropes.

When all the presents had been opened and exclaimed over and the wrappings cleared away, there was a big rush to get ready for the Christmas service at St. Cuthbert's Church just along Newnham Street near the church hall.

It was in this big, draughty place where first Joycey and then Shela joined the Brownies and both attended Sunday School and Shela collected bible texts every week to stick in her attendance book. In later years, she gave this tattered, old momento of her childhood to her own grandchildren, but sadly by then the concept of Sunday School had almost disappeared from their busy lives and she never saw it again. Shela loved to sing her favourite carols and afterwards gaze at the Christ-child surrounded by animals in the old manger beneath the altar and try to think for a short time of the real meaning of this special day.

Back at home, she knew that her mother and Gang-Gang would be busy cooking the big goose that Dad always brought home for Christmas dinner and that the house would smell of fragrant cigar smoke as he lit up the first of many Christmas cigar presents from his customers across the home counties. As the last morsels of goose and crumbs of stuffing were carefully cleared off the plates, Gang-Gang appeared in the doorway bearing aloft the Christmas pudding, doused in a spoonful of Dad's best brandy before being set alight in the kitchen with much giggling and false starts until it finally caught fire and was ready for the grand entrance. Inside the pudding the children knew they would find silver threepenny bits (this meant you would be rich), bachelor buttons (this meant you would never marry), silver lucky horseshoes (this meant you would be lucky in love), and tiny silver fairies which Shela liked best, all carefully wrapped in greaseproof paper and added to the pudding mixture that every child had stirred three times for luck around the big, yellow mixing bowl in the third week in October.

With all the wonder of Christmas Day, it seemed to Shela that the very best part was the day long presence of Dad, who on every other day was either at work travelling the roads or in his club every evening. For this one day in the year he played with his children and enjoyed the Christmas fun he had never known in his own childhood.

On the first day of the school summer holiday in 1937 the three older children were sent down to Russell Park for the afternoon with a packet of jam sandwiches and a big bottle of Tizer for their picnic tea. Joycey and Shela played on the swings for a while and then joined in with other children in a game of "sardines", which involved lots of hiding behind the thickly growing "snotty goggle" bushes whose fat, white berries made a lovely splat on the ground when they stamped on them. They were in an area of the park called the Valley, and one player had to stand on their own in the middle, waiting to be called to find the others.

Shela was the first one waiting for the call when she suddenly realised that she was not, after all, alone. A tall man with a black beard stood behind her and, as she turned to run, he grabbed her arm and forced her to stoop in front of him as he dropped his trousers round his ankles and slowly lowered himself down to her height. She stared in fascinated silence at another black beard between his legs and the long, sausage shape that slowly rose up to point at her as the man grabbed her other hand to place it firmly on the odd thing a few inches from her face.

"Why don't you stroke my little friend?" he whispered, as she smelled the sour odour coming from him. It reminded her of Susie, the family dog's smell when she needed a bath. "He'll like that," the man continued softly as he let go of her arm and put his hand quickly down inside her knickers and hurt her.

20

"Come here, Shela!"

It was John, still hiding with Joycey behind the snotty-goggle bushes, and she wrenched her hand away from the sausage and ran away from the smelly man as fast as she could. She did not understand why she felt so sore where the man touched her and she cried all the way back home.

"You should take her to the hospital, Mrs Winch," advised Pate-Pate later, after mum found a spot of blood inside Shela's white summer knickers. "She needs to see a doctor."

By tea-time she was lying on her back on a high bed on wheels, with both feet strapped into a harness high above her. A man in a white coat pushed her legs apart and began to poke painfully around inside her while a young nurse held her hands and told her that it wouldn't take long. Shela wondered fearfully what she could have done in the park that was so wrong. Was this the punishment? Was it all her fault? Why was everyone looking so serious? And why did this man have to touch her just like the other one had done that afternoon?

"No permanent damage done, mother," the doctor smiled at last, as he wrote out a prescription for zinc ointment, and Shela climbed quickly down off the bed and hastily pulled her knickers back on to hide the shame of it all.

"But the police should be informed," he continued, reaching for the big, black telephone and asking the switchboard operator to put him through to Horne Lane police station. "You must try to forget all about it," he said and smiled down at Shela and patted her on the head as she held tightly on to Mum's hand and tried to pull her towards the door. She longed to get out of that white, shiny room where strangers looked inside her small, secret places and somehow made her feel bewilderingly guilty and ashamed.

Next day, a policeman propped his bicycle outside the front gate and Pate-Pate came across the street to see if she could help while Shela was questioned about the man who had hurt her in the park. All she could remember was that odd beard and the smell. And the moving sausage. And how sore she was. Just before Christmas that year, Dad read out a small paragraph from *The Bedfordshire Times* and explained to Shela that the dirty man in the park had been caught and sent to prison. At last she could stop looking for the spots of blood, as she had done every day since it happened. But she didn't forget.

CHAPTER
TWO

Wartime Schooldays and a New Home

In May 1938 there was a new baby in the house. Her name was Beryl and she seemed to sleep all day in the big pram in the garden where Susie, the little Sealyham dog, stalked blackbirds while Mary toddled up the garden path and cried when one came too near.

"Thanks for the memory," sang Mum as she hung out another long line of nappies and Gang-Gang pounded bread dough in the kitchen. Shela had listened fearfully from under the bedclothes to her father and Gang-Gang having another row last night, and knew that her grandmother always kneaded the dough extra hard when she was cross with him.

"I think we are moving to a new house," confided Joycey during the walk to school on Monday morning. "Dad was telling Gang-Gang that this one is too small for us all now."

Shela wondered if that is what the row was about and hoped Gang-Gang could come with them when they moved, for she listened to her read at bedtime and sometimes let her sleep in her big bed in the attic bedroom. She also hoped that she wouldn't have to go to another school. She liked Goldington Road Junior School and in September she would be moving up into the big school across the playground and that smelly boy Gerald would go to the big boys' school on the other side of the lavatories.

"I'll miss Pate-Pate," she confided to her grandmother one day while licking the big, wooden mixing spoon clean. "And Mrs Stevens at the sweet shop," she added as she remembered how the kindly shopkeeper always found something good for her Saturday penny. Usually a gobstopper or a large, liquorice Catherine wheel curled around a shiny, hard, pink sweet in the centre.

"There'll be plenty of sweet shops where we're going, child," replied Gang-Gang, pulling a big tray of bread pudding from the oven in the back kitchen. Then she added with a smile, "You are always thinking about your belly, my girl!"

Shela was nearly seven years old and on her end of the bedroom windowsill was the blood marble that she'd found that day in the winter. Beside it was her tin of Ronuk furniture polish that she took to school every Friday for the desk-polishing lesson. The route to school was now much easier. The new house at 152 Castle Road, was just three doors away from the big, double-fronted shop on the corner of York Street, where Mr and Mrs Offa ran their Ladies and Gents Outfitters business. From there it was just a short walk along York Street and into the back gate of the school. Sometimes, when Shela came out of school at twelve o'clock, a rag and bone man was waiting by the kerb with his old hand-cart.

"Bring some old clothes for me when you return to school," he said to the children looking in awe at the display of cheap, celluloid windmills on sticks displayed at the back of his old cart. "Then you'll get one of these," he added. And somehow, Shela's busy mother and Gang-Gang always found enough cast-off clothes and old shoes for each of the Winch children to get a windmill. Shela placed hers carefully on the bedroom windowsill next to the blood marble and the tin of Ronuk polish. With the move to the new house came the problem of crossing the boys' playground safely, for in the winter they made long slides on the icy ground right down to the small field at the bottom of the slope and Mr Setchell grumbled and spread salt over them, but in those cold, 1930s' winters, another slide appeared as quickly as the last ones melted away.

John boasted that sometimes he and his friends sneaked out of the school back gate at playtime to buy sticky buns and doughnuts at Muncey's, the baker's shop on the corner of Denmark Street and York Street. And once, Mr Wignall, the headmaster, caught them and they all got the cane on their backsides.

"Was it worth it, John?" asked his mother as he told everyone about the caning that evening. Later he told his sisters that the doughnuts were the best and well worth the whacking. But Shela didn't believe him. Her new teacher in the big school was Miss Daughton and she liked to stand very close to her at the high desk because she smelled of talcum powder and peppermints, and she knew that inside the desk was a flat tin of boiled sweets, which would be handed out to the whole class on Friday afternoons.

"Come along, girls," Miss Daughton urged each week before sweet time. "Make your desk the shiniest in the school!" And Shela opened her old Oxo tin full of Ronuk furniture polish and rubbed happily away at her side of the desk. Her friend, Margaret Purser, who lived in George Street just down the road from the Winch family, polished away at her end and they nearly always finished their desk first. Later they sucked the boiled sweets until they crumbled up in their mouths while their teacher read "Tom and the Water Babies" aloud to the whole class just before they went home. For Shela, that was the most magical hour of the entire week. But she worried constantly about how those babies managed to breathe under water.

Several times during that quiet summer term, the classroom door opened to reveal Shela's younger sister, Joaney, dressed in an old sunhat with a soiled apron over her little cotton dress, wearing Wellington boots several sizes too big for her tiny feet. She was usually pushing an old doll's pram that had been Shela's and Joycey's before her ownership and carried a battered, old Winch teddy-bear under one arm. Each time this happened, Miss Daughton just smiled and gently told her to come in and sit next to her big sister for the rest of the afternoon. And each time, Shela was mortified that the whole class should see her little sister in that mucky state.

"She must have got out of the garden without me knowing," sighed Mum, when Shela marched Joaney firmly home again after the third episode of school visiting. "She is so anxious to start school, Shela. She won't be able to do it when she's in the infants class next term."

Years later, the two sisters laughed together many times over the younger girl's school visiting trips, escaping from the back garden and strolling so confidently down York Street pushing that battered, old pram. No-one else's little sister did it and Shela could only think that Joany was already possessed, at the tender age of four, with the free spirit which served her so well in later life.

Girls at school in 1938 were taught household tasks and polishing was one of them. Knitting and sewing were others. Shela didn't mind the knitting, but sewing was beyond her, and her efforts, especially in embroidery, always finished as a bedraggled, grubby piece of work, for she also could neither see well enough to thread the needle nor to make the neat stitches that all the other girls in her class seemed to do with ease.

"That child's inherited your weak eyes," her mother informed Gang-Gang regularly, whenever Shela complained about the sewing needles or the small print in school-books. Every year she was taken to the eye-clinic at Bedford General Hospital just over the railway bridge in Kempston Road. The dark waiting room, which served half-a-dozen clinics, always full of patients crowded onto long, shiny, wooden benches, were grouped into sections before tall, brown doors. On one door was the painted sign, "Mr Armstrong.

27

Consultant Ophthalmologist". Shela had no idea what that meant. She only knew that she would once again have to look at a bright light and smell Mr Armstrong's breath coming from the other side of it as he looked into her eyes. It always smelled of dinner.

"I'm afraid that she has in-growing eyelashes, Mrs Winch," he advised one day as Shela waited for the young nurse to put that horrible yellow eye ointment into her eyes again. "And there's not much we can do about that squint. We'll try her with a patch over the good eye. Hopefully that will strengthen the muscles in the weak one." On the way out, Shela tried to walk carefully between the benches, but everything was now very blurred and she kept tripping over outstretched feet. Later, the patch over her good eye made her feel sick and giddy and that night she dreamed of a man in a white coat coming towards her with a huge pair of tweezers ready to pull out her eyelashes. She wet the bed.

On her potty round that night, her mother found her asleep on all fours as Shela tried to avoid the wet patch in the bed, and she was still asleep as her nightie was changed and she was put back to bed in Gang-Gang's big, brass-knobbed one which always smelled of Elliman's Embrocation.

Eventually Miss Frodsham, the nice lady optician in Harpur Street, suggested that she remove the hated patch and prescribed new spectacles, and now Shela could thread those wretched needles on her own at last. On her next visit to the eye-clinic, the in-growing eyelashes had gone. Shela never told Mr Armstrong that she had pulled them out herself.

At the beginning of the autumn term a new girl appeared in the class and was seated next to Shela near the front because she also wore glasses. Soon the two quiet girls became best friends, and it was not long before Beatrice Cheeseman invited Shela to tea at her big house near Bedford Park.

"They had a big ornament with lots of candles on it — right in the middle of the table," Shela explained to Mum, "and they said a prayer in a different language before we could start eating," she continued as she thought of Beatrice's big bedroom, which she had all to herself, and her old grandmother dressed all in black and who did not speak English. Later, after the other children in the class started calling her "Beetroot and Cheese" and she cried, her mother explained to Shela that her new friend came from a Jewish family.

"We must all be very kind to her," stated her mother after she was told about the name-calling at the school. "Bad things are happening to the Jews in Germany."

Shela was not sure that she understood any of that, but she and Beatrice were best friends for the rest of the time they were at Goldington Road School together. The next year she did not come back to the school and Shela thought of her often and wondered what had happened to her. She never found out.

At Easter 1939, Dad gave each of the children a big Easter egg decorated as one of the gnomes in "Snow-White and The Seven Dwarfs", and Shela's was Doc because they both wore glasses.

"There you are, Agnes," he laughed as they all crowded round him after breakfast. "You're my Snow-White and these are our seven dwarfs!"

"What about Gang-Gang?" Shela asked as her grandmother appeared in the doorway with another plateful of eggy-bread to eat after their porridge.

"I couldn't get one for the wicked step-mother," he laughed, and even Gang-Gang smiled at this joke, but Shela saw Mum frown at him as he tucked into his breakfast.

The children didn't see much of Dad, except on Sundays, because he went off to his club every night after work. Sometimes he made everyone laugh when he came home just before bedtime and made silly jokes or dressed up in his old army uniform and marched up and down the living-room presenting arms with an old broomstick instead of a rifle. Gang-Gang always tried to usher the children up the stairs before he got home, for sometimes he wandered about the house half the night disturbing the babies and aggravating Mum or Gang-Gang. Shela loved the funny side of Dad, and it was not until she was much older that she understood what it was really all about. But to her he was just Dad.

Half way through the summer term at the school, workmen suddenly appeared in the small field at the end of the playground and began to dig long trenches with steps leading down to below ground level, and by the end of July Shela knew that they were air-raid shelters.

"What is an air-raid?" she asked Miss Daughton when the children were told to stay away from the field.

The teacher tried to explain, but Shela was only left with the very puzzling notion that somehow the air above the school could suddenly fall down and hurt the children if they were not inside the shelter. How would they know that it was about to fall, she wondered? On the third of September that year, all the family gathered around the heavy, polished radiogram in the front room to listen to a solemn voice belonging to someone called Neville Chamberlain, telling everyone that we were at war with Germany, and that night Shela's father went out to his club and came home later sillier than ever.

"It's his way of coping with things," Mum told her the next day. "He can't forget the last war."

And Shela remembered how Dad sometimes put on his old army uniform and acted the goat when he came back from his club and how he would never miss the Remembrance Day ceremony at the War Memorial on the Embankment when he wore a big, red poppy in his buttonhole. The only time she heard Dad talk about his time in the trenches in the Great War was when he came home one night earlier than usual and related how he'd met an old army pal he'd last seen in a big battle at Ypres, where the man had lost a leg. It was also the only time Shela saw tears in her Dad's eyes and she wished that he would tell her more about those days before she was born.

And now she was eight years old and the class play was to be "King John and The Abbot of Canterbury".

"I've been chosen to be the king," Shela said excitedly. "I was the first one to remember all the lines from the play! So I got the part!"

Later that day, her mother came in to the school to look at the chalk drawings of King John and all the other English kings that lined the walls of the classroom that year and promised to make her costume and any others that were needed. Shela knew that her mother was very good at sewing and that none of her girls ever wore shop-bought dresses. She watched her mother working away at her old Singer treadle sewing machine, and listened again to Gang-Gang's often told stories of how Mum had run her own dressmaking business before she married Dad and had all those babies. Shela's costume was wonderful. An old curtain was transformed into a scarlet, velvet cloak trimmed with cotton-wool ermine. Beneath it she wore a purple and green, shot-silk tunic and around her waist, a shiny brocade belt with a red and blue glass clasp. Mum and Gang-Gang sat up late into the night making her crown cut out from old shredded wheat packets painted with some of John's gold model paint and stuck all over with Rowntree's wine gums for jewels.

When the family didn't eat porridge for breakfast they always had Shredded Wheat, for Dad now worked for The Shredded Wheat Company in Welwyn Garden City and free samples were lined up all along the front hall of the new house in that autumn of 1939.

Before Christmas that year, ladies in green and red uniforms came knocking on the front door, asking Mum to take in evacuees from London. She was always upset to see those poor children standing at the front gate and knew she had to turn them away.

"I have seven of my own," she told the W.V.S. ladies as they ticked 152 off their long list of houses and moved on down the street. "Try next door," she called after them. "There's just one old lady living there and three empty bedrooms."

Shela never saw any children in the next-door garden, so the neighbour must have refused to take in any evacuees, and she thought that, although she was a very nice old lady, perhaps noisy children would be too much for her as she had none of her own.

At teatime, the family tucked in to thick slices of Gang-Gang's homemade bread spread with beef dripping from the Sunday joint and finished off with her lovely drop-scones and ginger parkin. Larry The Lamb made everyone laugh and Uncle Mac in Children's Hour told his listeners to be brave before signing off with, "Goodnight children — everywhere." By six o'clock, when Dad was home from his journeys obtaining orders for The Shredded Wheat Company around the Home Counties, the children were expected to be very quiet while he and Mum listened to the news.

"Here is the news and this is Bruce Belfrage reading it," announced the quiet voice coming from the bakelite wireless set with its sunrise motif front, newly installed in the big kitchen. And Shela tried to make sense of the reporting of "some of our aircraft are missing" and new government decisions on rationing and the evacuation of children from the big cities. On Thursday evenings, the three older children were allowed to stay up until nine o'clock to listen to ITMA and Tommy Handley, and they all became experts at repeating phrases from Arthur Askey in "Bandwagon" and in the next year of 1940 learned to sing "We Three in Happidrome", as Mr Lovejoy, Enoch and Me sang their catchy signature tune every Saturday night to cheer everyone up.

At school, Shela practised "air-raid drill" in those cold, damp air-raid shelters and now she understood about air raids and the damage they could do. But the smaller children cried all through the gasmask practice held every Thursday morning until well into the Easter term. When at last the hated exercises were over and everyone could escape back into their familiar and comforting classrooms, there were always wet patches left on those hard, wooden benches, and Shela remembered the dank smell for many years afterwards. The new baby had something called an incubator gasmask and when she was inside this contraption, Mum and Gang-Gang took it in turns to pump air in through a small tube. The first time she saw this performance Shela watched, horrified, as Beryl's little face got redder and her cries got louder until at last Mum could stand it no longer and quickly unzipped the big, black bag with a celluloid window and took her out to cuddle her.

"Better that than being gassed," commented Dad that night as he listened to Mum's account of it all. And later Gang-Gang told how he had been in gas-attacks in the trenches during The Great War and that was why he coughed a lot when he smoked his Player's cigarettes. And also why he went out every night to his club to drink with old friends from his army days.

The prospect of the baby in the incubator mask and her little brother, George, and sisters, Joan and Mary, having to wear their Mickey Mouse gas masks if there was a gas attack like those Dad endured during the Great War, gave Shela bad dreams all through that year of an expected invasion and uncertainty about the future.

During the first months of 1940, John began to recognise the sound of German airplane engines droning overhead as soon as the air-raid siren on the roof of East Hall in York Street had blasted everyone out of bed yet again. And so began a long succession of nights when all the children were bedded down on an old mattress in the meter cupboard under the stairs.

"The air-raid warden said it was the safest place in case of a direct hit," Mum explained every night as Shela settled down to sleep squashed underneath the electric meter and with Joycey's bony feet digging into her back. The family endured this cramped night-time ritual for several months and during that time an incendiary bomb hit the roof with an enormous thud just above the big, front bedroom where all the girls normally slept. Thankfully, it failed to ignite and slithered down the tiles, taking several with it on its way to unexploded ignominy beneath the laurel bush in the front garden.

"You had a lucky escape, Mrs Winch," said the warden as the bomb disposal cart arrived to lift the sandbag covering the unwelcome visitor and take them both away. "If that had gone off, you would have lost the house and probably next door as well."

In Russell Park that weekend, John discovered a long line of holes across the grass where a stick of bombs had fallen, and later that year the Town Council ordered a deep trench to be dug across the football pitch to prevent any enemy aircraft landing on that small strip of green.

"Aircraft landing?" laughed John as he and his friends searched for any stray bomb tail fins. "Nowhere near long enough for that!"

And Shela believed him, for he was now well versed in most things aeronautical and had steadily covered his bedroom walls with large posters detailing the intricate workings and recognition silhouettes of Supermarine Spitfires, Bristol Blenheims and Hawker Hurricane fighter bombers and other, strange-sounding German names of Messerschmitts, Heinkels and Dornier bombers, the engines of which made a deep, growling noise when the plane was directly overhead. On most of the nights when the air-raid sirens sounded, John insisted on staying out in the garden as he tried to count the number of enemy planes high above. His plane-spotting song was always,

"Whistle while you work,
Mussolini is a twerp,
Hitler's barmy, so's his army,
Whistle while you work."

And if he thought Mum couldn't hear him, he sometimes shocked the old lady neighbour on one side and made Mrs North on the other side laugh, as he sang a rude song to the tune of Colonel Bogey, one of Dad's old marching songs.

"Hitler, has only got one ball
And Goering has two, but very small.
Himmler is very sim'lar,
But poor old Goebells has no balls at all."

Already, although Shela did not realise it at the time, her older brother, then only thirteen years old, and an enthusiastic member of the Junior Air Cadets, was laying the foundations of a life-time interest in flying and a subsequent career as an airline pilot, which would eventually take him out of sleepy little Bedford and all around the world.

By the end of that year Doctor Chillingworth advised Mum that Shela was anaemic and prescribed Parrish's Food, spooned out from a big, brown bottle. She hated it, for it made her tongue and teeth black every day and tasted like sucking old pennies. Later, all the children were dosed up with cod liver oil and malt after breakfast every day, so that all the meals for the rest of it tasted of fish.

"It will do you good," declared Gang-Gang as Shela tried to swallow a full dessertspoonful of that awful, brown stuff and John twisted his head away and always seemed to get it dribbled down his school shirt.

"We're Going To Hang Out The Washing On The Siegfried Line," sang Mum every Monday morning while she and Gang-Gang emptied the old, brick-built copper in the corner of the scullery, and all three clothes lines in the garden would be full before the children came home for dinner at twelve o'clock. The newest baby, Beryl, was almost two in that spring of 1940 and, although the old brass-railed fireguard in front of the Ideal Boiler in the big kitchen always seemed to be draped with airing nappies, Shela noticed that Mum's tummy was not getting fat again as it had seemed to do for every year that she could remember. And Joycey informed her younger sister, with a knowing smile that she did not understand, that she'd overheard Dad telling Gang-Gang that he'd shot the stork. As, at that time, Shela firmly believed that babies came out of ladies' belly buttons, she wondered what on earth storks had to do with it.

Early in that summer term, when Shela was in Miss Hatfield's class and getting good marks for writing and reading, the four eldest Winch children began to make mysterious visits to the big hall in The Bedford Girls' Modern School across the river in Cardington Road. On the first journey to the school, John, as usual, decided to show off to his three younger sisters by demonstrating an emergency stop on his new bicycle right on the edge of the river near the Suspension Bridge. There was a loud yell and a big splash as his brakes failed, and the big brother demonstration came to a watery end as he went over the edge into the river, his bicycle sank to the bottom and all his school books floated away to end up at the Newnham Baths filter log a half-mile downstream.

"You little faggot!" exclaimed Gang-Gang later in her strong, Liverpudlian accent, as John stood dripping on the scullery floor, "and they are your only good pair of school trousers!"

Somehow Mum had managed to haul John out of the river and Sid, the park keeper, helped retrieve the sunken bicycle. The books were beyond saving, and later that day Shela's show-off brother had a lot of explaining to do when he presented himself at The Bedford Boys Modern School in his scout uniform minus his textbooks and homework.

"You must all have inoculations this year," Mum tried to explain one day after the third visit to the medical centre set up in the school. But each time, Shela's arm became red and swollen and the pain kept her awake at night. On one of these sleepless nights she crept downstairs to hear Mum crying quietly in the big kitchen while Gang-Gang tried to comfort her.

"It's for the best, Agnes," said Gang-Gang. And there was silence for a few minutes as Shela stood shivering on the bottom step of the stairs, trying desperately to understand what her mother could be so upset about. At teatime the next day, Shela watched Gang-Gang sprinkling brown sugar on the big slab of bread pudding she'd baked that morning from left over stale bread. And Mum told the children the reason for those puzzling visits.

"A man from the Town Hall came to see me a few weeks ago," she said softly as she held a crusty, homemade loaf against her chest and began to cut a slice across it with the bone-handled bread knife that had been used ever since Shela could remember.

"They think the Germans will invade this year and they want to get as many children as possible out of the country before that happens," she added. Shela watched the knife cutting towards her mother's apron and hoped it would not slip and cut her finger. The Winch children sat and listened in total silence as it was explained to them that they were to leave in a month's time and that was why they had to be immunised against all kinds of diseases before the New Zealand government would allow them in to their country.

"I'm not going," stated John firmly, though his mother tried to reassure them that they could all come back again when the war was over.

"But I'm going into the Royal Air Force when I'm sixteen," John persisted as little Joaney began to cry, and this started the younger children crying and Joycey and Shela did their best to comfort them. "And when I'm eighteen," he continued, "I'll be in pilot training and flying a Spitfire against the Jerries. And I can't do that in New Zealand!"

A few weeks later, after a Red Cross ship carrying British evacuee children had been sunk by German U-boats in the Atlantic, the government cancelled all further arrangements for future overseas evacuations. And Shela took back to the library all those books about New Zealand, because now she knew she would never find out what it was really like in that country on the other side of the world.

"I'm glad we're not going after all, Gang-Gang," she told her one morning, as her grandmother pounded the bread dough and allowed her to scrape the mixing bowl clean after a big, baking session. "They probably don't have ginger parkin over there."

All through those long weeks of the preparations to leave, Shela had become more and more apprehensive about leaving her family and Gang-Gang behind. When the mass evacuation was cancelled, she sat all evening on her grandmother's lap in the kitchen, covered herself with her soft, crocheted shawl and played with her thin wedding ring while the old lady told her about her own hard childhood in Liverpool and how she'd left home at thirteen to go into service in London.

"And they were good people, Shela," she said softly as the girl questioned her about those long ago days. "They let me borrow any book I liked from their big library. Your mother thinks that you take after me. She's probably right, too. Now it's off to bed with you. Your father will be in soon."

All through the early summer of 1940, the children kept quiet as radio bulletins told of the evacuations from Dunkirk and Shela looked fearfully at harrowing pictures in Dad's *Daily Express* showing boats crowded with exhausted soldiers being taken off the beaches just across the English Channel.

Later in that summer, John followed closely any items in the papers about the Battle of Britain. Just a week after Shela's ninth birthday, the skies above Kent became the new battleground, as young R.A.F. pilots fought the Luftwaffe to retain British air supremacy.

Soon, John's bedroom walls were covered with newspaper cuttings showing the skies above London and the south east, criss-crossed with vapour trails, and then disturbing pictures of the damage caused by the Blitz on London.

Shela was still in Miss Hatfield's class and nine years old, when she first came to the notice of Miss Slater, or Fanny Slater as she was popularly known, the fearsome headmistress of Goldington Road Junior Girls School.

"Anyone who is late three times in one week will be punished accordingly," she stated every Friday morning at assembly. "You all know the rules and must obey them," she continued, before conducting the hymn about forgiveness and love from the platform.

Shela watched, apprehensively, as the headmistress's raised hand waved before her and noticed how the chiffon handkerchief tucked into her watchstrap floated delicately backwards and forwards through the air in time with the music. Her stomach was churning and her mouth suddenly very dry as she realised that she had been late three times that week. And she was in no doubt as to what "accordingly" really meant.

"Which is your writing hand, Shela Winch?"

Shela indicated the right one.

"Raise the other one, then," the head snapped. "And stop snivelling, that girl at the back!"

Shela raised her left hand and shut her eyes tight as the thin cane came down on it with one swift stroke. At first she felt no pain, only a spreading numbness, as she held her hand tight against her chest and crept tearfully out of the head's dark, little office. Shame followed her back into the classroom and forty pairs of eyes watched it. Her teacher told her to hold her throbbing hand under the cold-water tap and Shela began to develop an intense dislike of a headmistress who ruled by fear and intimidation. Only when she learned of Miss Slater's death, many years later, did she at last begin to let go of the frightening memory of a short woman with piercing, brown eyes behind a pince-nez perched on an over-powdered, beaky nose. That well-corseted figure, invariably dressed in a lime-green costume and with swollen feet squeezed into high-heeled shoes, which clicked importantly as she walked around her little kingdom, haunted Shela for most of her childhood years. Today, she still recalls the woman's overpowering scent, which preceded her wherever she went and no doubt used to imprint her frightening personality on all the young children in her charge.

Later, that day of the cane, as Mum bathed her swollen hand with witch-hazel and she wet the bed again, Shela came to realise that the only way to survive in the puzzling world outside home was to keep quiet and stay in the background as much as possible. She also learned in those early school years how to protect herself against the Fanny Slaters of this world.

Try to be invisible.

The little windmill and the blood marble were still in place on her bedroom windowsill when the news of the battle of Pearl Harbour and America's dramatic entry into the war was the prime item on Pathe Pictorial News films at the Granada cinema in December. Shela had already left Goldington Road School to take up the scholarship she had won to Bedford Girls' Modern School with a new set of rules to be learned. The only comment made by Miss Webb, the scholarship class teacher, on her achievement, was that she should have won a place at the more prestigious Bedford Girls' High School and that she was Winch by name but not by nature.

Shela did not understand what she meant at the time but afterwards realised that she was probably right on both counts. Much later, she realised what an excellent teacher she was and thought fondly of Miss Webb's pink face and sharp tongue as she kept forty girls in order and opened their young minds to Dickens, Kipling and Wordsworth while she coached them across the bright threshold to a first-class education at one of the big Harpur Trust schools in the town.

In the spring of 1942, as more war news was reported from the Pacific, where the Americans were fighting the Battle of Midway, Shela's father rejoined the army after he was made redundant from his job as a commercial traveller at The Shredded Wheat Company in Welwyn Garden City.

"Your knowledge of French and German will be very useful," stated his C.O. when he joined the Intelligence Corps unit at a secret location in Yorkshire and on his infrequent leaves he would try to converse with his three eldest children to test out their newly-learned school French. Sometimes, after evenings at his club and to Shela's huge delight, her father sang old Mistinguette and Maurice Chevalier songs popular during the Great War and she caught a tantalizing glimpse of the man he must have been in his youth. When she asked him how he learned such good French, he tapped the side of his nose and grinned.

"Well," he replied slowly, "you'd better ask your mother that one, She-She."

"I think he had a French girlfriend in Paris after the war," Mum confided to her curious daughter one day after her father had been home on leave. Then she added hastily, "Of course that was before he came home and met me, you understand."

And now Shela understood her Dad's teasing over the years about someone called Martine and she remembered stories about his position as Passport Officer in the British Embassy in Paris. As she grew older, she learned more about this worldly man who now existed with a damaged lung and who for years, in nightly visits to his club, had tried to blot out terrible memories of the trench warfare. And here he was, back in the army again, and she hoped there would be no gas attacks this time and that her Dad would get safely back to his family when it was all over.

CHAPTER
THREE

Scholarship Girl

By the summer of 1942 it was three years since the family had been on holiday to their bungalow at Hemsby on the Norfolk coast. Every August, ever since Shela could remember, they had all packed into her Dad's big Ford car with their luggage jammed into the boot, with Gang-Gang holding the baby on her knee, and gone off on the long journey along Goldington Road, through Newmarket and down to the quiet little seaside town.

"You'd never get on to the beach, these days, Aggie," observed Dad one Sunday morning when he was on a rare weekend leave looking through the snapshots of the last holiday taken in 1939. "It's all ringed with barbed wire now and probably mined as well. Anyway," he sighed, putting the snapshots carefully away, "we can't afford it on my army pay." And John looked up from his book on "Airplane Modelling" and asked anxiously if the Germans were going to invade after all. And Shela remembered the wide, sandy beach with its mysterious dark, rock pools and the smelly, ancient Elsan toilet in a shed behind the bungalow and the long, sunny days when all she had to worry about was not getting too sunburned and what Gang-Gang was cooking for supper.

The family never went back to Hemsby and, when she visited it many years later, it had changed so much that Shela wished she'd not been so keen to see the summer place of her childhood and left the memory of those far-off happy days beside the sea forever intact. But if the family couldn't get to Hemsby during that hot summer, they could still go swimming at a place much nearer home.

"Here you are then," said Mum cheerfully as she handed each of the older children their individual season ticket for Newnham Swimming Baths at the corner of Newnham Avenue and The Embankment. "Take care of them because they cost fifteen shillings for a family ticket and I can't afford to pay that again this year."

The swimming baths was really just a part of the river Great Ouse as it flowed out of Bedford and on towards Willington and Great Barford. At the top of the waterfall, which took the murky, green water into the big, round pool, a chain-secured, surface filter log was in place, but this did not stop all kinds of rubbish turning up in front of your nose as you practised swimming in the shallow end or jumped clumsily off the lowest diving board into the deep end. Shela loved going "down the baths" in the hot summers of the early forties, but what she didn't enjoy were the changing facilities which were nothing more than canvas sheets slung at right-angles from the boundary walls, with girls on one side and the boys opposite.

There they stood, her two sisters and herself, shivering, on old, wooden duck-boards in those draughty places, and Shela was always worried that the slightest breeze would blow open the canvas sheets to reveal her to the world in a humiliating state of half-dress or, even worse, completely naked once she had stripped off the soggy, woollen bathing costume handed down to her from her big sister. It had, she recalled with a smile many years later, a permanent hole worn in the rear caused by repeated slides down the dirty, old, brick waterfall, and eventually she developed another abscess on her bottom and that, for her, was the end of that season's fun at the swimming baths.

She didn't find out until the end of the summer, that the proper changing rooms had been commandeered by the government to serve as an emergency mortuary, should the existing one at Bedford General hospital not be sufficient to deal with fatal casualties from possible air-raids. She steered well clear of those grey, concrete buildings from then on and, even when people were allowed to use them again after the war was over, still shivered every time she handed in her heavy, metal clothes basket and received a green, rubber, identity wristband in return. She wondered if the expected dead bodies would have been identified in the same way and if these same wristbands would have been attached to one of their cold, dead arms as they lay stretched out in the changing rooms. But, apart from morbid thoughts of dead bodies and what might have been, those were happy days and even the absence of ice-cream or sweets from the little kiosk by the back wall of the baths could not dim the enjoyment of thin, ice-cream wafer-biscuit jam sandwiches sold at a penny each to hungry children in those days of shortages of everything.

There were now evacuees in Shela's home. Not just children but two families. The big, front bedroom was home to a couple from Southend-on-Sea and their two small children, while the tiny back bedroom was taken by a soldier's wife who had the same shape tummy that Mum had showed before Beryl arrived.

"It's just for a few weeks," Mrs Saunders explained cheerfully as she hauled a big suitcase up the stairs and along the passage to her room. But the few weeks turned into months and suddenly there was another baby crying in the night and never enough room on the three clothes-lines in the back garden, so that Mum had to ask Mrs North, next door, if she could use some of hers. When the tummy shape appeared again the next year and the lodger's husband was still serving overseas in North Africa, it was tactfully suggested that she try to find better accommodation and Gang-Gang complained regularly that three families did not fit into one small kitchen.

"I'll just have to do the baking at night," she grumbled, and often Shela heard her creep quietly out of the little, downstairs bedroom she now shared with two of the girls, to pick up the big, white bread bin where the dough had been proving by the kitchen fire, and soon there came the familiar thumps from the back kitchen where Gang-Gang was kneading the dough and she knew there would be fresh bread for breakfast the next day.

"I heard Gang-Gang crying in her sleep last night, Mum," Shela whispered one morning soon after the new upstairs baby arrived, and when she arrived home from school one day a week later, the back bedroom lady had gone and Gang-Gang was able to return to her precious brass-knobbed bed and put all her photographs and ornaments back in her old room again.

"She went back to London," Mum explained, and Shela wondered if she had found a nice room there, for she liked playing with her baby and liked even more the barley-sugar sticks she sometimes gave her after helping her with her shopping.

Joycey thought that she had found her own solution to the shortage of chocolate when she secretly shared with her sister a small bar of chocolate Ex-Lax bought from Mr Jones, the chemist in Castle Road. The next day both girls suffered the consequences as the laxative did its work.

"Don't tell Mum," she ordered every time one or the other of them made a hasty visit to the outside lavatory. And it wasn't until the chemist himself enquired about the frequent purchase of laxatives and hoped that all was now well with her children that Mum found out and both girls were both punished for being so stupid. Afterwards, Shela thought she had been punished enough by all those visits to the lavatory and the belly-aches that syrup-of-figs made even worse until Mum found out the real reason for them.

On one weekend leave that summer of 1942, Dad brought home two army blankets and new records of the "Forces Sweetheart" singing the latest hit songs of the year. Mum sang along with Vera Lynn as the tunes of "The White Cliffs of Dover" and "Bless 'em All" came faintly up to Shela's bedroom from the big radiogram in the front room. It was well past midnight but she was determined to finish her library book that she read by the dim light of an owl night-light hidden beneath the bedclothes. When the owl-light battery ran out, it was not replaced, and Mum made the excuse that the shops had sold out. Although Shela knew that her mother worried about her reading by such a poor light with her weak eyes, she missed those late-night reads almost as much as she missed her father when he went away into the army. This second daughter, who always had her nose in a book, got through at least four of them every week, and it became an escape from the noisy family life going on constantly all around her.

On Saturday mornings in the Winch household, you could choose to do one of three things. You could take the baby down to Russell Park accompanied by Pauline Luff from York Street, who was a regular baby-walker. Or you could go to the Saturday morning matinee at the Granada cinema in St. Peter's Street or the Empire cinema in Midland Road. The third option was a visit to the Bedford Public Library. For the bookworm in the family, Saturday mornings meant time spent in the children's department of the library looking for the latest Arthur Ransome, Enid Blyton or Mazo de la Roche books. The happiest hours of her childhood were those "helping" the Children's Librarian in that elegant old building at the top of wide steps opposite the Bedford Boys Modern School in Harpur Street, where John had been a pupil for nearly five years.

Another Saturday morning stop for her was the bookshop near Timaeus' shop on the High Street where, before the war, her father bought ordnance survey maps. It was in F. R. Hockliffe's that she browsed among the second-hand books piled onto wooden stalls on the pavement outside the shop, and, if it was raining, climbed up the rickety stairs at the back of the shop to the used book department smelling of damp and old paper, looking for cheap paperbacks of her favourite children's authors. If Shela had enough pocket money left over, she bought an iced bun at Joe Lyons on the corner of Silver Street on her way back to the library to help the Children's Librarian.

The summer of that year passed quickly for Shela and, one memorable morning in early September 1942, she cycled off to her new school with Mabel, the girl next door who was in the second year at Bedford Girls Modern School.

"She will keep an eye on her, Mrs Winch," assured Mrs North, Mabel's mum, as the two girls set off on their journey along York Street and across Russell Park past "Tizzyboms" café at the corner of the park and Bushmead Avenue. It was hard work dragging their bikes up the steep steps of the Suspension Bridge and bumping them down the other side. But the ride over the green Engineers Bridge crossing the old river presented no problems, before they pedalled their way quickly along the narrow path to the back gate of the school.

Mabel's bicycle was very modern compared to the younger girl's. For Shela was riding the old Winch family child's bike, first used by John when he was six years old and they were still living in Newnham Street. It was also a very bright blue and Shela was wearing a coat made by Mum from a beige army blanket. So the rest of the school must have seen her coming, with her new school bag, shaped like a music case, and made of a pale, pink pigskin with side pieces that refused to stay taut and flapped around her legs as she walked along the terrifyingly long corridor to her new classroom where the teacher awaited the new intake of Class 3 Lower A1.

"Please stand up, Shela Winch."

Miss Gratton, the class teacher, who was also to teach the new intake phonetic French before they could tackle the intricacies of French verbs and all the imponderables of the tenses and genders of that language, looked searchingly at her over her spectacles as Shela rose to her feet wearing the wrong school uniform.

"Take this note home to your mother, Shela. It is important that your school uniform is correct. We must uphold the honour of the school."

Shela sank, red-faced, back into her seat beside another girl who grinned as she passed a sherbet satin sweet to her under the desk and later, at break-time, told her that she was wearing her older sister's cut down gym slip because Braggins, OVR BOYS and OVR

GIRLS, the big school outfitters in Silver Street had run out of the proper uniforms for the new school.

"Well, and what am I supposed to do about it?" exclaimed Mum at teatime after she had read the note from Miss Gratton. "That's a perfectly good gym-slip and the last one they had in stock at Braggins!"

Shela looked miserably at the square-necked, velvet trimmed gym-slip she had been creeping round in all day at school, trying to be as invisible as possible, and told Mum that it was a Bedford Girls High School uniform and she must wear the correct one by the next day.

"What nonsense!" said Gang-Gang sharply as Shela cried at the memory of the humiliation of the morning and Susie, the little Sealyham dog, licked her hand in sympathy.

As she lay in bed that night, Shela remembered Gang-Gang's tales of Mum running her own dressmaking business before she started her family, and listened to the old Singer sewing machine treadling away in the front room. When at last she turned over to sleep, she knew that she would go to school the next day dressed like everyone else, with the exception of the beige, army blanket coat and the awful, pink pigskin schoolbag!

"They are dreadful snobs at that school, Mrs Winch. But they offer an excellent education."

Mrs West, the grocer's wife, stood behind the counter of H.T. West, Groceries and Provisions in Castle Road, where the family was registered for grocery rations, and smiled sympathetically as she cut out the coupons from the two beige and seven blue ration books and then helped Mum load up the big pram with the week's rations.

"How on earth do they expect parents to dress their children in the correct uniform when clothes are rationed and there are queues for everything?" Mum asked in exasperation.

"Well," replied Mrs West sympathetically, "if my Nancy had been a year or two younger when she started at that school, I'd have been faced with the same problem. As it is," the kindly woman continued as she counted out Mum's change, "I think I have some of my girl's outgrown school things that would just fit your daughter."

Then, calling to her husband, Harry, enjoying his morning cup of tea in the back room of the little shop, she bustled away and returned a few minutes later with a big bundle of school clothes, which lasted Shela for the rest of her time at the big school across the river. In later years, Shela remembered with distaste those ugly school gym-slips with elasticated waists and the pale blue P.E. dresses and matching knickers and the darker blue hockey stockings held up around her podgy thighs with elastic garters. But she also remembered kindly Mrs West for helping to make her invisible in the place where the honour of the school must be upheld at all cost. The beige army blanket coat was reserved for weekends only when, one cold Saturday morning, the games mistress refused to take its wearer to an away hockey match, leaving her standing in tears outside the school gates as her sub grinned at her from the back of the coach bearing the team to the rival school. To Shela, who loved hockey and always worked really hard to retain her position in the under twelve hockey team, it was the ultimate betrayal and afterwards she lost interest in the sport and resorted to her beloved books again for comfort.

On Monday morning she hung her brother's outgrown and altered navy-blue school mac on her peg in the cloakroom known as The Tunnel and she thought how clever her mother was to have changed the buttons and button-holes to opposite sides of it to make it into a girl's garment. One suitable for any future school event and the strict demands of a Harpur Trust School originally endowed by Sir William and Dame Alice Harpur to provide a good education for all Bedford children, fee-paying or scholarship, no matter what their background or circumstances might be.

She remembered with deep affection the school headmistress, Miss Tonkin, who went calmly about her business in that big school making sure her girls learned something about the Holy Bible and the life of Jesus by teaching them Religious Education with a quiet authority born of a kind but firm disposition and a willingness to listen to every youngster in her charge. It was Miss Tonkin who stood before the whole school one foggy November morning to warn the girls against using the riverside path while the Canadian army unit was based there under canvas. They must, she insisted, go the long way round by the town bridge on their way to school.

56

"Do you think she saw him?" Shela asked her friend on the way home that afternoon.

"Of course not, silly!" Mabel replied. "She comes to school in a car, so how could she? And anyway, I expect she would have fainted on the spot if she'd seen what we saw."

What Mabel and Shela saw on that dark morning near the Suspension Bridge was a young Canadian soldier looming at them out of the fog to open his greatcoat and reveal all of his naked body to every schoolgirl taking the short cut to school. Half-buried memories of the dirty man in the park returned to haunt Shela for the rest of that day, and that night she had a bad nightmare about black beards and army greatcoats and awoke the next morning with a sour-dog smell in her nostrils. Shela never knew whether Mabel reported the incident to her teacher but, many years later, reasoned that there must have been many other reports of it made on that distant day in 1942, when units of troops from various commonwealth countries were gathered in the town to practise crossing the river on pontoon and Bailey bridges.

Later that year, Miss Tonkin discovered Shela sitting disconsolately in the cloakroom one day after she became lost yet again in the bewilderingly big school and who held her hand in her long, cool one to lead her back to the right classroom.

"Ask your teacher to help you make a chart of your lessons and where you should be for each one, Shela," she said quietly as she left her at the classroom door. "Then you won't get lost again."

Miss Window, an elderly history teacher, inevitably nicknamed Mlle. Fenetre by all the girls, smiled vaguely at Shela over the top of her half-moon spectacles as she sat down thankfully at her desk, and someone laughed as she made her excuses for being late for the lesson. Shela liked this teacher who was the butt of many jokes, mainly because of the way she was always dressed in a long, grey coat and a dark red, wide-brimmed hat that she wore in school whatever the weather. Much later, Shela learned, with some compassion, that this clever, but somewhat unworldly woman, had been called back from retirement by the shortage of wartime teachers and obviously found it difficult to maintain discipline over the overlarge classes of the nineteen-forties. Shela always enjoyed her lessons and it was Mlle. Fenetre who first awakened her interest in things of the past and subsequently inspired her long ago pupil to research and write articles and stories about local historical events and how they have helped to shape lives today.

It was her English teacher at this good school who carefully and patiently taught her how to use the English language, in all its diversities and sometimes eccentricities, to achieve a decent piece of writing, and she remembered Mrs Long with deep appreciation and a well-deserved respect.

Shela eventually made the lesson chart and it helped. But by the end of that term she was taken under the wing of a tall, self-confident girl named Pat Simpson who had been with her in the scholarship class in junior school. And life became easier as she joined her little group and she was protected from big, pushy girls and the few toffee-nosed ones who, together with one or two teachers, considered scholarship children to be beneath them. At Christmas that year, the hated, pink pigskin bag disappeared, to be replaced by a leather, school satchel bought second-hand from the newly opened W.V.S. depot in Bromham Road, where Mum and Joycey often went to exchange children's clothes and to buy much needed school shoes for the large family with never enough clothing coupons to go round.

"Mrs West passed on these for you, Shela," smiled Mum one day as she parked the big grey pram in the hallway and handed her daughter a pair of black, canvas hockey boots, one size too big, but that didn't matter, and best of all a triple-sprung hockey stick. "Her Nancy's left school and gone on to college, so she won't need them again."

Now Shela looked just like everyone else at Bedford Girls' Modern School while she made new friends and coped happily with her lessons and looked forward every day to eating halfpenny, sticky buns in The Tunnel at break time and even to eating watery stew and tapioca pudding for school dinners.

"Your father is coming home next week," announced Mum one summer's day in 1943. "And this time it's for good!"

Dad was invalided out of the army after a long spell in Sierra Leone had left him with recurring bouts of malaria and black water fever, and Shela hardly recognised the thin, gaunt face of the man who stood in the hallway to kiss Mum as if he would never let her go and all his children crowded round to give him a big hug after so long away from them.

"You must all be very quiet," explained Gang-Gang that night after Dad had gone early to bed and while everyone drank their cocoa in the big kitchen. "He has been very ill and needs plenty of rest. Just you remember that."

It was to be many months before Dad returned to anything like the cheerful man he had been before the war and many more before he managed to obtain work to help support his family, now relying solely on a pitifully small army pension and Mum's hard earned income from dressmaking alterations which kept her up far into the night to finish a garment for the next day.

"Take this round to Mrs Curtis," she instructed Shela, one day in 1944 when Dad had been off sick again from his job at the American Red Cross G.I. Club dormitories in Ashburnham Road. "And make sure you give her the bill and wait for the money. I'm relying on that," she added as Shela took the neatly wrapped parcel and began the short journey past Miss Linford's grocery shop on the corner and down Denmark Street to Rosamund Road and finally into George Street, where Mum's customer lived in one of the big houses near Goldington Road.

Mrs Curtis was a regular customer of Mum's and always had the correct amount of money ready when one of the Winch children delivered her newly made up or altered garment for their hard-working mother. Sometimes she gave them sixpence to spend on their sweet ration at Lawrence's confectioners shop just across the road from the house. So Shela never minded delivering her parcel. A lot of the sewing work in those hard days came from Mrs Baylis who, together with her husband, had recently taken over Offa's, Ladies and Gent's outfitters, just a few doors along from the house in Castle Road.

"It is so convenient having a dressmaker near the shop, Agnes," she confided as she regularly passed over her customers' alteration needs every week to Shela's hard pressed mother and allowed her a 10% discount on reels of Sylko and lengths of petersham ribbon, bias binding or knicker elastic.

By February 1944 the war had dragged on for over four years and Shela had become familiar with the sight of slogans of "Open The Second Front Now" appearing on blank walls and along fences all around the town and Bedford seemed to be full of servicemen and women of all nationalities. Then, one day towards the end of that cold month, when everyone was tired of eating dried egg for breakfast and trying out every sweet shop in the vicinity in the vain hope of finding precious milk chocolate, Dad came home from work with some exciting news.

"There's a job going at the Red Cross Officers' Club at the corner of Kimbolton Road," he announced. "It's just right for you, Aggie. They are advertising for an experienced tailoress to start after the Easter holiday. The money is quite good too," he added as everyone helped themselves to Gang-Gang's drop-scones at teatime. "And you wouldn't have to work such long

61

hours as you do at home." Later that evening, as "Lili Marlene" was played over and over on the radio and John prepared to go back from leave to R.A.F. Halton where he was now an Aircraft Apprentice, Shela sat pretending to read her latest library book as the new idea was discussed. As she listened intently to the conversation between Mum and Gang-Gang, she suddenly realised with apprehension that, if her mother got the new job, it would be the first time in her young life that her Mum would not be there when she arrived home from school.

And she remembered those years when she was little and Dad held down a well-paid job and the family always had a car and she wondered, incongruously it seemed, what had become of Mum's beautiful, silver fox fur that she always wore draped over a tailored costume she had made herself. And how smart she always looked whenever she accompanied Dad to Conservative Club occasions or on visits to Bedford County Theatre in Midland Road. Now Shela had a mother who had to "go out to work" and the idea seemed so strange to her that she kept asking Gang-Gang about it until she at last told her to stop worrying and that Mum would probably enjoy being out of the house for a change.

"It will do her good," Gang-Gang said quietly. Then she added firmly in her Liverpudlian accent, "You and Joycey will just have to pull your weight when your mother is at work."

Joycey had left the Harpur Central School the year before and now worked at Harry Hills Gents Outfitters in Silver Street. So Shela realised that this meant mostly herself to keep an eye on the younger children after school and in the holidays. Her younger sister, Joaney, who was nearly three years her junior and about to start at the Girls' Modern School had already developed a firm mind of her own, and would not be at all willing to fall in line with the new arrangements. Gang-Gang was always there, of course, but she was getting on in years and needed her rest in the afternoons.

"Thank God those evacuees have all gone home," she repeated to herself and reminisced constantly about the times when she was obliged to do all the family baking in the middle of the night, as there was no room in the small back kitchen during the day. A week later, Mum had her interview at the Officers' Club and came home with the news Shela secretly dreaded to hear. She had obtained the job and was to start on Monday morning. Shela hated the idea of Mum being at work all day and when she was at home at the weekends she took to following her around the house and regularly sat on the top stair, waiting for her to come out of the bathroom so that she could follow her into the bedrooms as she made the beds. Shela simply would not let her out of her sight and it was only when Gang-Gang sat and talked to her about the money problems that she at last began to accept the painfully changed situation in the family. But she still hated it. All through that year of 1944, through the drama of the D-Day landings and Mum worried that John would soon be old enough to be on active service, she worked even longer hours at the American Officers' Club than she had done at home.

"I'm earning good money, Ted," she told Dad one day in August, while he was listening intently to the news of the liberation of Paris. "And we need it now that you can't work full-time any longer."

It was true, because the Yanks paid well for their uniform alterations and there was the added bonus of gifts of Hershey Bars, jelly-beans and American doughnuts and sometimes, lovely chewing gum, unobtainable in wartime Britain. But for Shela, the sudden appearance of glossy American comics was better than all the other gifts put together. Just before Christmas that same year, the family heard the sad news that one of Mum's customers at the club had gone missing on a flight to newly liberated Paris. Major Glenn Miller had been at the Christmas party that all the Winch children enjoyed only the week before his disappearance and Shela thought sadly about the quiet man with the smart spectacles who poured out a big glass of juice for her and afterwards gave each child there a big bag of almost forgotten oranges to take home at the end of the evening.

Toad-in-the-hole made with Frankfurter sausages was now a regular Saturday dinner for the family. Although Gang-Gang sometimes grumbled about "that strange American stuff" Mum often brought home, everyone knew she was secretly glad that her only child and all those grandchildren were eating well in those years of shortages of everything, from cheese to make a decent macaroni cheese pudding, to dried fruit to put in her homemade Christmas cake.

And then it was Easter again and Shela thought longingly of those pre-war Snow-White Easter eggs as she tucked in to her breakfast of a precious egg boiled by Gang-Gang in cochineal water to make it bright pink. On the B.B.C. Home Service, Alvar Lidell told a waiting Great Britain that the Allies had crossed the Rhine and were now fighting on German soil at last. And Shela thought of all those people killed in the big Dresden raid the month before and tried hard to understand what this horrible war was really all about.

"It will all be over soon," commented Dad as he finished his breakfast and picked up the *Daily Express*. "And when it is, Aggie," he continued, "we will both be out of work. The Yanks will go home and our jobs will go with them."

At that moment, on Easter Sunday morning in 1945, as she saw Dad wink at Mum across the table and she answered with a small shake of her head, Shela first realised that plans were already being made for the future. And now she recalled hearing whispered conversations between Gang-Gang and Mum and mysterious, official looking letters that arrived regularly and how both Mum and Dad sat up late, night after night, long after everyone else had gone to bed. She could not know, on that far-off, spring day, that those plans, already under way as she finished her pink egg and helped Gang-Gang with the washing up, were eventually to change the course of her young life and trigger the start of all that came after.

PART TWO

1945–1963

CHAPTER
FOUR

A Family Business

Dad was venturing into business. Somehow, between the two of them, Shela's parents had managed to save enough money to open a small café in Castle Hill, Bedford.

"I was lucky to secure the lease on that place, Aggie," he enthused, on that memorable Easter Sunday in 1945. Shela sat near the old Ideal Boiler fireplace in the big kitchen, listening intently to all that was going on. "Old Filby had two other offers before mine but they apparently considered he was asking too much rent for it."

"But, Ted," interrupted Mum while he was in full flow. "Four pounds a week! That's a lot of money!"

"Which we can afford if it's managed properly," Dad replied. "And," he continued with his old, familiar grin, which Shela had not seen very often since he came back from the war, "we can keep it in the family. The Yanks will have gone home by Christmas," he told her confidently. "Then you can open your own dress-making business in the rooms over the shop, just like you did in the old days."

Recent hurried, whispered conversations and the strange, official-looking letters at last made sense to

Shela and she began to get just as excited as Dad with the idea of being "in business". Castle Hill Café opened on April Fool's Day, just six weeks before V.E. Day, and right from the start it was a success. In those early months, Dad and Mum ran the business between them while Joycey and Shela helped out at really busy times. The double-fronted shop, owned by Filby's Garage, directly behind it, had previously been the coal order office for C.A.E.C. Howard, the coal merchant, or "Cacky" Howard, as he was known to most Bedfordians.

The rooms were small and the rent substantial, but within a short time the business was up and running and Shela's Dad was once again the happy man she remembered from her early childhood. The new business thrived on the juxtaposition of so many others. For it meant that every morning and afternoon, brown paper bags of fresh buns and doughnuts, delivered daily by the Co-op bakery in Midland Road, together with jugs of tea and coffee, were sold to the workers in workshops and repair yards in Castle Lane and Castle Hill.

H. H. Bennett, Ladies Clothes Manufacturers in Castle Works; The Consumers Tea Company, later to become The Bedford Gallery on the opposite corner; George Ford, Upholsterer and Mattress Maker, just across the road; Keech's Billiard Hall at one end of Castle Hill and T. C. Ginn, Furniture Removers at the other. Henry Bacchus, the electrical goods shop and Wells, the big furniture store in the High Street, both had workshops in Castle Lane, while further along Castle Hill, Gents Mineral Waters occupied extensive premises at the rear of John Bull, the Jewellers, whose big, imposing shop on the High Street with its golden bull standing over an ornate clock was a landmark for everyone in the town.

The café traded with all these firms and their workmen and sold Gents Mineral Waters and also Boswell Ice-Cream, manufactured by Jimmy Fitzpatrick in his cramped little factory in Boswell Place in the Black Tom area of the town. In later years, his premises would never have passed the Health and Safety regulations. But in those days of post-war austerity, when ice-cream was a rare treat, he continued in business until the big names in the ice-cream world moved in and, eventually, J. Lyons and Walls took over all his trade. Boswell Court flats now tower over the site of the tiny factory where the brave, little business once thrived and later that enterprising man became a Lyons Ice-Cream franchisee and opened a larger factory and café at Honey Hill Lido in Queens Park, Bedford.

By August that year, when Shela was fourteen years old and considered herself to be quite grown-up, Castle Hill Café was doing well and she had not seen Dad so cheerful since the days before he went back into the army. The bouts of malaria that so weakened him all through the previous two years had subsided and, as the business began to take up all his time, the number of visits to his club declined. For Shela, the memory of those puzzling and sometimes frightening nights of disturbed sleep and crying babies began to fade as her dad regained his pride and started to provide for his family once again.

71

All through the school summer term, Shela worked every evening and weekend in the café, sometimes until eleven o'clock at night.

"You must make sure that you finish your homework before you go down to help your father," insisted Mum, as her daughter settled down to a hurried homework session in the new dressmaking workshop above the café. But Shela already knew that her heart was no longer in her school work. Her old life at school and her long-held ambition to become a teacher began to take second place in her life and she learned to keep Dad's business accounts and negotiate all the necessary paperwork required by the Ministry of Food office at the town hall, and she told her mother that she did not want to go back to school in the new term.

"Just try for this term," her anxious mother pleaded. "You'll probably change your mind again by Christmas."

On an unforgettably humiliating first day back at school in September, Shela realised that she would not be going up into the fourth year with her contemporaries. She was to be kept back in the third year with all those kids coming up from second year until she had caught up with her neglected studies. And she finally rebelled.

"I'm not going back," she told her mother tearfully as she arrived back home. "I'll have to do all the year's work again and all the other kids are younger than me!"

So Mum at last and very reluctantly gave in and went off to the school to see Miss Tonkin to explain that her daughter was needed in the family business and would not be returning to school. Shela had no deep regrets about leaving school so early at fourteen. But over the years since that hasty decision was made, she came to realise just how much she had missed in that crucial time between fourteen and eighteen years when her youthful ambitions could have been realised.

So the pattern of her young life was firmly set as she worked long hours with her father. Upstairs, Mum also worked hard to establish her dressmaking business, which was well advertised in the *Bedfordshire Times* and the *Bedford Journal*. Various ladies' outfitters in the town displayed discreet notices recommending her dressmaking and alteration skills. Dusts Ladies Outfitters and Arthur Day Costumiers, both in the High Street, recommended her services. Mrs Baylis, in Castle Road, who provided most of Mum's work in her early days there, also passed on her name to grateful customers wearied by clothing shortages and endless make and mend attempts to produce decent clothes from old, pre-war garments and hand-me-downs for their children.

Clothes rationing was still in force in those spartan years after the war but as this was eased by a new Labour government voted in by a nation more than ready for change, despite Winston Churchill's inspiring leadership through the war years, good materials began to appear once more in the town shops. E. P. Rose and Son, later to become Debenhams, Dusts in the High Street, Braggins and Sons in Silver Street, later to be taken over by Beales, and Blotts Haberdashers opposite The Arcade, further along High Street, began to stock up on materials not seen since 1939. Mum's business expanded accordingly and soon she was employing two apprentices as well as Joycey, who sometimes helped out with rush orders after her own day's work was over. All through 1946, the year when bananas were on sale for the first time since before the war and Mr Churchill warned that "an iron curtain has descended across Europe", Shela worked happily in the family business. She was untroubled by the news that America was carrying out nuclear tests on Bikini Atoll in the Pacific Ocean but intrigued by the sight of women wearing daring bikinis on the cold beaches of Cornwall.

"How are those two things connected, Dad?" she queried, as she deftly sugared and jammed six dozen doughnuts every day and then poured endless cups of tea to be stirred with a large teaspoon tethered to the counter by a length of string.

"Its just a fashion gimmick," offered one of the Filby boys. "And very nice too!" he added, picking up the large enamel jug of tea for his brothers waiting in the garage behind the café for their morning tea break. Wednesday afternoon was the only time that Shela could take a break from the café and not even then if one of the girls now employed on the afternoon shift failed to appear.

"I've not been to the pictures for over a month, Mum," she protested one afternoon in late autumn. "And I did want to see that new film," she complained as her mother tried to placate her frustrated daughter. "It's just not fair!"

The new film was an adaptation of Charles Dickens' *Great Expectations*, starring John Mills and Valerie

Hobson, and Shela had been looking forward to it all that week. The next day, as she often did both at the time and in later life, Joycey stepped in to do the afternoon shift for her sister on her own afternoon off from her own job and Shela was able at last to use the complimentary ticket presented by the Granada in exchange for displaying film advertisements in the café window.

After many quiet afternoons spent in the little shop, where Shela often sat behind the counter with her head bent over a small exercise book, creating impossible romances involving handsome boys and virginal girls who always lived happily ever after, one short story was accepted by *Oracle*, and another by *Red Letter*, girls' magazines of the day but now discontinued for many years.

From the beginning of December 1946, Britain experienced its coldest winter for nearly half a century. Heavy snow fell just before Christmas and lay frozen on the ground until late April the next year. Buses crawled along roads banked high on either side with dirty snow and children skated on Longholme boating-lake and slid on enormous ice slides nearly two feet thick. On Christmas Eve, the Filby boys from the garage dug a path from the road to the shop door through snow shoulder high. And every morning at eight sharp, Shela opened the door for custom after a weary trudge through frozen streets and decided that the little café, smelling of freshly brewed coffee and great quartern loaves, still hot from the Co-op Bakery in Midland

Road, was the only warm haven in that frozen world beyond.

In the three small rooms where she worked for up to fifteen hours a day, Dad's little radio, perched high on its shelf above the cigarette cupboard and permanently tuned in to the B.B.C. Home Service, became a familiar feature of café life. Shela listened avidly to "Housewives' Choice" and "Forces Favourites" and customers sang along to the current "big band sounds" of the Glenn Miller Orchestra, so familiar to recent wartime Bedford where the great bandleader played many times at the Bedford Corn Exchange. The volume was always turned up at eleven-fifteen every morning to listen to Mrs Dale's Diary and again at a quarter to seven every evening for Dick Barton — Special Agent.

Thursday nights brought the Land Army girls into the café to stock up on rolls, cakes, tarts and buns to take back to their billets at isolated farms, where they also worked long hours at unfamiliar and dirty tasks previously unimaginable to the city dwellers amongst them.

"Charge a penny for the paper bags," instructed Dad, when the girls lined up at the counter. "They are hard to come by and cost me a packet," he continued. Shela protested that no other shop ever charged for the bags, and the good-natured girls laughed at his cheek as they called a cheery "goodnight" and rushed to climb back onto the two covered lorries waiting for them beside the huge, static water tank, a leftover piece of wartime defence, just outside the café.

On Saturday nights, the little shop was filled to bursting with R.A.F. boys from Cardington and there was always a terrific rush to get them all served in time to catch the 11.15 bus back to camp. At just fifteen, Shela enjoyed the company of these youngsters who were mostly National Service boys away from home for the first time. But her father kept a close eye on their behaviour and a sharp ear for any bad language that they occasionally let slip. Several times he reminded them, to her deep humiliation, that his daughter was "just a baby, lads, so watch your language".

"I'm not a baby, Dad," she protested every time this situation arose and Dad just grinned and told her that she had a lot of growing up to do before she could handle a bunch of lads like the R.A.F. boys. A year after the café opened, Mum's dress-making business on the floor above closed to make way for Dad's newest idea. Within weeks, the new restaurant opened and the dozen or so tables covered with smart blue and white checked tablecloths became crowded at lunchtime and every evening until ten o'clock with eager customers. Soon, the word spread that you could always get an extra egg with your sausage and chips at Castle Hill Café.

For Shela, the opening of the restaurant meant a far more hectic life than the routine of the first year in the little snack bar. For Mum it meant working much longer hours, for she coped with all the cooking and eventually two more employees were taken on to help. Dad continued to run the snack bar alone but on very busy evenings Shela divided her time between upstairs and downstairs as trade expanded and a greater variety of food became available to the catering trade.

"Don't forget to record everything you sell, Shela," Dad reminded her every day, as he left her in charge in the afternoons while he went home for his regular "forty winks" before the busy evening rush started. And Shela knew this meant marking down on the till roll all the requirements of the Food Office at the Town Hall. She became used to marking each item with "main meal", "snack meal", or "tea meal" and meticulously noting a tea or coffee sale to be counted at the end of the day. Without these records to return at the end of each month there would be no further allocation of food vouchers to purchase food still strictly rationed in the late forties. The one unrationed luxury available was ice-cream. Always eager to exploit every business opportunity, Dad installed a big chest freezer in the corner of the snack-bar and Shela quickly became expert at serving up cornets with a round scoop and wafers with a "clicker-disher", both supplied free from Boswell Ice-Creamery. Today, that low level of food hygiene would never be allowed but, in those days of rationing of everything from chocolate to dolly mixtures, customers were glad enough to taste something sweet for a change and the café sold ice-cream throughout the year.

Shela did not fail to notice that the boy delivering regular supplies of ice-cream was, in her opinion, a dark-eyed, quietly spoken and handsome younger version of the film idol Ronald Coleman; from the first day that this paragon appeared in the shop, the sixteen- year-old girl was aware of a new and disturbing feeling that she had never experienced before.

"Dad keeps pulling my leg about my 'heart-throb'," she told her mother one night on the long walk home. "But he's not!" she protested, when Mum just laughed and replied that she was far too young to know about such things. And so Shela kept her feelings to herself but she looked daily for the arrival of Johnny, who was later to play such a momentous part in her life and set in motion all that came after.

Regular customers in that year of 1946 were members of the B.B.C. Symphony Orchestra that had been evacuated from London during the V1 and V2 raids at the end of the war and now rehearsed in the Bunyan Meeting Rooms in Mill Street and broadcast regularly from the Corn Exchange and The Bedford School Great Hall. Shela attended these concerts regularly, for the gentlemen of the string section always had spare complimentary tickets to hand over in exchange for an extra cup of coffee.

"I never knew that classical music could be so good, Mum," she enthused after every performance, and Gang-Gang smiled and reminded her sixteen-year-old granddaughter that it was not only Glenn Miller and jazz that made the world go round. Those early awakenings to wonderful music and the great composers remained in the girl's mind long after the appeal of dance music and modern cinema themes had faded. In later life, the memory of those live concerts inspired the considerable collection of classical albums and later CDs which she treasured more than any "hit" of the day.

The hours at the café were long and hard and there was a constant turnover of staff. They seemed to come and go with depressing regularity, with the exception of one girl who stayed for three years and another, older woman who worked the evening shift when the restaurant opened. On one awful Saturday in December, Mum was busily chipping potatoes for the evening meals and Shela was working alone in the snack-bar, missing her father who was off sick with the recurring chest complaint which had begun to trouble him every winter. At seven o'clock, she glanced up at the big clock behind the counter and realised that yet another girl had let them down on the busiest night of the week.

"What are we going to do, Mum?" she said, as the queue waiting to be served got longer by the minute, and she was fast running out of clean cups and saucers. It was when Johnny walked in a few minutes later that she knew help had arrived, and soon he was helping her in the snack-bar and a lady living opposite came in to help Mum with the upstairs customers. On Monday morning a notice appeared in the labour exchange offering wages above the regular rate for two more assistants. Within a week things had returned to normal, but Johnny continued to give a hand occasionally and Shela secretly loved those evenings when he was there. At sixteen, she had not yet learned the difference between love and infatuation and was content to let this exciting, new relationship continue for as long as she could retain his interest.

There was great excitement in the family when Joycey announced her engagement to the young soldier she had been writing to for the past year.

"He's being demobbed soon," she announced one Sunday, just before Shela set off to open the café at three o'clock. "And then we'll start arranging the wedding."

Privately, Shela thought that her older sister was far too young to be talking about marriage at just eighteen, and it was not until she met the clean-cut and polite man who was to become her first brother-in-law, that she changed her mind.

"I'll soon have a home of my own," Joycey confided to her sister, as she paraded in their bedroom in the slipper satin wedding dress that Mum had made for her. "But first, Johnny and I will stay here. Mum says we can have the front bedroom as a bed-sitting room and use of the kitchen. I've already put my name down on the council list for a flat."

A few months later, Dad decided the family would be better off living nearer to the business, and the move was made to number four Castle Road, a big, gloomy house with no electricity and badly in need of paint. Shela hated the place. The gas-lit rooms made reading difficult and the lack of any kind of heating apart from the old-fashioned kitchen boiler meant cold bedtimes and a hasty exit from the bathroom in the winter months. Joycey stayed on at the old house with Gang-Gang, whose increasing infirmity meant that she needed more care now that she was in her middle seventies. But the old lady rarely complained and as the time for the girl's wedding drew nearer, the two sat together in the evenings while Gang-Gang talked about her own youthful dreams and how she had met Grandpa Thomas and how her Agnes was born after four late miscarriages.

It was towards the end of that year of 1947, when the newspapers were full of the drama of the end of British rule in India, that Gang-Gang suffered her final stroke. No amount of care at home or nursing in Bedford General Hospital could prolong the life of the dearly loved grandmother who had been a second mother to all the children for as long as they could remember. And Shela remembered the difficult scenes from her childhood when the puzzling tensions between her father and grandmother sometimes resulted in divided loyalties, for she loved them both equally.

Gang-Gang was laid quietly to rest in the old cemetery in Foster Hill Road one blustery October afternoon as the light faded from the sky and petals from late summer roses blew across the newly turned soil at the graveside. And this third grandchild, who was so like her grandmother in her love of books and a natural curiosity about the world, grieved for the loss of the warm lap of her childhood and the comforting words of her Gang-Gang who had worked so hard for the large family.

A few weeks later, the first of the Winch girls was married and Joycey and her new husband settled down happily in the old home. Shela increasingly wondered if she also would have the chance of starting married life in familiar surroundings and secretly hoped it would be with the boy with dark eyes and wavy hair who constantly occupied her daytime thoughts and her dreams at night. The first unravelling of those hopes and dreams began on the day in 1948 when Dad fell ill once again.

"Your father and I have decided to sell up and buy a smaller business that is easier to run, Shela," explained her mother. She closed and locked the café door behind them after another long day on aching feet that not even a regularly visiting chiropodist could relieve. "And once it is sold, we'll move back to the old house," she added wearily, and Shela looked closely at her mother's white face and decided that it could not be soon enough, for she had seen that strained look before and knew what it meant.

"My mother's going to have another baby," she confided to Johnny a week later. They were watching the film of The Third Man, starring Orson Welles, at the Granada Cinema in St. Peter's Street. "And the business will be sold by the end of the summer," she added quietly.

There was no answer from the young man beside her, but from then on his visits to the café grew less frequent. Three months later, with the business sold and the Winch family living solely on the capital gains that diminished alarmingly with every week that went by, Shela was despatched to Brighton on her father's behalf in an abortive attempt to buy a half-share in a small hotel on the sea front. When the accountant realised that the hotel owners had "cooked the books" for a quick sale, Dad settled instead for a small confectionery shop in Bromham Road in Bedford. Once again and to Shela's immense delight, Johnny again began to drop in to "Daphne's Confectioner and Tobacconist", where she had rapidly learned to cut out "E" and "D" coupons from post-war ration books for sweets and chocolate and hide precious milk chocolate under the counter for regular customers.

"I see that he's not given up, then," was Dad's sour comment one day. The sole object of Shela's desire had hurriedly left the shop when her father drew up outside in the new Citroen car bought from the proceeds of the café sale. "What is he doing here at this hour of the day?" he added, as Shela flushed and tried to avoid his eye. "He should be at work like the rest of us!"

Shela had no answer for her father, for she also was increasingly puzzled by the erratic working pattern that Johnny seemed to follow. It was not until she met him at eight-thirty one morning on her way to open the shop and he was on his way home to bed that she realised he had been out all night.

"I'll see you later," he said shortly, then turned quickly into Queen Street where he lived, and Shela was left wondering all day what he was up to and hoped it was not something illegal.

"I lost a packet last night, Shela," the pale-faced young man confessed to her later that evening. "I just hope those Greeks give me a chance to win it back, that's all!"

Johnny was an inveterate gambler. Every penny he could scrape together was chanced on nightly games of poker against older men, mostly restaurant owners in Midland Road, who could well afford to lose the equivalent of a week's wages every night of the week.

"That young man's only out for what he can get, my girl," her father warned her several times during the two years that the Winch family traded in the confectionery business. It was only, once again, when the accountant warned Dad that the business was not paying and that he was steadily losing money on a ridiculously low allocation of confectionery passed to him by the previous owner, that the decision was made to sell up as quickly as possible and move on.

Mum too was anxious about the relationship between Shela and her questionable boyfriend. But she was now middle-aged, coping with her latest child, worried about her eldest daughter's pregnancy and overwhelmed by weariness. Though she tried several times to talk seriously to her second daughter, her brave efforts were ineffectual. Wasted too, for Shela was deaf to any advice. She chose also to ignore her father's gloomy view of her deepening regard for Johnny. Soon the pair were meeting every night and she was introduced to his family in the tiny, terraced house in the Black Tom area of the town.

"It's awful, Mum," Shela explained one day, after closing and locking the shop door behind her and walking home to Castle Road with her mother and sister, both now pushing their prams. "His mother committed suicide on his fourteenth birthday. He's lived with his grandmother ever since, and they are really old and don't understand him at all. I feel sorry for him."

Beware of pity. It comes in many guises and love is the most convincing. For when Johnny admitted he had dodged the National Service draft for the last year and now the government had finally caught up with him and he was to go into the army the next month, Shela knew that she would wait for him for as long as it took and however hard it might be.

The little confectionery business was finally sold in 1950 and Shela found work in the office of Tucker's Dairies in St. John's Street. She missed Johnny to walk her home on dark evenings but never missed the last post on Friday nights when she sent him a ten-shilling note to enable him to come home for the weekend from his army base in London. On Sunday evening, another ten-shilling note was handed over to take him back again.

She never questioned the appearance of packets of twenty cigarettes he always seemed to have in his pocket or the money he spent on the cinema or café meals on weekend leaves. She only knew that she was happy and would do anything to keep things as they were. At nineteen and so much in love that sweet reason presented no obstacles, Shela began the first tentative moves away from the family unit where she had been loved and protected for all of her young life.

CHAPTER
FIVE

Marriage and a Different World

The two-up, two-down terraced house in Queen Street was not at all what Dad expected. He and Mum stood on the doorstep of number 23 with Shela, who stood nervously beside them waiting for the door to open.

"Come in. Come in," said Grandpa Warner, with the crooked smile that Shela was to come to know so well. The hare-lip and broken nose were explained as being the result of a kick from a horse in his youth, when corrective surgery was beyond the reach of working class men. "Young Johnny is out with his friends. I expect he will be home soon."

The following hour passed painfully slowly as Shela listened to the talk between her parents and Johnny's grandparents.

"Yes, Mrs Winch," sighed Granny Warner. "That's right," she continued, then poured another cup of tea for Mum from her best rose tea service. "We've looked after the lad since he was born. His mother had four others after him. And she was so young."

"And still young when she died, our Grace," added the old man. "In 1946 that was and the lad only fourteen and still at school."

Later, as Dad parked the car in the rented garage on the corner of George Street and Castle Road, he at last spoke his mind.

"Well, my girl," he stated, locking the garage door behind him, "if that's what you want, go ahead. But I expected better things for my daughter."

Shela could not understand why her father was making such a fuss about her planned move to the small house in the Black Tom area of the town. The deciding letter from her boyfriend had arrived unexpectedly the previous week proposing that they get married in the summer, and the excited girl began to make preparations for the wedding in August 1951.

"I'll get two weeks compassionate leave," Johnny told her on his next 48-hour leave pass. "And afterwards we can go down to Brighton for a few days to stay with my friend's aunt who keeps a guest-house there. When we come back we'll have time to settle you in to Queen Street before I have to report back."

Shela knew that "reporting back" meant to Catterick Garrison in Yorkshire and that there would be no more weekend leaves from there. Woolwich in London had been a short train journey away but Yorkshire was out of the question for a quick weekend pass.

The wedding at Christ Church in Denmark Street, known locally as "The Tin Tabernacle" because of its corrugated iron roof, was a quiet affair compared with Joycey's big day three years previously. Shela wore her sister-in-law's beautiful wedding dress and veil made by her mother for John's new wife the year before, and the Juliet cap trimmed with artificial pearls from an old necklace sat well on her newly permed hair. Mary and Beryl were her bridesmaids and Johnny's young sister, Sandra, and his grandparents made up the wedding group outside the little church as they posed to be photographed by the *Bedfordshire Times* photographer for the Friday newspaper.

There was no money now in the family for the lavish reception that followed her sister's wedding in 1948 and, after a basic meal at the Co-operative Rooms in Midland Road with short speeches from the best man, and Jimmy Fitzpatrick, Johnny's last employer before the army draft caught up with him, the newly-weds returned somewhat lamely to Queen Street to pack for their short honeymoon in Brighton.

Shela was half-way up the narrow, winding staircase to the back bedroom to change into going-away clothes, when she first heard the raised voices that were to become a regular feature of her future life in that small, cramped house.

"That's all I have! I told you this morning!"

Then the front door slammed hard and Granny Warner's little dog Podge began to whimper. Shela peered from the bedroom window to watch Grandpa retreat to the lean-to at the end of the narrow garden with a rolled cigarette hanging from his twisted lips. As she stood there, uncertain what to do and already absorbing, against her will, the unhappy atmosphere in her new home, she heard Gran call softly to the old man cowering in his hiding-place.

"Come back in, father. He's gone out."

89

Johnny stayed out of the house for the next three hours and only arrived back just in time to catch the six-fifteen train to St. Pancras Station and then across to Victoria Station for the short journey down to Brighton. Shela never knew where he had been during those hours out of the house on their wedding day, but she was to learn over time that it was best not to question the comings and goings of her new husband.

"You must come and go as you please, my dears," the kindly landlady smiled as she helped them up to their room at the top of the three-storey house in a back street of the town. And Shela's uneasy thoughts about the events back home in Queen Street were firmly put to the back of her mind. The long, sunny days and newly-experienced passion of the nights in the big, old bed soothed away her doubts about the man she had married. Overwhelming love blinded her to his faults. Shela did not see much of her new husband once they were back home. For the whole of that second week of his leave, he left the house every evening after supper and returned in the small hours the following morning. By noon each day, Johnny was at last out of bed and remained affable and good-humoured towards his grandparents and loving and helpful to his new wife as he cooked supper for them all in the tiny scullery.

"He's winning at poker," stated Grandpa one evening. Then sighed in resignation when his grandson left the house once more and Shela kept the old couple company to listen to the news on the B.B.C. Home Service about the newly opened Festival of Britain.

90

"The Festival of Britain is just what our people needed," intoned Gerald Barry, the director of the festival. "It is a real tonic to our nation. The drab, grey days are over and now Britain can get back to normal."

But in the little house where Shela now lived, things were far from normal. On the wall beside the old fashioned, carefully black-leaded kitchen range, the blurred photograph of a narrow faced, dark haired young woman looked unsmilingly down at her ageing parents and her new daughter-in-law. Shela tried in her small way to dispel the palpable sadness left in this place when Grace, the beloved mother and daughter, had died so tragically on Johnny's fourteenth birthday. It was a strange relief when Johnny returned to his army base. The late night, puzzling, loud whispers of Grandpa to his wife, who was partially deaf, ceased and an uneasy peace returned to the little house.

But Shela had heard it all quite clearly through the thin, bedroom walls as the old man urged Gran to go to the doctor for treatment to the bruises on her face and angry, red weals on her arms. And with the whispers came the horrifying confirmation of what the girl suspected but could not bring herself to fully believe. Something terrible was happening in this place. Each Friday, as she set off for her new office job at the Igranic Electric Works in Elstow Road, a very confused girl both dreaded the arrival home of Johnny that evening and yet hoped she would see her new husband again soon. She still sent a ten-shilling note to him every week out of her meagre wages of three pounds, and soon he was posted back to Woolwich again and home for three weekends a month.

On a dark December morning, whilst standing barefoot at the stone sink in the scullery, she saw her surroundings with a clarity that plunged her into misery and forced her to admit the reality of her predicament.

The glare of the bare light bulb illuminated the brick walls. The rough surfaces, though whitewashed, were grimy with aged cobwebs, dust and grease. A mouse behind the ancient food cupboard squeaked, sending a shudder through her slight frame. The lean-to room reeked of long-past meals cooked on an old gas-cooker and overhead a row of black saucepans brooded darkly. In a dim corner stood the dolly tub and copper in which dirty clothes were steeping in a slimy brew of soda and soap and producing a nose-stinging odour that made her stomach heave.

She tried to quell the gall that rose to her throat and reached for a glass to fill from the single cold-water tap. As she stepped off the duck-board onto the flags she stood on a fat slug which squelched between her toes. Desperately she turned to the sink, just managing to lower her head over the stained, enamel bowl before she threw up. She could hear herself, between the sounds of her retching, gasping repeatedly.

"It shouldn't be like this. It shouldn't be like this!"

No money had been spent on this house for many years. It was like living in a house from the last century. God! How awful this place was and how could people live in it in this state? And where had all Grandpa's hard-earned money gone over the past few years? In her heart she knew the answer. She also knew that things were about to get a great deal worse. The revelation came to her clearly in those few, frightening moments, that she had made a mistake. That, for her, the years ahead would be difficult. That the future was never going to be other than making the best of a bad job. Johnny would be home that evening and she would have to tell him that she was pregnant. And now she knew that the man she had married in ignorance of his violent temper would be unable to cope with the prospect of fatherhood.

CHAPTER
SIX

Babies and Bruises

February of 1952, the month of the sudden death of the king, was as cold and raw as any Shela could remember and the works office at the Igranic Electric Company equally cheerless. A long room of filing cabinets with rows of desks occupied by busy clerks dealing with stock control and other mind-numbingly boring office procedures. Working hours were 8.30 a.m. to 5.00 p.m. and Shela hated every one of them.

Her belly, already swollen in pregnancy and a source of some amusement and ribald comments from the younger men at the work-benches on the factory floor below the office, made it difficult and increasingly hazardous to pedal the old bicycle through icy streets to and from work. On dark mornings and afternoons, she became one of a great swathe of cyclists surging over Elstow Road Railway Bridge like some vast ship in full sail to disperse as if by magic at the junction with London Road Bridge and the roads leading to St. John's Street on the left and the sprawling London Road housing estate on the right.

A fall from her bicycle, which resulted in bruised knees and a restless night, with the child inside her kicking out in protest, and another bout of sickness the next morning when she vomited helplessly into the waste-bin shared with the girl at the next desk, meant several days off work and Shela handed in her notice. She was to dream of that place for many years afterwards and always, in those dreams, she saw the horrified look on her office colleague's face as she retched into that bin and the dreary office spun round and round. She always awoke sweating and breathless at the never buried memory of those miserable days.

Johnny took the news of the pregnancy surprisingly calmly and Shela tried to believe what his grandmother repeated every time he left the house at weekends to join his friends at the snooker hall above Burtons in Silver Street or at Poole's Milk Bar in the Broadway. There was never any suggestion now that Shela might like to go with him to the cinema or even for a walk in Bedford Park on fine days. And she guessed that he did not want to be seen with a pregnant woman, for he was desperate to keep up his image of a carefree bachelor about town for as long as possible.

Granny Warner was very kind to the young woman who had come to live in her home and full of reassurances that things would change when the baby arrived.

"You'll see, dear," she tried to comfort the girl after yet another row over money. For there was now only the meagre army wives' allowance to pay for her keep and no money to spare to buy the things she so desperately wanted for the coming baby. "He will be different when the baby arrives and soon he'll be out of the army and things will return to normal."

But what is normal? Shela thought bleakly, watching her husband's handsome face reflected in the small oval mirror above the fireplace. She knew how vain he was about his dark, wavy hair that glistened with the Trugel hairdressing he applied as soon as he came home on Friday evenings and then washed off again before returning to barracks on Sunday. It was one of the first things about this immature man that had so attracted her to him when they first met and he told her the facts about his mother and she felt so sorry for him and fell in love with the boy with wavy hair.

"Don't say anything to your parents about the rows, Shela," pleaded the old lady who still, although now in her late sixties, worked at a cleaning job at a big house in Park Avenue for five mornings every week. And sometimes returned to more work in the afternoon, for there never seemed to be enough money to go round.

At seventy, Grandpa Warner, or "Plum" Warner as he was known at W. H. Allen's Engineering works in Queens Park, still worked full time as a tool-grinder, and now Shela knew where all the money went. Not into this small, shabby house, of that she was certain. But into her feckless husband's pockets, to be squandered at poker or whatever else he got up to on his nights out on the town.

Across the road from 23 Queen Street, the small, general shop run by Win Hutchings and her young assistant became a regular refuge for Shela during that summer of 1952, and often she was invited to the small flat above the shop for a cup of tea and precious chocolate biscuits which she could never afford to buy for herself. The kindly spinster always allowed the hard-up young woman to buy small items "on the slate" every week until she could get down to the General Post Office in Dame Alice Street to draw the small army allowance on Friday. By Sunday, most of that money had gone into her husband's pocket to keep him in cigarettes for the next week, and his wife was left to rely on the goodwill of Granny and Grandpa Warner until the next army pay day.

Vera Lynn sang "Auf Wiedersehen" on the B.B.C. Home Service on the morning that Shela went into labour. She was alone in the house and very frightened, for she had no means of getting to the hospital on her own. It was old Mrs Burden, the next-door neighbour at number twenty-one, who went across to Win Hutchings' shop, to ask her to phone for a taxi from the taxi rank in St. Peters Green. And it was the kindly shopkeeper who paid the five-shilling fare to the Maternity Wing at Bedford General Hospital North Wing in Kimbolton Road.

Shela's mother, who now worked in the sewing room at the hospital, met her frightened daughter at the hospital door and settled her into the narrow bed in the maternity ward, promising to come back in her lunch break.

"Don't worry, dear," she smiled as a young nurse approached bearing all the familiar paraphernalia of hospital enema equipment. "You'll feel better after that."

Christopher John weighed in at a hefty nine pounds at two o'clock the next morning, and at breakfast time Matron Ball held him up to the window for Shela's mother to see her new grandson from the hospital sewing room across the courtyard. Joycey visited her sister later that day, bringing with her some of her own little boy's baby clothes. When she went home to Queen Street after ten days on the big ward, Shela thankfully laid the twelve new terry nappies, bought by her mother, in the small drawer that Granny Warner had lined with fresh paper, and her little son in the old clothes basket on the low cupboard next to the fireplace in the tiny front room.

"His father lay there when he was a new baby," she confided as she brought Shela a fresh cup of tea. "But he had thick, dark hair. Not a bit like this little man," she continued, smiling down at Christopher's fine, blond hair.

"You will probably get a council flat now, dear," her mother comforted on the day that her daughter left hospital. But the only advice the housing officer had to give the new, young mother was not at all comforting.

"Go away and have another baby, Mrs Warren. Then you'll have enough points for a housing allocation."

The bond between the two women in the small house in Queen Street, one old and careworn and the other young and hopeful for the future, was forged during the first few months of Christopher's life. When she fell pregnant again in early 1953, Shela hoped that the year would end with her little family installed in a council house. But she knew that the housing allocation would not be granted without the tenant being in regular work. With Johnny now finished with National Service and two years in The Army Catering Corps, the need for work in September 1953 became imperative, but still he did not settle for a job in any of the many restaurants and cafés around the town.

"You are a qualified cook, now," observed his brother Roy one day, when he visited with his own new wife, Doris. "Get out there and start to support your family properly. You can't do that messing about on ice-cream vans and toffee-apple sales ventures."

Later that day as her husband prepared for his nightly visits to the snooker hall in town, Shela repeated her brother-in-law's remarks and received a bruised eye and nose in return as Johnny head-butted her twice in the dark scullery before leaving quickly through the back door.

"I had no money left to give him, Gran," she wept. The older woman said nothing but bathed her bruises with witch-hazel while Grandpa raged about his good for nothing grandson.

Shela knew that her parents were deeply concerned for her, and John, her older brother, threatened more than once to give that Warren chap a damned good hiding if he ever got hold of him. On her regular weekend visits to the old family home in Castle Road, where she could have a real bath in the familiar bathroom of her childhood, Shela talked to her worried mother about walking out on her disastrous marriage.

"If I could stay here, Mum," she tried to reason, "I might be able to get a job locally and, after the baby is born, go for a legal separation. Then he would have to pay me an allowance by law."

Her mother looked anxiously across to where Dad sat wheezing away in his old chair by the kitchen fire. Shela knew that her father was now extremely ill with emphysema. She did not want to give either of them any more worry, but she was desperate for them to agree to her plan for her little family.

"No, my girl," Dad interrupted, as she tried to persuade her mother that her plan could work. "You made your bed and now you must lie on it."

That was all her father ever said about the disastrous state of Shela's marriage, but in later years Mum confided that he was worried sick about this daughter who had chosen the hardest start possible to her adult life. Shela's second son, Barry, was born with no complications less than thirteen months after the first, and the placid, brown-eyed child slept peacefully all through the night beside her in the old wicker clothes basket used by his older brother the year before. The longed-for keys to a new home came a month later and, with Johnny now working as a grill cook out at Chicksands USAF base, Shela began to make preparations for the move to the newly built two-bedroom council house in Barton Road, near to where Joycey lived in Hereford Road on the other side of the town. Granny Warner sorted out spare sheets and towels and Grandpa brought home odd pieces of furniture picked up from second-hand shops in Tavistock Street and offered by kind neighbours.

"Give me the window measurements," suggested Joycey as the two sisters drank tea together in the kitchen of her now overcrowded flat. "I'll make up some net curtains for you. Mum has loads of that spotted muslin stuff left over from my move here and Phil Starkey upstairs has offered some old thick ones she no longer needs. You can have my old bedroom curtains too."

The move to the house on a rawly-new estate off Harrowden Road was made early in January 1954. Shela waved to her new neighbour on that first morning, and her hopes were higher than they had been since the early days of her marriage that at last things were improving. Inside the small, two-bedroom house, she was astonished to find a sparkling, new three-piece suite and dining furniture already installed in the long, living-dining-room and upstairs, new beds and a new, drop-sided cot for the baby.

"I ordered them last month," stated Johnny shortly. Shela stood open-mouthed at all the sudden opulence. "Jays Furnisher's in St. Peter's Street do hire-purchase. It was just a matter of finding the deposit and the rest can be paid off in monthly instalments."

Hire purchase, she thought uneasily as she settled the baby down for the night and tucked Christopher's old shawl around his tiny form in the unheated bedroom. She knew about the system of buying goods "on the weekly", for her sister had explained it to her, but she thought this was just from clothing catalogues like Great Universal Stores and Littlewoods.

"You must make sure the payments are kept up," remarked Joycey, when she visited and saw all the new things in her sister's house. "Otherwise they will come and take it back and you will lose the furniture and the deposit."

The job at Chicksands seemed to be going well as the cold early months of 1954 slowly gave way to a warm spring and Shela realised that she was pregnant once again.

"Why on earth didn't you get help from the doctor?" questioned her mother, as her pale-faced daughter held back the tears and pretended that everything was alright at home now that Johnny was working regularly. But everything was far from alright. Shela now stood shivering on the toilet seat every morning to look out of the bathroom window that faced down Barton Road. She was watching for the returning figure of her husband who regularly missed the early morning bus out to the big American Air Force base at Chicksands. She dreaded to see that hurrying figure turn in at the gate, for she knew his foul temper would erupt as soon as he closed the front door behind him.

"Why the hell didn't you call me in time, you stupid bitch!" he yelled. "I've been late once already this week and now I'm on a warning! This was my last chance. If I lose this job it will be your fault!"

Johnny had begun to stay out late again every night and Shela was nearly always in bed when he returned, smelling of tobacco and complaining about the poker or snooker game he'd just lost. The late nights resulted in a heavy sleep from which he could not be roused by six o'clock the next day, and the inevitable row when he at last came down the stairs meant crying children in addition to the nausea which now overtook her every morning. There never seemed to be enough money for food for her children, let alone the clothes they needed as they began to grow out of babyhood. If it had not been for her sister, still living on the next estate, who passed on all her own children's outgrown clothes, Shela knew she would be reduced to appealing to the National Assistance Board for any handout they would allow her. Johnny was gambling regularly again, and Shela suspected that the smartening up procedure he performed every evening before leaving the house meant that her good-looking but immature husband was also betraying her in the worst way she could imagine. Her fears were confirmed when an old school friend admitted that Johnny was seeing a young girl who worked at Paulo's Milk Bar in the High Street.

"He must be mad," said Hugh as he left the house after a visit with his own new wife. Then, after a pause and a warning look from Mavis, "I've never thought that he was good enough for you. And you may as well know, for everyone else does, that he was only so keen to get married in order to get two weeks compassionate leave from the army. The bastard!"

When the concerned couple had gone, Shela climbed slowly up the uncarpeted stairs to look at her two beautiful babies. Inside her newly swollen belly another life stirred as she put her head down beside her sons and cried herself to sleep.

CHAPTER
SEVEN

Starting Again

On the new radio, also acquired on hire-purchase from J. P. Simmons and Sons on the corner of Queen Street and Tavistock Street, Norman Wisdom sang mournfully, "Don't Laugh At Me, 'Cos I'm A Fool," and Shela smiled to herself as she rinsed out the last nappy in the big, white sink.

"These are going home," her sister Joycey chided as she took them into the small square of garden to peg them out on the washing-line. "You'll need new ones for the new baby."

But, on this day in August 1954, the sun shone and Shela was happy watching her older son toddle down the path towards his little brother, now sitting up in the old pram. The job out at Chicksands lasted for a few more weeks but at Easter the ice-cream merchant, who had supplied Castle Hill Café and gave Johnny his first job after leaving school, offered him work for the summer at his new premises in Honey Hill Road in Queens Park. At weekends, he became a familiar sight on the estate as he pedalled an ice-cream tricycle around the streets or pitched beside the Suspension Bridge on Bedford Embankment. The job meant long working hours, finishing only at dusk in the height of the summer, and often Johnny stayed the night with his grandparents in Queen Street. Shela was only thankful that the work was regular and that there would be up to two shillings and sixpence left on the mantelpiece every morning to buy food for the day.

With the small family allowance of eight shillings a week, she could just about manage the daily needs for herself and the children, for seven pence halfpenny bought a small steak and kidney pie and one shilling and nine pence bought a pound of beef sausages from Canvins the butchers in Harrowden Road every Thursday. Then, for two days of the week she and the children ate well, but their meals for the rest of it consisted of baked beans or potatoes with Oxo gravy and occasionally a bowl of custard with a blob of jam on top. The rent for the new house was just over one pound a week and Shela knew that it was paid only very intermittently. Each Friday morning, when she had no money to give the rent collector, she tried to keep the children quiet when the man knocked repeatedly at the front door, and then watched fearfully as he went on down the road to her neighbour, Mrs Ponsonby. One Friday morning, she found an official looking letter on the front door mat stating that the tenant was now three months in arrears with his rent and that unless the full amount was paid within one week, steps would be taken to evict forthwith.

"What am I to do?" she pleaded with her older sister that evening as the children were fed yet again with Joycey's children around their kitchen table.

"He's working, Shela," was the terse reply. "Tell him to pay it. He must be earning good money now."

Yes, and spending most of it in town, Shela thought desperately. The next morning, while Johnny prepared to leave for work after an unexpected night at home, Shela handed him the letter left by the rent collector the previous day.

"We can't go on like this," she said quietly and then waited nervously for his reaction. None came. "We've paid no more instalments on the furniture either," she continued doggedly.

Then she watched in apprehension as her husband's face darkened and he lit up another cigarette and blew smoke into her face. Suddenly, anger overcame her fear. How could he buy cigarettes when there was hardly any food in the larder and his children were living on such a meagre diet and handouts from her sister and mother?

"I need more money, Johnny," she screamed as hysteria threatened to overwhelm her. Her young husband lounged back on the new sofa and took another drag on his cigarette and smiled at her. The next instant, a hard, clenched fist pounded low into her stomach and she was knocked backwards off her feet to land with a crash against the table behind her. The baby within her turned quickly over. Shela clutched her swollen stomach and nausea engulfed her. Then she fainted, with her spinning head now underneath one of the new dining chairs. From a long way off, she heard Johnny's voice calling back over his shoulder as he left the house.

"I'm going to work, now," he snarled. "Perhaps that will teach you not to whine at me about money all the time. There is none!"

Then he was gone and Shela lay stunned and sick on the floor, watching blood seeping through her cotton skirt. And upstairs, the babies began to cry. The room seemed suddenly full of people as the Ponsonbys from next door rushed in through the back door. The older woman looked with concern at her young neighbour's white face and called to her husband for help, and Shela knew that the time had come to leave her bright, new home and once again seek the help of her mother. She was eight months into her third pregnancy when her sister put her into the taxi she had called on that awful morning in August.

"You can stay until the new baby arrives," her mother comforted, helping Shela and her children with her few belongings and the dozen ragged nappies into the old family home in Castle Road. "After that, we'll see."

A hastily summoned Doctor Finch confirmed that the blow to her stomach had not harmed the baby. "But the police should be informed, Mrs Winch," the old doctor advised as she prescribed medication for her young patient.

"That's no use, Mum," Shela pleaded later, while her mother comforted the two little boys and told her daughter to drink the strong cup of tea beside her on the old kitchen table of her childhood. "The police won't do anything about it. Domestic violence is not a crime, apparently."

Shela knew that her father was unhappy with her sudden arrival in the house, which, in the last few years, had settled comfortably into the routine of Mum working at home while he kept an eye on young Robert, now six years old and at the old school round the corner in York Street. Shela also knew that her younger sisters, Mary and Beryl, openly resented her unexpected presence in their home, which was, at last, after years of overcrowding and babies, now comfortably roomy and afforded them the luxury of their own bedroom. An advantage that their older sister had never enjoyed during her own childhood and growing up years in the big house at 152 Castle Road.

When Shela's new baby arrived in early September and her father came to the big maternity wing at Bedford North Wing Hospital to see her, she was thankful that some of the old affection between the two of them had re-established itself.

"Well, my girl," he commented, peering into the cot at the end of the narrow hospital bed, "I hope that this is your last one." Then he continued as he gently stroked the fair-haired baby girl's face with a tobacco-stained finger, "You've made a proper mess of things so far. I just hope it will improve from now on."

After ten days of the "lying-in" period in the hard hospital bed, Shela was more than ready to go back to the big house in Castle Road where her two little boys had been cared for so well by their grandmother. The weeks stretched into months and Shela regained her strength, while the previous pressure on her to return to her own home lessened. For Mum enjoyed having a baby in the house again and, when his weak chest and laboured breathing allowed, Dad tried to play with Christopher and Barry in the warm, old kitchen, with the Ideal boiler and the brass-bound fireguard once again draped with airing nappies.

Only her two younger sisters remained opposed to the idea of babies in their home again and many harsh words were exchanged that, although forgiven in the years that followed, were never entirely forgotten by Shela as she observed the very different paths from her own that they had chosen. Many times during that winter of 1954, with her children settled into a daily routine and Shela earning money at an evening job at Poole's Milk Bar in The Broadway, she thought about returning to the house in Barton Road. But how could she go back to an unheated house in the middle of winter and no work for Johnny? The man she had married with so much love and hope for the future. And the man she now recognised was too immature to support his wife, let alone his children.

Her own, familiar bed, from the days before she left home, had been hastily moved into her mother's small dining room together with Robert's old, drop-sided cot for Barry and a borrowed crib for Deborah, the fair-haired baby conceived with fading hopes for the future in that cold house on the other side of the town. At just over two years old, Christopher slept peacefully on the old sofa that had also been a fond part of Shela's childhood. Every night, her body ached for sleep, but her restless mind denied her that one blessed escape from the daily reality that she was trapped in a humiliating situation from which there seemed to be no escape. For Shela and her children were now almost completely dependent on the goodwill of her sympathetic mother and not so sympathetic father. When sleep finally came towards dawn, she dreamed constantly of the past, with all its memories of her own secure childhood and, on waking, grieved for her three little ones who had so cruelly been denied the same. For with waking, her terrible dilemma returned daily as she tried desperately to face up to her shattered illusions.

Gradually, tiredness and worry began to affect both her physical and mental health. Shela found herself going through the motions of caring for the children and trying to cope with her desperate situation inside a comforting, invisible bubble protecting her and from which she could observe, oddly dispassionately, the detached world around her.

Just before Christmas and with the new baby nearly four months old and thriving well on the loving care given so willingly by Shela's hard-working mother, the question of returning to her own home was once again raised by her younger sister.

"Why should we help to keep someone else's kids?" Mary demanded crossly one morning over breakfast, before leaving for work as a telephonist at the big GPO Telephone Exchange in Harpur Street. All that day, Shela thought about and worried over the angry outburst from her sister and came reluctantly to the painful conclusion that she must soon make the move back to her own home on the other side of the town.

She knew her sister was right about the money situation, for Johnny had not given anything towards his family's keep since the day they left home. But, Shela fretted, as sleep refused to come that night, she gave every penny she earned from her evening job to her mother for her keep. Ten shillings of the fifteen shillings a week family allowance was also added to her wages and paid over promptly towards her mother's small household budget.

"You must keep something for yourself," Mum protested, the first time Shela gave her all of the allowance. But the five shillings were never spent, for how could she go anywhere or do anything when she worked every night and cared for her children all day?

On one cold, Saturday morning in February 1955, Mary came running into the kitchen demanding that her sister answer the front door.

"That useless husband of yours is trying to knock the door down!" she shouted angrily. "And you'd better open it before the neighbours complain!"

Her parents tactfully left her alone with Johnny and the children in the front room. But behind them in the big kitchen Shela could still hear Mary's shrill voice as she told Mum in no uncertain terms what she would like to do to that hateful man and how dare he make all that commotion on their doorstep.

"Look, Shela," pleaded Johnny softly as he knelt in front of her and looked up into her face in the old, endearing way she remembered so well from their first days together. "Come back to Queen Street with me. I've given up the house and the furniture's paid for up

111

to date. Gran says you can come back there to live for now."

Christopher, now just two years old, climbed on to his father's knee. The pleading continued and Shela tried to harden her heart against this weak man who had caused her and his children so much misery already in their young lives.

"I'm working regularly now," Johnny continued hastily. Shela turned her head away from those brown eyes so like her younger son's. "I'm driving cabs part time and working for Jimmy Fitzpatrick during the week in the ice-cream factory. By Easter I can take over one of the new vans and make good money. He has just taken over the Lyons Ice-Cream franchise in Bedford."

Still Shela did not answer as he continued to plead, and she wondered why and how this sudden concern for his family had come about. There must be a reason for it, her mind told her, even as her heart tried to persuade her to give him another chance. Deborah cried in the old Swan pram by the big bay window and Johnny went over to her to pop the rubber dummy back in her tiny mouth. Perhaps he really has changed, she thought frantically. She tried to still her racing mind into some semblance of order. And tried to imagine what it would mean to live back at Queen Street again.

"The old man's retired and Gran only works three mornings a week now. And," he continued, with a confident smile as he saw that she was wavering, "I give them regular money and they want to see the children again. Come back, Shela. I've really changed, you'll see."

Shela knew that the decision she was about to make would affect not only herself and her children. If she gave way to her husband's pleadings, the animosity between herself and her sisters would surely dissipate in time and her sick father would find peace again in his old chair by the kitchen fire. Her mother, she knew, would never pressurise this daughter in need to leave the safe sanctuary she had found in the old family home. And what of the old people in Queen Street? Was it fair to have a young family thrust upon them again at their age? Here, in this big house, where only three of her mother's large family remained, she had hoped to make a new start for her own little ones. But she also knew that the present repeated recriminations from her sisters and the recent, dreaded coldness from her much loved father weighed heavily on her conscience.

"What happens during the winter months, Johnny?" she asked quietly as he picked up Barry and settled him on his knee. That's the first time I've ever seen him bother to do that, she realised. "You'll earn nothing from ice-cream sales then!" Shela spoke sharply to the kneeling figure before her, confident in the knowledge that he did not dare to show any violence in her parents' home.

"I can do full-time taxi work," he answered quickly. "I got my driving licence last month and Jim Spencer has offered me work on his cabs. If I can save enough money by next winter I will apply for my own borough taxi plate and drive for myself. And with three children we will have enough points to qualify for another council house very quickly."

Shela looked around her mother's comfortable sitting room and tried not to think of the cramped and drab conditions to which he was begging her to return. She knew that her proper place was with her husband and that, as her father regularly reminded her, children should have their own father to support them. But her heart ached as she made the hard decision to go back to that other, tiny house she thought was left behind when the move to the brand new one was made just over a year ago. And still she had to take her husband on good faith and again rely on his varying moods and far from certain earnings to pay for their keep.

"Go straight down to the Housing Department," advised her worried mother. Shela nodded and packed the last of the children's clothes into the battered, old suitcase, which, she reflected sadly, had been used for her honeymoon just over three years ago. "With your three so young, they are bound to find you another house quickly."

It was only as she stood before the little window in the dark council housing office in the town hall in St. Paul's Square, that Shela learned the devastating truth. Her husband had vacated the house in Barton Road leaving behind him arrears of six months' rent and rates.

"I cannot put you back on the waiting list until these arrears are paid off, I'm afraid, Mrs Warren."

The middle-aged man behind the counter looked sympathetically at the pale, thin-faced young mother and asked her where she was now living.

"I'll see that the Housing Officer comes to visit you as soon as possible," the man continued, "but I can't hold out any hopes until this debt is cleared. I'm sorry."

Christopher began to cry and pulled at her hand, while Shela bent down to comfort him, almost in tears herself. It was to be three, long years before Bedford Town Council offered housing accommodation to her family again.

CHAPTER
EIGHT

Queen Street and Kind Neighbours

Shela never forgot the kindness shown to her by the neighbours when she returned to the tiny, two up, two down, terraced house in Queen Street. When the two boys were safely tucked up in the newly acquired, second-hand iron bunk bed and Deborah slept quietly in the old, wicker clothes basket on the floor beside them, she often stood in the narrow back garden to talk to elderly Mrs Burden at number twenty-five or the Cassels at number twenty-one. Mrs Burden regularly gave her sweets for the children, and the childless couple on the other side offered cast-off clothing from their own relatives' families.

In time, Shela was invited in to both neighbours' houses for tea and a friendly chat and always, as she looked around their cosy, well-maintained homes, she was made even more aware that Granny and Grandpa Warner's home must once have been just like theirs. Small but comfortable and well decorated, with modern furniture and kitchen conveniences. Why, then, had number twenty-three become this drab, dark place with everything fifty years out of date and paintwork to match?

"Now don't go having any more babies, my dear," advised both neighbours in turn. "The doctor can help you there. Go to see her before it's too late."

Shela now relied on the contraceptive device supplied without question by Doctor Finch in her surgery in Wendover Drive. She hated the thing. At best, it was inconvenient and, at worst, nastily smelly.

"Look at it!" she exclaimed one afternoon to her mother, soon after the move back to Queen Street. "It's horrible!"

"Better than unwanted children, Shela," her mother replied calmly and then told her astonished daughter about her own reliance on the Dutch Cap after Beryl was born.

"It works, my dear. Just don't take any chances," she advised. Shela nodded and kissed her ailing father goodbye before leaving the house for the long trek back home.

"Goodbye, She-She," he called and Shela smiled to herself at the long ago, affectionate name he had called her when she was little. In illness, her father had mellowed and the recent animosity between them had now given way to a few kind words and anxious enquiries about her new situation.

On quiet evenings in the little house, when Johnny was out working on the cabs or with his friends, his grandparents sat with Shela playing cards or recalling the young years of their only child, Grace, who had died so tragically when she was only twenty-nine years of age. And Shela began to understand what the work-hardened, older woman had endured while she struggled to bring up the wayward first child of her beloved daughter.

On the wall above the table in the tiny dining-room, the picture of Grace, a dark-haired, narrow-faced girl, looked down on everything that went on below and her eyes seemed to follow Shela as she moved around in her old home. On Sunday afternoons, Shela sometimes accompanied Grandpa on his regular visits to his only child's grave in the old cemetery at the top end of Foster Hill Road.

On the way, she stopped to let the children play on the swings in Bedford Park or took them across to the peacock house near the big lake, where peacocks she remembered from her own childhood still strutted and displayed to their small, insignificant hens. The regularly scrubbed, marble headstone on Grace's grave, and the pretty border of blue lobelia and white alyssum surrounding a small rose bush, had become a shrine to the daughter Grandpa had lost. And often Shela thought uneasily that there might be something unhealthy in the amount of time the old man spent there. Then wondered why her husband never visited his mother's grave and wished she had known Grace. For things might have been so different for all of them in that sad house in Queen Street.

"The trouble is," remarked Johnny's younger sister, Jean, when she met her sister-in-law outside Woolworths in Midland Road, "Gran spoiled him something rotten. He never wanted for anything. They even paid his school fees for the Bedford Boys Modern School after he kicked up a fuss when my other brother, Roy, won a scholarship there. Johnny had failed his the year before, but he was not going to allow any of the others in the family to have something better than him. And this," she added bitterly, "is how he repays his grandparents." Then she added, "I don't expect he will change now, Shela. So I wish you the best of luck. You'll need it!"

On Friday evenings, with her husband out of the house again and no money in her purse to buy food the next day, Grandpa Warner bought fish and chips home from Tucker's Fried Fish Shop in Tavistock Street for the three of them. The old man knew that his grandson gave hardly any money to his own wife or his grandmother for the family's keep and that Shela was often desperate for the money to buy National Dried Milk for the baby from Herbert and Herbert's, the big chemist on the corner of Adelaide Square.

Although the worst violence of the earlier days had subsided and Johnny worked intermittently on the cabs or ice-cream vans, Shela knew that he was still wasting money on gambling and in the snooker hall above Burtons in Silver Street. The money, she thought bitterly, that should have been for his family and saved towards paying off the rent and rates debts from the council house. She had not been back in Queen Street for many days when she found out the real reason for Johnny's determination to get his family back there.

"He was boasting that he could get you to come back at any time," explained Johnny's old school friend, Hugh "Knocker" Brice. "I heard him place a large bet with his mates that he could just walk in at any time and persuade you to return," he continued, one time when Shela stood with her children outside Hugh's mother's house just round the corner in Albert Street. "And he won, didn't he? One thing is for sure. He's no friend of mine, after that!"

For many weeks, Shela tried to think of ways to earn money and it was only when Grandpa came up with the idea of a job at the offices of W. H. Allen, the big engineering firm where he had worked for over fifty years, that she thought she had found the solution.

"There's a cleaning job going there," Grandpa told her one Friday evening as he carefully shared out the fish-and-chip supper. "Some of the women have been there for years and I know them all well. You'll soon learn the ropes."

A cleaning job! Was she to be reduced to that? The girl, who since childhood had harboured ambitions to become a teacher. An office cleaner! As she lay in bed that night, waiting for sleep to come, Shela faced up to herself and her life. She knew she could take the job offered and earn enough money for food for herself and the children. It was not fair or right that the old couple should pay for their grandson's family's keep out of their pensions and Gran's meagre earnings from her own cleaning job at the big house in Park Avenue. Before she slept, Shela made up her mind to give it a try. She also made up her mind that her parents must never know what she was doing. Her mother would be horrified and her father, in his present poor state of health, was now too frail to be given any more stress.

On Monday morning she left the house at five-thirty, leaving her children and husband still asleep. Then cycled quickly through dark, quiet streets to reach the big, engineering works just over the railway bridge in Queens Park.

"You can borrow my bike as long as you are back for eight o'clock," Mrs Cassels told her over the fence when she discussed the new job with her kindly neighbour. "But is there nothing else you can do? Surely not cleaning work, Shela! And such an early start, too." Then she added quickly, when the younger woman's face flushed painfully, "Good luck. I hope all goes well."

At six o'clock on that cold December morning in 1955, Shela stood outside the men's toilets gazing down at a heavy, galvanised iron bucket. Floating in the hot water, a bar of strong, yellow soap gazed back at her as she slowly knelt on a rubber mat to lower a big floor cloth and long scrubbing brush down into its soda-harsh depths.

"Put your back into it, gel!"

The rough voice came to her from the next cubicle. The harsh soap stung her hands and beads of perspiration dripped from her face into the bucket beside her.

"We'll never get finished at this rate!"

Six toilet cubicles each. Six urinals each. The reception office and entrance lobby made filthy each day by office staff arriving for their jobs in the main office behind them. And all of this to be scrubbed every day for two pounds, nineteen shillings and sixpence a week.

"'Ere, come on gel!" the loud voice came again. "You'll still be 'ere when the toffs come in. I'll finish up 'ere for yer. Take yer bucket and empty it down the drain. I'll be finished sooner without you 'indering me!"

The big, rough woman, with hands to match, grinned up at the girl beside her and splashed dirty water on the last square of floorboards. When she had finished, Shela watched, fascinated, while her workmate expertly rolled a cigarette between fingers thickened and coarsened by years of hard work, then took a long drag on it before she waved goodbye.

"See you tomorrow. Don't be late." Then, more gently, "You'll get used to it, gel. Like I did. No 'usband, yer see. Only kids. Six of 'em at the last count. 'Bye."

The cleaning job at W. H. Allen's lasted until mid-summer 1956 and Shela made new and unexpected friends as the rough women helped her through the hated two hours' work every day from Monday to Saturday. But in August of that year Deborah was already showing signs of the asthma that was to trouble her all through her childhood and teenage years.

"Look at this child," exclaimed Doctor Finch one day, when her worried mother took her youngest child in to the old doctor's surgery in Wendover Drive.

The shrewd, older woman knew all the circumstances of Shela's life and always tried to offer advice when it was so desperately needed.

"She has a very swollen abdomen and her arms and legs are like matchsticks. Is she eating properly?"

The questions continued, and Shela tried to tell the doctor how she found it so difficult to cope with her little girl who cried constantly with stomach ache and was always on the little, enamelled potty which she filled each time with evil-smelling, pale yellow stools.

"Bring me a sample in tomorrow, mother," Doctor Finch stated firmly. "I'll get it tested. Then we'll know what treatment she needs."

By the end of the week, the diagnosis was through and Shela was gently told that the little girl was suffering from coeliac disease.

"She is allergic to the wheat-germ in flour," the doctor advised. "You must make special bread for her and don't let her have biscuits or custard. Here," the doctor continued, busily writing out a long prescription. "Take this to the outpatient clinic at Bedford South Wing Hospital. They will give you a seven-pound tin of gluten-free flour. You can get free, regular supplies from there from now on."

By Christmas of that year Christopher was four and Barry was three and the song sung repeatedly by Doris Day on the old radio, "Whatever Will Be Will Be," brought a distracted frown to Shela's face as her youngest child deteriorated rapidly.

"I'm worried to death about her, Mum," she wept, while her mother looked with concern at the child's thin arms and legs, the grossly swollen stomach and the peaky, little face beneath soft, fair hair.

"She looks like one of those starving babies in Africa," exclaimed Beryl, kneeling down before Shela's little girl. "Her breath smells acidic, too. That's a sure sign that something is wrong."

"Leave her here for a couple of weeks," her mother suggested, and the child started to wheeze again while Shela applied the asthma spray, which sometimes helped.

The two weeks lengthened into two months, then three and by the spring of 1957 the constant love and care given to this granddaughter who had such a poor start in life was beginning to take effect. Deborah was now almost back to normal and the child's arms and legs were beginning to lose that awful, stick-like appearance that had so shocked her grandparents. Young Robert, an unexpected addition to the Winch family when his mother was forty-five years old, was now almost nine and quite used to the comings and goings of his older sisters' children when their mothers fell on hard times.

"This place is getting more like a hostel for the homeless every day," commented Mary sharply one day, looking in disapproval at one of Joaney's youngsters left with her mother for the weekend.

Shela usually managed to ignore these cutting remarks but, on days like these when everything seemed so hopeless and she longed to take her little girl home, it was hard not to resent the comfort and security her younger sisters took for granted in their ordered lives. Mary was now engaged to a hard-working and kind young man and due to marry later that year. Beryl, meanwhile, was occupied with setting up her own hairdressing business in small premises in

Foster Hill Road a few streets away from Shela's home in Queen Street.

"Come in to get your hair done," said Beryl, when Shela visited the new shop soon after it opened. "But I can't do much about those nails!" she added, taking her older sister's hands and looking in dismay at the nails bitten down to the quick.

Deborah had now been staying with her grandmother for just over four months and Shela was so thankful that her little girl was recovering so well that she at first failed to notice when the child started to call her grandmother, "Mummy". It was only when she began to call Shela by her first name that she realised the time had come to take her daughter back home to the cramped little rooms in Queen Street. The routine of gluten-free bread and hard biscuits baked in the old gas cooker in the lean-to kitchen became a daily nightmare and often her mother baked extra for her to collect on Shela's still frequent visits to her old home.

On most mornings in the little house Shela listened to "Housewives' Choice" or "Music While You Work" on the B.B.C. Home Service, and, when the news of Grace Kelly's fairytale marriage to Prince Rainier of Monaco was broadcast, thought longingly of that other, happy marriage, and tried to keep the children amused and quiet while their father slept the morning away in the tiny bedroom above. And Grandpa Warner played marbles with the children and made cat's cradles from old bits of string for the boys. Deborah always hid behind her mother in fear of the cobbler's hobbling foot when the old man mended their shoes with bits of worn out, rubber tyres. The move back to Queen Street, undertaken the previous year with such a tenuous hope that life would improve, now seemed to the distraught girl to be a very ill-judged one. But she had no choice, she tried to reason with herself as the days dragged by and she could see no end to the situation in the little house.

On a cold evening in November 1956, when the Suez crisis was coming to a head, Shela stood outside the entrance to the North End Working Men's Club in Russell Street, waiting for someone to take a message in to the secretary, Mr Simmons.

"I was told that you might know of a small house to let in Boswell Place," she told the kind man who came to the door to speak to her.

"I'm sorry, my dear," the man replied, while Shela hugged her arms close to her body for warmth. "Those properties are empty but they are all condemned and soon to be pulled down. Why don't you try the Housing Department at the Town Hall? They can probably help you."

His words echoed in Shela's head all the way home, trying to stop the tears, for she knew his suggestion was hopeless. The arrears of rent were no nearer being paid than they had been when she moved back to Queen Street. But how could she have done otherwise? Torn between concern for her parents and the desperate position of her little family in that other, alien place where they now lived.

Grandpa and Granny Warner and Shela and the children were fast asleep one night in late April when

Johnny arrived home in the small hours in one of his foulest moods to rouse the old couple from their bed demanding money. Shela listened in horror as he informed them that he had lost heavily at a poker game that had been going on all day behind one of the Greek restaurants in Midland Road.

"I owe them money," he shouted, waking the children, who started to cry, and Shela hid behind the bedroom door in fear of the violence that she knew was coming.

"I've got until five o'clock to get back to the game. Otherwise they will be after me. I need money. And I need it now!" he yelled at the old man. Mr Cassells, next door, banged on the wall and Shela ushered the frightened children down the narrow stairs and out into the dark garden.

"Bring them in here, my dear," whispered old Mrs Burden on the other side of the fence. "They'll be alright with me for a while."

Inside number twenty-three the shouting continued and Grandpa tried to stand up to his bullying grandson. When Gran cried out in pain as her arm was twisted viciously behind her back and the old man punched twice in the face, the old couple gave in and watched, trembling, as every penny in the house, including the fifteen shillings family allowance that Shela had collected that morning from the post-office, was stuffed into Johnny's Humphrey Bogart style mac pocket. The mac that she had bought for him only the week before from a Littlewoods catalogue and still owed money on; the mac that a week later he would lose to one of his friends in yet another poker game.

"I'll win it all back, you'll see," Johnny snarled as Shela tried to comfort the old woman and Grandpa called him every name under the sun.

The front door slammed behind him, and Shela ran into the garden to next door to bring the children back to their beds. It was almost four o'clock and the children were asleep again as Shela dressed quickly and went downstairs to where the old couple were still sitting, too upset to go back to bed.

"Please listen out for the children," she asked Gran. "I'm going to the police," she added quietly. "He's not getting away with it this time."

Grandpa tried to stop her and Gran began to make excuses for her wayward grandson, but an unexpected strength born of great anger and overwhelming despair drove Shela out into the dark night and soon she was talking agitatedly to a young police constable on duty in The Broadway, just a few hundred yards away from the house. The children were still sleeping upstairs when later the policeman questioned Shela and the old couple in the tiny front room.

"It's nothing, officer," replied Gran as the constable took notes. "Just a row between a man and his wife. That's all."

Grandpa hung his head and said nothing. Shela pointed out the bruises on his wife's arm and signs of recent bruising round her old eyes.

"See here! Look at me, officer," she protested as Johnny's stubborn and proud grandparents refused to admit to any knowledge of his bullying behaviour towards them.

Then she pulled back her sleeve to show the marks of her own ill treatment, while the policeman looked thoughtfully around the little group before him.

"It seems to me that there is a lot of mistaken loyalty going on here," he commented, closing his notebook and replacing it in his pocket. "But we know the young man in question. He's one of the local lads about town, although I didn't realise he had a wife and kids to support. We keep a close eye on his comings and goings and any involvement in those illegal poker games is well recorded. However," he paused, looking keenly at Gran and Grandpa Warner as he prepared to leave, "if you are not making an official complaint we will leave it at that."

Then, looking directly at Shela who stood in disbelief on the doorstep, he added, "As for you, young lady, we must have witnesses to any assault between man and wife. Just tell that husband of yours to watch his step in the future and that I, personally, will be watching him."

A very cocky young man tried to laugh off the events of the night before, when he finally came home at breakfast time to throw a bundle of notes on the table.

"There you are!" he laughed, handing round a few notes from the bundle, "I told you I'd bring it back. Here, Granddad, buy yourself some extra tobacco and we'll all have a good dinner tonight."

An angry scowl, that turned the handsome face into something very ugly, was the only response to Shela's calm statement that, if he ever laid hands on his grandparents or herself again, she would go back to the police and lay charges of assault against him.

"And they will listen next time," she added. Behind him Gran shook her head in warning and Grandpa left the house for his usual hiding-place in the outhouse.

For a time the warning seemed to have taken effect. Johnny's behaviour moderated, and the money situation eased. Work was obtained on the ice-cream vans once more. But all this changed one day in early April, when Shela heard the distressing news that her father was in hospital and not expected to live more than a few days. Since the incident of the police visit, Gran had hardly spoken a word to her grandson's young wife. To the old lady, keeping up appearances meant far more than seeing justice done, whatever the consequences might be, and Shela and the two youngest children increasingly suffered from this misguided attitude. Another, and to Shela a far more disturbing, effect on her family was Gran's increasing display of favouritism towards the older boy. Harsh words were exchanged between the two women, because the boy was given special treats, while the younger children looked on in tears, and Christopher learned to run to the old lady when his mother attempted to discipline him.

"That child will end up just like his father if this goes on much longer."

Shela was visiting her mother yet again after another week of silent hostility from Granny Warner had almost driven her to distraction. With Dad now so critically ill, Shela was reluctant to give her mother any more worry.

But the recent disturbing memory of the night she stood weeping silently on the edge of the dark river by The Embankment while her children slept in their tiny bedroom on the other side of the town, now made her desperate. That late night walk around the familiar streets of her childhood and across Russell Park, where so many school holidays had been spent in happy ignorance of what was to come, comforted the distraught girl. The raised flower bed opposite Russell Park Café depicting the Bedford coat of arms and the shallow steps of the old Suspension Bridge from which she cheered on the rowing eights gliding beneath on successive Regatta Days, all reminded Shela of happier times.

At midnight she sat on the worn bench opposite the big houses facing the river and thought of the countless Sundays of the past when her parents and Gang-Gang brought the whole family there to listen to the Bedford Town Silver Band, playing on the moored raft pushed out into the centre of the Great Ouse. Sometimes on one of those distant, summer Sundays, the Winch family took a trip aboard one of the canopied pleasure boats plying between the Town Bridge and the old, rustic Newnham Bridge, a mile or so down river. When her brother John was old enough, he and his friends regularly hired a canoe from Mr Bryant's boatyard near The Picturedrome cinema to paddle upstream to Honey Hill Meadows in Queens Park and return just before the two hours' hire ran out. The younger children were content to spend Saturday afternoons on Longholme Boating Lake, paddling round the island in its centre in the heavy, wooden paddle boats hired out by the town council from the small, square tea kiosk next to the Bedford Rowing Club sheds. The tiers of graceful rowing boats on display by the river's edge and the practised discipline of the rowing crews as they performed their pre-launch routines, fascinated the youngsters while they waited for their little paddle boats to be called in by number from the far end of the lake.

From where she sat, Shela knew that in daylight she would be able to see the huge stone plinth near Russell Park Café, on which had once stood a long-barrelled gun dating from The Great War. On the opposite side of the road was another, smaller plinth once bearing a squat, Crimean War cannon. And Shela remembered the war games her brothers and hundreds of other Bedford youngsters played on those symbols of violence before the guns were taken for scrap iron during the last conflict.

Shela shivered, and a chilly wind stirred across the dark green water, interrupting her comforting thoughts of the past. Then she turned slowly away from the river's beckoning depths and began the long walk back to Queen Street and her children. She never told anyone about that dark hour beside the river, or how she found the strength to resist the temptation to bring her despair to an end.

"Granny Warner spoiled Johnny from babyhood," Shela agonised. "And see what's happened! She was good to me at first but now she just wants Christopher.

The others don't count! I must get away from there, Mum. I must!"

And her mother tried her best to comfort her weeping daughter as Deborah ran in from the garden, with her little chest wheezing from the asthma which now seemed to trouble her every day. On the following Wednesday evening, Shela met her mother at the chest ward at Bedford North Wing Hospital, where her father lay struggling for breath through the oxygen mask that made his gaunt face look like that of a stranger. Shela bent to kiss him goodbye, and he squeezed her hand but was too breathless to speak the words she longed to hear.

The next day, Win Hutchins from the shop across the road came over to tell Shela that her father had died early that morning and would she get in touch with her mother as soon as possible. The enormity of what had happened on that cold day in late April 1959 seemed to drive all other worries from her mind and Shela asked Gran to care for the children so that she could attend her father's funeral. When she returned, distressed and grief-stricken over the loss of her beloved dad, she was surprised to find that the old lady had tea ready and was doling out peaches and cream to all three children. The long silence was over, and she began to speak normally to their mother once again.

"Dear old pals, jolly old pals!" jeered Johnny that evening as he brushed his thick, dark hair before the front room mirror. And Shela wished with all her heart that things would change and that the old couple could be left in peace to live with the memories of their daughter in that small house where so much tragedy had overwhelmed them.

Six weeks after Dad died, a letter arrived from the Housing Department stating that a Housing Inspector would call shortly to assess the Warren family's accommodation needs. Johnny made sure that he was not at home to face the elderly man who stood in the doorway looking slowly round the tiny bedroom at the top of the spiral staircase.

"Do you all sleep in here?" he asked incredulously, looking at the bunk bed where all three children now slept and the double mattress on the floor, where it had been placed after the old bedstead collapsed the year before. Across one wall, a thick string, supporting a row of children's garments, hung suspended from nails above a fly blown mirror and a small chest of drawers, which held Shela's few belongings. The man looked closely at the great patches of damp on the wall opposite the door and the green mould growing in the corners of the crumbling window-frame and made notes on a long form attached to his clip-board.

"How long have you lived like this?" he asked. Then listened attentively to Shela's dismal story of her return to the little house and how she had tried and failed to get on to the housing list again some three years previously. The man, clearly shocked at the cramped and squalid conditions, assured Shela that a housing offer would be made by the end of the month.

"I understand that those rent arrears were fully paid up last week by a relative," he stated, as Shela followed him down the narrow stairs and tried to tell him about

Deborah's asthma and the coeliac condition that disturbed her little girl's sleep in the tiny room above.

"Don't worry, Mrs Warren," assured the man later on the doorstep. "You will have the keys to a new home quite soon and then I hope your girl's health will improve."

"Thank God for that!" exclaimed Joaney, when her older sister called in to see her with the good news at her own small council house in Goldington. "You will probably get a house on this estate," she continued. "They are allocating all those beyond Elliot Crescent this year."

Shela's children went out into the small patch of garden to play with their cousins, and she added slowly, "Did you know that the last thing Dad asked before he died was for Mum to pay off your outstanding rent arrears on the house in Barton Road?"

"It was his last wish, Shela," her mother confirmed, when she heard the news of the Housing Inspector's visit. "You father's life insurance money left me enough to do that for him. It was what he wanted more than anything."

And Shela wept as she remembered the faint squeeze of her hand as her father lay dying in the hospital bed, unable to speak but doing his best for his She-She at the very end.

CHAPTER
NINE

Another Start

The longed-for keys to a three-bedroom, terrace house in Fieldside, Goldington, were handed over to Johnny in June of that year.

"I just wish it could be in your name, Shela," commented Mum, busily making up curtains for her daughter from old ones recently discarded by one of her dressmaking customers. "Then that hopeless man of yours could be left behind."

Shela sighed. She was standing in her new living room, sparsely furnished with second-hand items donated by family and friends and remembering the lovely, new furniture of the previous council house. Then shook her head at her own foolishness, when she also remembered the hire-purchase debt, which was never paid. She was not told what had happened to that furniture but suspected that it had been sold off cheaply to pay for Johnny's gambling habit. Now, here she was, starting all over again and hoping with all the strength and optimism she could muster that things could only get better from now on.

Johnny still worked only intermittently and the money he handed over to her each week barely covered the family's needs. But with the two boys now at Goldington Green Junior School and Deborah due to start there in September, Shela had hopes of finding work on the small industrial estate just down the road from the new house.

"We are looking for office staff that can start as soon as possible, Mrs Warren," stated the young manager of Sanger's Wholesale Chemists, at her interview one morning in late August. "Have you made arrangements for your children in the school holidays? You must understand that we are offering a full-time position only."

Hugh's wife, who now lived just a few doors away, decided not to accept the offer, but Shela jumped at the chance to earn regular wages and she had already arranged for either Joycey or Joaney to look after the children during the school holidays.

"Wouldn't a part-time job be better, Shela?" queried Joycey. "Then you could be home for the children when they get in from school."

But Shela knew that she needed a full week's wages to make ends meet for her family, for she could never rely on the handouts from Johnny who sometimes gave her no money at all.

"I can't start until September, when my youngest goes to school," she explained to Mr Lushington in the office block attached to the big warehouse. "But then I'll be free to start full-time," she explained confidently, looking round the bright, new general office and exchanging smiles with other young women waiting to be interviewed.

"Right," the manager stated briskly. "If that's all sorted out, you can start on September the fifth. The wage is seven pounds a week. Nine to five, Monday to Friday, with one hour for lunch."

The summer of 1959 drew to a close and with it the work on the ice-cream vans. Johnny again began to stay out all night on casual driving jobs and slept all day when Shela was at work. Sometimes he did not come home for several days or nights and Shela knew he would be sleeping at his grandparents' house or out on the town, spending any money he earned from taxi work. When she herself started work, earning a regular wage, she grew accustomed to not relying on any money at all from her husband and soon began to look on him as a casual visitor who contributed little or nothing to the meagre household budget.

Early in the New Year of 1960, when Deborah had been at school for just one term, her condition suddenly worsened. The boys were already on their way to school, where they were now staying for school dinner, but their little sister had not yet woken up. All through the previous night Deborah had struggled with violent chest pains, which had kept the asthma spray in constant use. Now, utterly exhausted, she was deeply asleep and Shela was trying to rouse her. As she looked down at the child's peaky, white face and watched her poor little chest heaving away in the battle to breathe, Shela knew that something was terribly wrong. Suddenly, the harsh breathing stopped and she panicked.

"Oh my God! She's gone!" she screamed and rushed down the uncarpeted stairs to the woman next door, who tried to reassure the distraught girl that her child was only sleeping and urged her to ring for the doctor.

"I'll stay with her until you get back from the phone box," she called after Shela, now running down the road to her sister's home in Elliott Crescent.

"Quick," she gasped as Joaney opened the door to her frantic banging. "It's Deborah. I can't wake her up!"

"Go back with her, Joaney," exclaimed their shocked mother, who had just arrived for a visit. "I'll phone the doctor. Hurry now. Perhaps you can do something!"

The two sisters turned and raced as fast as they could back to Fieldside, where the worried neighbour was still sitting beside Deborah's bed talking to the little girl, now awake and staring at everyone with her big, blue eyes wide with astonishment. Half an hour later, Doctor Finch arrived to set up an oxygen cylinder and a small mask for the child and promised to come back later with a long-spouted asthma kettle, which Shela was to keep boiling when her daughter had difficulty breathing.

"But you must get some heat in this room, mother," Shela was told as the doctor looked round at the bare floorboards and the empty fire grate. "A coal fire is best. Not paraffin. That's not good for chest complaints."

Shela looked hopelessly into her empty purse and knew she could never afford to buy coal. And the only heat in the house came from the paraffin heater in the living room. That evening, Beryl arrived with three big sacks of coal and three bundles of bedding for the children's beds, after her worried mother related the drama of that morning to her shocked and angry younger daughter.

"Where is he, then?" she demanded sharply, when the fire in Deborah's cold bedroom was finally lit and the new eiderdown pulled up under the child's chin. "Where's that husband of yours? I'd just like to get my hands on him — the useless pig of a man!"

Two days later, Doctor Finch arrived with a startling proposal for Shela to consider by the weekend.

"I have made enquiries about a place for your daughter in a residential hospital school, where she can benefit from nursing care and keep up with her education," the old doctor stated calmly. Shela's heart raced and wild thoughts about children's homes and her child being taken into care whirled round and round in her head.

"A few weeks in there will set her on her feet again, mother. And you will be able to go back to your job. I know you need the money, my dear."

"It's for the best, Shela," comforted her mother as they waited for the ambulance to arrive for the journey to Winifred House at Arkley near Barnet in Hertfordshire. But neither of them could realise, on that cold morning in January 1960, that the big, rambling hospital was to become her little daughter's home for the next five years.

With the two boys now well settled in at Goldington Green School and Shela working full time at Sanger's, the money situation was eased and she was able to visit her daughter twice a month. Every second Sunday morning, with the two boys cared for at Joycey's house, Shela caught the yellow Birch Bros. coach on St. Peters Green for the hour-long journey to Barnet. From there, a local bus took her almost to the gates of Winifred House, where she knew Deborah would be waiting anxiously for her mother's arrival.

Over the months since coming to this large, echoing building, which had formerly been a children's home, the long dormitory where the child slept with five others with varying degrees of disability had become Deborah's home. And Shela tried to be cheerful when she looked at the small, hospital bed and listened to the kind words of the young nurse telling her that her little daughter's health was improving but she needed constant care in the future. The care that Shela could not give this youngest child who had had such a difficult start in life and now looked up at her mother with those big, blue eyes filling with tears every time she kissed her goodbye. The sight of that small, white face, peering through the fence at her mother waiting for the local bus, was to haunt Shela for many years. And it was to be half a life-time before she finally forgave either herself or Deborah's father for those lost years of her beloved daughter's life.

Shela had always been puzzled as to why her husband was unable to sign on at the Labour Exchange for benefit during his frequent spells of unemployment. It was Beryl who came up with the answer.

"He's probably invisible, Shela," she explained one day. The sisters sat together in their mother's comfortable living room. "If he has been self-employed or done casual work since he left school, the authorities will have no record of any payments towards National Health Insurance or Unemployment Benefit Insurance, because he's never made any. That also means he pays no Income Tax," she added coldly. "What a stupid man you married. And a selfish one," she continued as Shela listened in astonishment to her sister's words.

She knew Beryl must be right, for her sister was now a business woman and well versed in all the intricacies of government forms and obligations to her employees.

"And that leaves you and the children completely unprotected by any kind of insurance."

The new house, still only barely furnished with neighbours' cast-offs and her mother's old cooker, was one in a newly built row on the edge of Goldington Council Estate. The only shop was the Co-operative Grocery Stores in Elliott Crescent, where everyone bought their weekly groceries and customers could run up a weekly bill to be paid off on Fridays before any more purchases were allowed "on the tick". This system was a godsend to Shela, who shopped there regularly for the family's small needs. With her regular wages and family allowance, she could just manage to pay the rent, save a few shillings for the electric meter and have enough left over for food. It was a tight squeeze and without the regular loan of ten shillings every Thursday afternoon from a friend in the office, Shela knew she would never have managed.

Often, very early on Thursday mornings, she made the long trek along Queens Drive to her older sister's house in Overdale on the adjoining estate of Putnoe, to beg for a shilling for the electric meter so the children could have a hot drink before setting out for school. Joycey always sent her back with the shilling and a small parcel of bread and any other left-overs from her own family of four growing boys. She also had harsh things to say about her sister's wayward husband and constantly advised that Shela would be better off without him.

"Phil Starkey tells me that you go in to work with no breakfast inside you, Shela," accused Joycey early one Thursday morning. Shela put the shilling in her purse and hastily finished the slice of toast her sister always made her eat before leaving the house.

"Sometimes I do," she admitted. "When there's not enough for all of us. But Phil often passes me a cheese roll from the canteen on the way into the office. She's a good sort."

Mrs Starkey, who had been one of Joycey's neighbours when she lived in Hereford Road, now lived locally and worked in Sanger's canteen, where she kept an eye on her old friend's sister.

"We all know you are having a hard time of it, Shela," she often said as she passed the girl a cheese roll or a few biscuits early each morning. And in later years, Shela remembered with affection the kind-hearted people at the firm who tried to help with small offerings of sweets for the boys or cast-off clothes for their hard-pressed mother. Sometimes, her friend Peggy

Quinn stopped on her way home to buy bread and a tin of beans for Shela from the Co-op shop. Often there would be a freshly baked Irish soda loaf left quietly on Shela's desk as she went to her own to begin the day's work.

When the two boys were in bed and the little house was tidy, with school clothes laid out neatly, ready for the next day, Shela sat quietly with her secret exercise books. There were now more than a dozen of them, gradually filled over the years since her days behind the counter at Castle Hill Café and added to on quiet evenings when she sat alone in the house.

Short stories. Impossible romances. Love poems. Poems of anguish and betrayal. Dark, gothic pieces depicting nightmare situations beyond her control. And in contrast, word portraits of her children as they grew from babyhood into two sturdy young boys and the delicate little girl now missing from the small family circle.

Shela thought long and often of the constant advice given by her family to separate from her husband. She knew that everything they said about him was true, but during those early years, when her children were so young, the thought of becoming one of the increasing number of single mothers on the estate where she lived, weighed heavily on her mind. At weekends now, she tried to keep the boys quiet while Johnny lay in bed until mid-afternoon and often stood at the window watching other couples with their children walk past on their way to town or on a day's outing. Gradually, an unfamiliar and frightening feeling began to take shape in her mind. It was unrecognisable at first but, as it grew, Shela at last acknowledged that any lingering affecton she had for the boy she had married, had turned to bitter resentment.

"I am no better off than those women whose husbands have deserted them." She spoke the words aloud, and looked around the humble home she had tried so desperately to keep together. "And at least they have the law on their side."

Shela knew that the option of applying for help from the state meant a visit to The National Assistance Office in the ugly, grey building in Ashburnham Road. She also knew that several women on the estate made regular, weekly visits there to beg for money.

"Go on, Shela!" urged Joaney. "That man of yours gives you next to nothing. Ask for help, for God's sake! That's what we pay our taxes for!"

Not my husband, Shela thought bleakly as she made her one and only trip to the hated office on the other side of Bedford. And this is the result. Begging for money for food. The humiliation of standing in line before a small window and being quizzed in public by a tired, overworked man who had encountered her circumstances many times before, only served to make her determined never to do it again.

"We can allow you one pound, Mrs Warren," the grey-haired clerk told her. Shela tried to make herself invisible to the queue behind her. "Go home and buy some food for your children. And tell that man of yours to get regular work."

145

As she turned away from the window and the sympathetic shake of the head behind it, Shela knew that everyone in the room had heard the entire interview, and she hung her head in shame before hastily tucking the one pound note carefully away in her empty purse.

"Never mind, gel!" remarked a scruffy woman in the queue. "Come back next week," she continued. "You'll get another handout then. I'm a regular here and it always works better after the first time."

Shela had been in her job at Sanger's Wholesale Chemists office for nearly a year, when Joaney suddenly announced that she was moving off the estate to a larger house that her husband had bought at Barton Seagrave near Kettering.

"So I'm afraid that I can't help with the children any more," her younger sister stated, and Shela listened with a heavy heart to the news, for her sister, despite all her own family worries, always tried to lend a helping hand when she was able. And Shela knew that Joaney's position, with five children and a tight-fisted husband, was not much better than her own. Apart from the violence, that is, thank God, she thought. For when she asked for money or complained about his frequent disappearances, Johnny still lashed out with his fists, and Shela carried constant evidence of his bullying behaviour on her arms or shoulders where the bruising did not show.

"Why don't you ask the housing people for a transfer to this house?" Joaney queried. "I can leave you the curtains and some bits and pieces I won't need in my new home. You will be better off here, Shela. For a start, it's a lot warmer than that cold place of yours. And much nearer to the shop and your work."

By Easter, the Warren family was installed at eight Elliot Crescent, Goldington and Shela found a new friend in her neighbour, Doreen Boulton, who had a growing family of her own but was still willing to keep an eye on Christopher and Barry when their mother was at work in the school holidays. A few months later, Shela's older sister, Joycey, told her gently that her husband had secured a new job in Plymouth and they would be moving away in time for the new school year in September. And now Shela was really alone as she tried to cope with her job and find care for the boys and enough money for the bus fare to see Deborah twice a month. All through that winter, when a shortage of coal and constant electricity cuts meant a cold house, Shela walked twice a week to the garage in Queen's Drive for paraffin for the old paraffin heater in the living room.

On increasingly rare occasions, Johnny showed up with taxi-driver colleagues to play cards all night, and these kindly family men usually brought a fish and chip supper with them to share with Shela and the boys.

"Why don't you get your wife a washing machine?" they asked Johnny one evening as Shela stood at the big, white sink wringing out the sheets from the children's beds.

"I've already got one," was the reply. "She's standing over there doing the washing."

There was much laughter from the men at this cruel joke, but a week later a second hand twin tub washing machine was delivered, and the week after that Shela was as astonished as she had been at Barton Road to find new furniture in the small downstairs rooms and rugs on the bedroom floors above.

"I got it on hire purchase again from Jays Furniture Stores in St. Peters Street," Johnny announced. Shela looked with a strange mixture of apprehension and delight at the new things and the boys clamoured for their father to turn on the sixpence-in-the-slot, black and white television set in the corner of the room.

"That came from Radio Rentals in St. Loyes Street. No down payment. Just keep feeding it with sixpences," was all Johnny said. And then scowled at the worried expression on Shela's face, when she enquired who was to pay the instalments on the furniture. "Because I can't," she said shortly. "I earn barely enough to live on as it is."

Alone again in bed that night, Shela wondered if her wayward husband had been shamed into providing more for his family by the taxi drivers from the cab rank on St. Peters Green, who occasionally dropped off a Chinese take-away or fish and chips for young Warren's wife and kids over in Goldington. With both sisters now moved away and her mother planning her own move from the old family home in Castle Road to a newly built house at Bromham with Beryl and young Robert, Shela felt more isolated than ever. It was Beryl, now in business in a new hairdressing salon in Brickhill Drive, who occasionally called in to see her older sister to pass on clothing and small luxuries that she knew Shela could never afford.

Beryl was always in a great hurry when she hugged her sister goodbye, and it was to be many years before she told Shela the real reason for the rush to get out of the door and climb back into her Ford Prefect car.

"I didn't want to meet that man of yours," she confessed. "I would certainly have given him a piece of my mind if I had. And you were upset enough as it was."

As the cold months of winter gave way to an early spring and her boys played happily with the Boulton boys from next door, Shela tried to count her blessings. At nine and ten years old, these two were healthy. But her thoughts were constantly with her girl so far away from home and, although Deborah came back for short holidays, her continuing health problems meant that she always had to return to the hospital school so that her mother could go back to work.

"I thought that I would always be there, Mum," she confided in later life. Then, with a little sigh she added, "At first I thought I had been sent away because I had done something wrong. Later on, I thought I would grow up there and become a teacher in the school."

And the heartache continued as Deborah turned nine years old and still there seemed to be no end to her absence from family life in Goldington. On Saturdays, Shela often stood by her front window, now curtained with red and white striped curtains purchased from the Great Universal Stores catalogue, to watch as friends and neighbours walked past with their husbands and children. And she both envied those happy families and grieved for her own when they asked to do the same and she was unable to give them even that simple pleasure. On the black and white television set, which she could now afford to switch on for up to two hours each night, Shela began to tune in to the world again after so many years absorbed with her own problems.

On Mondays and Wednesdays, the antics in "Coronation Street" became a regular topic of conversation at tea break in the office canteen and, later in that year, the Great Train Robbery at Linslade near Leighton Buzzard in Bedfordshire made headline news, and the B.B.C. televised shows featuring Cliff Richard and a heavily eye-shadowed Dusty Springfield. One evening in November of that year, Shela's television stayed switched on for four hours as the appalling scenes of the assassination of President Kennedy were broadcast repeatedly on B.B.C. television and the image of Jackie Kennedy's bloodstained suit was everywhere in the next day's newspapers.

Once every month, the Radio Rentals collector appeared to open the coin box attached to the television set and take the month's rental due. Any sixpences over were returned to the renter but Shela rarely had any returned, for she did not have the money to feed the box for several hours a day.

"Brian's parents have their telly on all day," complained Christopher one Saturday afternoon when the sixpences ran out and the boys wanted to watch football on the box. "Why can't we, Mum?"

Why, indeed, thought Shela later, sitting alone with her books and trying to finish a piece of writing. The solution came a few weeks later, when Beryl offered her sister a Saturday job at her new salon making up the wages for the three shops she now owned in Foster Hill Road, Brickhill and Kempston. Occasionally during those years in Elliot Crescent, Shela was able to take her children to visit their Gang-Gang at the new house in Bromham. Beryl usually gave them a lift back home after her day's work in the shop, and one evening she put the proposal to her sister who was so hard up all the time.

"We'll get your hair done regularly, Shela. And try to do something about those nails!" Then she added, as if it was an afterthought, "I can book driving lessons for you from next week. That will save me having to call at the other shops every week. See you on Saturday then. About two o'clock. You can bring the boys with you. They can sit and watch television in my flat as you work."

So the money situation was eased. Her two jobs kept the family afloat and, in the big hospital in Hertfordshire, Shela's girl benefited from good nursing and an excellent education, and two years turned into three and then it was suddenly four years since Deborah left home. Johnny's intermittent visits continued unchanged, while he worked odd hours on the taxis and Shela heard gossip about him seeing younger women and Hugh kept telling his old schoolfriend's patient wife to throw her husband out.

"He only comes here to stay when he can't get sex anywhere else, Shela. Why do you put up with it?"

There was no sensible answer to Hugh's question about her husband's unacceptable behaviour. Yet still, on cold nights, when she lay down to sleep, Shela thought about the early days with Johnny and often ached for the touch of a warm body beside her in the big bed. How had it all come to this? What had she done that was so wrong? And above all, how could she rid herself of the dreadful feeling of guilt about her little girl? On the rare occasions when Johnny stayed overnight, the bed became a place shared with a stranger. There was no friendly kiss goodnight. Only the cold formalities of sex, swiftly accomplished before he turned over to sleep. And for Shela, still only in her early thirties, these moments slowly became an ordeal to be endured by her body, even as her mind grieved for a lost love and the comforting touch of an affectionate man.

One Sunday morning in spring, Shela tried to keep the children quiet while their father slept upstairs after a late night and a surprise visit to the house, for she knew he would be short tempered when he awoke. At nine o'clock, she tried to rouse him, remembering the last thing he said before he fell into a deep sleep.

"Make sure you wake me up by nine o'clock. I have a taxi job at ten and it means good money. It's an airport run."

Then he added, just before he turned over to sleep, "Don't let me down — or else!"

152

Several times over the next three hours, she tried to wake her deeply sleeping husband, but each time she failed. By one o'clock he was still in bed and Shela dreaded the moment when he realised he had missed his fare. The two boys sat quietly at the new dining table waiting for their dinner. Shela tried to stop her hands from shaking as she poured Bisto gravy on to the plates of Tyne Brand tinned stewing beef, for she could hear Johnny coming down the uncarpeted stairs.

"Why the hell didn't you wake me? You useless cow!" he shouted in her face as the children hid behind their chairs and the younger one began to cry.

The next minute, the checked tablecloth was ripped from the table. Dishes and plates crashed to the floor and the remains of the Sunday dinner skidded after them. Shela braced herself for the beating she knew was coming. The severity of the first blow had her cowering in the corner of the kitchen, with arms folded across her head trying to ward off the closed fists hammering down on her crouching body. Barry, the younger of the two boys, tried to run to his mother, calling out to his father to stop.

"Leave her alone! You're hurting her. Stop, Dad!"

"Get out! Get back in there," Johnny shouted, taking a swing at the terrified child and hitting him on the back of his head.

In that moment, all fear left her. Shela stared at the contorted features of the violent man before her. And the crying child clung even tighter to his mother as Christopher tried to drag his brother back into the dining room to safety behind the chairs. Suddenly,

153

Shela was no longer afraid of this bullying man. Something inside her mind changed in that moment to a cold hardness. She reached for the greasy kitchen knife and lunged towards the retreating back of the man who had caused her and her children so much misery for the past twelve years.

"Stop, Shela! Put the knife down!"

It was the urgent voice of Bernard Boulton, her neighbour, who stopped her, and her wrist was held firmly in the air before the long knife clattered to the floor.

"He's not worth it, my dear," consoled Doreen Boulton later. She looked with concern at the shaking girl beside her on the sofa and told her own husband to take the children back next door with him. Johnny had long left the house when the kindly woman helped Shela clear up the mess in the dining room and then took her into her own home to make her a strong cup of tea.

"I'll give evidence for you, any time," stated Bernard, and Shela cried quietly into her tea as the two boys stood silently beside her.

"We heard it all," he continued. Then he explained how he had climbed over the fence between the two gardens. "Thank God your kitchen door was unlocked," he added with a short laugh. "Otherwise I dread to think what would have happened."

"And it's not the first time, is it, Shela?" Doreen questioned quietly. "But if you have any sense at all, it will be the last. That man is useless. You'd be better off without him. That's my advice!"

The next morning, as the bruises on her face began to turn purple and yellow, Shela took the day off work and the bus out to Bromham to see her mother.

"I've had enough, Mum," she replied calmly to her mother's anxious questioning over her appearance. "I'm seeing a solicitor tomorrow and suing for a legal separation. The court will make him pay me a regular allowance and, if he fails, it will mean prison for him. And," she continued, even more calmly as her mother listened in astonishment to her daughter's suddenly determined voice, "I hope he does fail. A spell inside is what he deserves."

It was to be almost three years before Shela obtained a divorce from her unstable and violent husband on the grounds of cruelty towards her and wilful neglect of his infant children. The events of that awful Sunday in 1963 finally brought to an end the disaster years. But they also hardened the heart of the easy-going girl she had been when she first met Johnny. There was hope at last for the future, even though Shela knew, with an almost unbearable sadness, that never again would she feel that first, overwhelming love she had lost when the handsome boy with wavy hair grew up into a weak and immature man.

PART THREE

1963–1976

CHAPTER
TEN

No Going Back

"Make sure that you go to the Housing Office today, Mrs Warren."

Shela sat opposite the kindly solicitor who had dealt with all her father's legal needs, and nodded silently as she was advised to have the tenancy of her home changed to her name.

"Show them the copy of your legal separation petition," continued Mr Culpin. "And, if it becomes necessary, ask them to change all the locks."

The heavy doors of Phoenix Chambers in Bedford High Street closed solidly behind her as Shela made her way across St. Paul's Square to the Council Offices in the town hall. The same middle-aged man who had dealt with her first housing application, twelve years previously, glanced swiftly through the document on his desk and assured the young woman sitting nervously before him that from the next rent day the tenancy would be in her name.

"If there is any trouble from Mr Warren, contact me again and we will certainly change all the locks," the concerned man stated quietly. "But in my experience that will probably not be necessary," he continued with a comforting smile.

So life without her husband began. And Shela was torn between apprehension about the present and excitement for the future. Tentatively at first, but with an increasing confidence, she began to cope with single parenthood and a steadily growing hope that once again things could only get better.

The driving lessons that Beryl had promised were completed by the end of the summer. The driving test was passed at the second attempt and now Shela began to visit her sister's shops regularly for banking and wages purposes. Beryl was also as good as her word about looking after her sister's hair and soon it was cut and styled into a neat chignon with added, blonde streaks and Shela was able, at last, to wear decent clothes for her office job at Sanger's.

"We are about the same size," commented Beryl every time she passed on barely worn dresses and skirts to her sister. "You have lost such a lot of weight in the last few years. Are you eating properly?"

It was always the same question from both Beryl and her mother whenever Shela visited them at their new house in Bromham. But with Johnny and the fear of violence now out of her life, Shela's health improved, and she was able to join in the office fun and attend the firm's social events, confident that she looked good and knowing that she felt better. When she was promoted to supervisor and her wages increased accordingly, the girl who had lived on beans on toast and gratefully accepted canteen cheese rolls, began to buy better food for herself and the two boys, now rapidly growing towards teenage.

Sometimes, when she was in town, Shela made a detour to the Black Tom area to visit Granny and Grandpa Warner in Queen Street. She was no longer afraid of meeting her husband there, for the she knew that the separation order gave her some protection, although his maintenance payments were intermittent and invariably late. It was no surprise to her, therefore, to learn on one visit to the drab, little house, that it was Grandpa who paid the monthly instalments on the new furniture recently installed in her home in Elliot Crescent and that Johnny had reverted to his old bachelor lifestyle.

"Why don't you take him back, Shela?" pleaded Granny Warner. "He's learned his lesson, this time. I'm sure."

But there was no going back for Shela, who was now making her own way in life and who had vowed never again to risk dependence on the weak man who was content to let his children go hungry and who had so nearly driven his young wife to suicide. In later years, Shela thought often about the reasons for Johnny's behaviour and eventually forgave him. But the twelve years of their marriage left a scar that would never fully heal.

CHAPTER
ELEVEN

A New Life

At Sanger's Christmas dinner and dance in that year of 1963, Shela discovered a renewed enthusiasm for dancing as she waltzed to "Stranger on the Shore" and twisted energetically to "Let's Twist Again". And she remembered, with nostalgia, the Thursday night dances of her youth at the Assembly Rooms in Grafton Road and a quick and daring drink at the Grafton Hotel opposite, during the interval. At thirty-two, life was improving. Although the sadness over the absence of her youngest child was never far from her thoughts, Shela began to emerge from the bubble of self-preservation in which she had survived for so long.

"I've been invited out to dinner," she explained nervously to her surprised mother one day soon after Christmas. "Will you have the boys to stay for the night?"

The dinner date was the first of half-a-dozen with the nephew of one of the firm's directors. The well-spoken, polite, young man, several years her junior, made her feel like a princess and showed her a glimpse of another world far removed from her daily life of careful budgeting and making ends meet. Shela knew that the affair could not last, but, when it was over, the process of re-establishing her self-esteem was almost complete. She was to look back on those few, short, magical weeks with a genuine affection and a sense of quiet satisfaction that she was no longer a cowed and timid reject, but a newly-assured woman in charge of her own destiny.

It was in the same week that John Profumo, the Minister of Defence, resigned over his affair with Christine Keeler and the news filled television bulletins and made daily headlines in the national press, that Beryl quietly bought tickets for her sister and mother for a five-day holiday in Paris.

"It will do you good to get away for a few days," she insisted as she handed Shela the air tickets and told her that their brother would meet them at the small pension in Montmartre, where the two of them were booked in for bed and breakfast. "I'll look after the boys. You go and enjoy yourself."

The short flight from Heathrow to Charles de Gaulle airport was a new experience for Shela, although Mum was already a seasoned traveller, having flown to the West Indies the previous year to visit her eldest son. As the aircraft finally left the ground, Shela knew a strange feeling of unreality as she looked down at the rapidly diminishing airport buildings below. Was she really sitting here? In an aeroplane? Going to Paris? And for five whole days? She closed her eyes and then opened them again to find Mum looking at her with concern from the seat beside her.

"Are you alright, dear?" were her anxious words. Shela nodded and smiled, then hugged herself tight and tried to keep her tumultuous thoughts steady, while the plane banked and headed for the channel and Paris, just over the horizon.

All through those next five days, the mother and daughter explored the beautiful, old city, drank fresh coffee at a pavement table outside the Café de Paris, and watched, fascinated, the artists along the Left Bank painting watercolours of Notre Dame. At night, they saw the great, illuminated sails of the Moulin Rouge as they turned high above the narrow streets of Montmartre and Mum recalled some of Dad's old stories about his youthful adventures in the bohemian quarter of the city. From the small, balconied window of their bedroom, with its lumpy, old-fashioned beds and hard pillows, they laughed at the Madame of the brothel down the street when she accosted passing men, trying to entice them into her establishment.

This was a world that Shela never knew existed until that day. She had only read in risqué novels and magazines about the strange goings on that she now watched with fascination, as all around her the great city went about its nightly business. Her schoolgirl French proved to be quite inadequate when she daily tried to ask directions from traffic gendarmes, who invariably answered, with slight grins on their faces, in perfect English. Her one attempt at ordering a mixed salad resulted, to her brother's huge delight, in a large plateful of raw vegetables and much laughter all around the restaurant table. But Shela didn't mind. At last she was experiencing life outside the narrow confines of her small house and job and she made the most of it. Now she knew that there was another world out there after all. A world only read about or imagined before that short trip across the Channel, when Mum found the small club where Dad had been a member in 1921 and Shela felt the stirrings of a long-stifled curiosity about the world and her own place in it.

A week after returning home, she received an invitation to the wedding of a work colleague's young son.

"Treat yourself to a new dress," advised Beryl. "I'll lend you some shoes and a handbag. Come up to the shop early and get your hair done."

On a beautiful summer's day Shela sat quietly at the back of St. Mary's church in Goldington to watch the young bride come down the aisle and to listen again to the wedding vows that she herself had made thirteen years previously. Where and why had it all gone so wrong? she thought distractedly, as the bride and groom stood smiling for photographs in the churchyard and Shela hoped with all her heart that this marriage would be a success. At the reception later, Shela found herself seated next to a short, cheerful man, some years older than herself.

"Old George fancies you," laughed the groom's mother, Mary, as Shela was led out on to the dance floor yet again by her neighbour at the table.

But I don't fancy him, she thought to herself. When the dance ended, he escorted her back to the table, where he rapidly downed yet another pint of bitter and told his partner to drink up and asked if she'd like another. As the evening wore on, Shela watched in fascination while her dance partner drank his way through the reception but remained steady on his feet, laughing and joking his way around the room.

"He's a widower," Mary told her, when Shela prepared to leave. "And he's lonely."

"I lost my wife to cancer three years ago," George Porter confided later, as he walked her slowly home across the green towards Elliott Crescent. "Poor girl," he added softly, "she was only thirty-nine. And left me with a young daughter to bring up."

Shela did not know what to say to this kind man who was obviously still grieving for his wife. And the sudden thought came that she had heard all this before. The thought that Johnny's mother had died young and the memory of the overwhelming pity she had felt for him all those years ago. A pity that had fallen on hard ground. And here she was, faced with it all again. Walk away from it, her newly found independence demanded. But her heart reached out to this man who had suddenly found himself alone when his only child married.

Shela looked at him more closely in the fading light of the summer evening and saw a middle-aged man with a round, pink face, a broken-toothed, cheerful smile and a twinkle in the blue eyes that could not quite conceal his loneliness. At forty-five, he looked much older, and she guessed that hard drinking and smoking had added to the lines on his face and that the thinning, fair hair had once been thick and curly. As she

166

said goodnight and watched him walk away to his car, Shela thought about the young wife who had died and hoped that he would find happiness again before it was too late.

During that summer, circumstances began to change in the big office at Sanger's. Shela was offered the position of wages clerk, which meant higher wages but also the loss of the company of the work colleagues which she had come to value so much over the last three years. She now spent most of the day alone in a small, secured office dealing with wage packets, National Health Insurance and Income Tax deductions. She did not find the work difficult, for she had been dealing with all these issues now for nearly two years in her sister's business.

"I miss being with the others," she complained to her friend, Peggy, who had taken over her old job as supervisor on the Adrema system of invoicing in the big office. "If I could afford to do it, I might try for another job locally."

Easier said than done, she thought anxiously. For the small industrial estate had not yet expanded into the spread of small businesses it was to become in later years. With her smart, blonde hairstyle and now fashionable clothes, Shela began, much to her annoyance, to attract the unwanted attention of regular callers at her front door.

"If you invite me in for an hour, we'll forget this week's instalment," grinned the first tallyman, when Shela paid him the five shillings due and watched in silence as he marked the payment card. When the same thing happened with another tallyman later in the week, Shela suspected that the word had gone round that she was a vulnerable woman living on her own.

"Don't worry, my dear," sympathised Doreen from next door, who also paid the two collectors each week. "I'll pay yours with mine and you needn't answer the door to either of them. The cheeky devils!" Then she added with a laugh, "I've been told that they try it on with most of the single women on the estate. If you have any more trouble, Bernard will deal with them."

Shela was to learn the hard way that single motherhood could be full of pitfalls, and when a pair of over-sympathetic Jehovah's Witnesses began to call twice a week with well-meant but irritating solutions to all her problems if she would only join with them in prayer and their Kingdom Hall church, her solution was to hide in the coal shed until they had gone. That was where George Porter found her one Saturday afternoon, after Christopher had let the pair into the house and then gone out to play, telling them that his mother would be back shortly. When George knocked at the back door, Shela emerged from her hiding place with her finger to her lips to whisper to him about the people in the living room.

The next minute, the front door slammed shut behind the pair of them and George stood in the kitchen with a big grin all over his face.

"They won't be back for a long time. If ever," he told her, and Shela went to switch off the television set which the pious pair had switched on to watch as they waited for her to return.

The other regular caller was the council rent collector, who called fortnightly for the carefully saved sum of almost six pounds, which Shela always put away each week from her pay packet before spending the money on anything else. This man was courteous and efficient and, each time she handed over the money, Shela remembered her father's wise advice. "Always keep a roof over your head first, my girl." And then recalled the haunting trauma of hiding from the rent man at Barton Road.

Sometimes, Shela found it difficult to follow her father's advice to pay the rent first and buy food afterwards. Her two boys, now growing up fast and with voracious appetites, always seemed to be hungry, and there was never a biscuit left in the house by Friday. Their growing interest in the new Beatles group meant that Shela tried even harder to find more sixpences for the television set in the corner of the living room. But even she sat down to watch "Sunday Night At The London Palladium" as the Fab Four performed there for the first time.

By the end of June, George was calling in to visit regularly, and on most Saturday evenings his old Hillman California car drew up at the door to take Shela and the boys over to Shortstown Social Club for the evening.

"I don't like the bingo very much, Peggy," she confided every Monday morning in the office, "and I don't care much for the drinking either. But it means that the children can be taken out every week, like their friends. And he's always cheerful and generous with them." Then she added, with the smile that Peggy rarely saw on her old friend's worried face, "On Sunday, he is taking us to visit Deborah at the hospital in Barnet."

Shela's younger boy, Barry, took to George right away. But it was a very different story with Christopher. This oldest son, who would be twelve years old in September, had begun to visit his father every weekend, where he still lived with his grandparents in Queen Street. Sometimes he stayed overnight and then arrived back home late on Sunday afternoon with comics and sweets and occasionally a new shirt or shoes bought for him by Granny Warner. There was never anything for the younger boy and Shela watched with growing anxiety as the two children began to grow apart.

"The old lady's spoiling him again, Mum," she sighed in exasperation one day after an argument with Christopher, when she made him share his weekend sweets with his younger brother. "She's up to her old tricks again. Just like before! She's trying to take him away from me."

A month later, after another visit to see Deborah at the big hospital school, George suggested that Shela should give up her job and bring Deborah home.

"Before she becomes too institutionalised and forgets what family life is like," he added softly.

"But how will I manage for money?" she demanded crossly, even as her heart tried to persuade her to do the one thing she most wanted to do. Get her girl home again.

"I'll see to that, my dear," George assured her quietly.

170

Then, before she could answer and as the possibility of at last bringing to an end the painful separation from her young daughter began to filter into her troubled mind, he took her hand, with its still bitten nails, in his big, work-hardened one and murmured, very gently, "I'll look after you all from now on. If you will let me, that is. Just get that child home."

CHAPTER
TWELVE

Changes

In early June 1964, in the same week that the U.S.A. entered the Vietnam War, Shela handed in her notice at Sanger's to take a weekend job with T. Wall and Sons, the ice-cream merchants, based in Cauldwell Street. For the rest of that summer, she drove a small, left hand drive vehicle, shaped like the house from Grimm's fairy tale, "Hansel and Gretel", around the streets of the sprawling housing estates of Goldington, Putnoe and Brickhill, selling ice-cream. On fine Sundays, as George looked after Barry, she served Mister Whippy soft ice-creams from the Wall's van parked high on Dunstable Downs and watched as the gliders from Dunstable Gliding Club took off and landed far below.

"I earn more over the weekend than I can all week in the office," she told her bemused sister, when Beryl came out of her shop to buy ice cream for the staff. "And I'll still be able to come to you on Fridays to make up the girls' wages."

It was during those few short weeks in the summer that a strong bond was forged between George and Shela's second son.

"I always wished that I'd had a boy," George explained as the two of them prepared to go fishing every Sunday morning. "And he needs a father."

Every week, Shela watched the man and boy go off down the road with their fishing rods, and was content in the knowledge that at least one of her sons was able to benefit from the growing relationship between his mother and the new man in their lives. She still grieved for the other boy who, at that difficult age poised between childhood and young manhood, was making the choice that was to affect the rest of his life. Within a month and with George's help, the young daughter who had been away from her family for nearly five years at last was brought home.

The asthma that had troubled her for so long was now under control with the inhalator that Deborah had been taught to use at the hospital. And the debilitating coeliac condition, which had made the little girl so ill in her first year at school, now seemed to be a thing of the past and she was once again enrolled at Goldington Green Primary School. She was nearly ten years old. But with the return of one child, Shela faced the trauma of the loss of another. For Christopher told his distraught mother that he wanted to live with his father in Queen Street and start the new school year in September at Goldington Middle School in Haylands Way.

"Never mind, lass," sympathised Beryl's husband, Geoff Millman, on one of Shela's frequent visits to his jeweller's shop in The Arcade, "Two out of three is not a bad average."

Shela was to remember those optimistic words much later in her life when her gentle brother in law helped her out of money difficulties more than once and always quietly enquired about her family and changing circumstances over the years ahead.

"It's the coughing. I can't stand it. And he always smells of beer."

Christopher tried to make his mother understand his longing to leave his home in Elliot Crescent to move back with his father, who had recently started up a new business in Foster Hill Road. The "Condeli Café" was doing well and Christopher now helped Johnny there on most weekends.

"But your father smokes," objected Shela, when she attempted to talk the boy out of leaving. "And heavily," she continued, as Christopher, with all the bravado of a twelve year old, revealed his dislike for the new man in his mother's life.

"You can take that back! I don't want your old fishing rod!" he shouted one Saturday afternoon when George drew up outside in his car. Then he threw the rod, given to him earlier in an attempt to win him over, at the door of the car before George had a chance to get out and stop him.

"Let him go, my dear," he advised, after the harsh words and the tears were over. "Just tell him that he can always come back if he changes his mind."

Then he got back into the car to drive Shela's eldest son out of her life and back to the old house in Queen Street where Granny Warner and his father waited for him. For his birthday that year, Shela bought

Christopher the new Beatles record, *From Me To You*, and, to her great relief, he at last began to visit his mother and brother and sister again in his old home. Although an uneasy truce was called between George and the boy in that autumn of 1964, Shela realised that the incident of the fishing rod was a defining moment in her relationship with the man who could provide a secure future for them all. And she grieved for the boy who chose to leave, the same way she had grieved for her little girl when the child went away to be nursed back to health five years previously. The break in the family unit was never to be fully resolved, and, in later years, the memory of that day of decision returned remorselessly to torment her whenever she thought about the past.

"I'm Into Something Good", sang Herman's Hermits on the day that Shela began to turn her thoughts to the move away from the present in Elliott Crescent and into the future with George in Lovell Road. The disquieting knowledge that Barton Road, with all the old associated bad memories of her short stay there, was just around the corner from his home, at first made her reluctant to move.

"You must try to put the past behind you, Shela," advised Mum. "You have been offered a new start. Try to make the most of it."

And Shela knew that she was right, for that was the philosophy her mother had followed for all of her own eventful life. The move was swift and efficient, as just before Christmas, George helped her to pack her few belongings and, on the last day, piled all the new furniture in the porch for Johnny to collect before nightfall.

"Goodbye, my dear," smiled Doreen Boulton as Barry and Deborah climbed into the car with their mother. "Be happy."

And now Shela's little family could begin a new life with no money worries. For George held a secure job with the Ministry of Public Building and Works at R.A.F. Cardington. There could be no question of marriage until the divorce from Johnny was finalised and Shela knew that neighbours gossiped about the young woman "living in sin" with the older widower just down the road. But with her two younger children flourishing and now settled in at Kingsbrook Junior School just across Silver Jubilee Park behind the house, Shela was at last able to enjoy the love and support of a good man. She loved him in return but it was never to be the kind of overwhelming passion that comes only once in a lifetime. Instead, it grew slowly into a loving and affectionate relationship, which promised to sustain both those lonely people as they made a new life together.

Shela quickly made friends with George's daughter, Judith, and her new husband, Jim, and the Saturday night outings to Shortstown Social Club became a regular feature of the family's weekend. During those first few months and years with George, Shela and her children enjoyed the protection of a secure family unit, something they had never known before. It was a happy man who left for work each morning and returned each day with a big smile on his face to the house in Lovell Road.

"I've not seen Dad so happy and cheerful for a long time," commented Judith, and Shela smiled as she listened to George playing cards with the youngsters in the living room and she sang the words of "Those Were The Days My Friend", along with Mary Hopkin on the radio. There was, however, one ongoing and puzzling reason for concern in Shela's new relationship. George was distressingly, and very obviously, almost totally impotent.

"His liver is damaged," explained Doctor Fitzmaurice, when she tried to answer Shela's questions about George's health. "He is also a very heavy smoker and that has not helped over the years."

The kindly woman doctor looked keenly at her new patient's worried face, and added gently, "You already have three children, my dear. It is highly unlikely, although not entirely impossible that you and George can have a child. But I would advise that, under the circumstances, you consider being sterilised as soon as possible."

"If that's what you want," agreed George later, when Shela told him of her conversation with the doctor. "Just in case," he added quickly. "You have three children and that's more than enough."

There was a strange mixture of regret and relief in his quiet answer and, for a long time afterwards, while she waited for the date of the sterilisation procedure, she questioned whether she was doing the right thing. And what were those circumstances the doctor had mentioned, but never fully explained? The operation, performed with keyhole surgery, was carried out the next year and Shela settled into a quiet life of looking after her family and enjoying the weekend outings and short seaside holidays that the children had missed when they were so young.

In those first years together, Shela came reluctantly to terms with the missing element in her new relationship and, when they finally married in 1966, when she was thirty-four years old, she told herself, quite firmly, that that part of her life was over and she must be grateful for what she had. But she often wondered, as she looked at her new husband's ageing face, if he regretted the loss. She was to find out, much later, that he did.

CHAPTER
THIRTEEN

Second Chance

The quiet wedding ceremony took place at The Bedford Registry Office in Brereton Road on a cold February day in 1966. The small, dark room, filled with rows of chairs for family and friends, grew even darker as snow threatened outside, and Shela thought longingly of her warm, winter coat left outside in George's old car. Her blue, two-piece suit fitted her slim figure well, but when George placed the ring firmly on her finger and kissed her tenderly on the cheek, Shela prayed silently that the formalities would soon be over. She knew that her new husband was not entirely sober, for he had downed several large scotches at the Coach and Horses public house in Commercial Road before driving on, fifteen minutes late, to park outside the drab little registry office.

"You are very late, Mr Porter," frowned the receptionist. Then, to Shela's acute embarrassment, George bent forward to kiss the woman's outstretched hand and grinned his broken-toothed grin at her before making his apologies.

"We had to stop for a warmer, my dear," he explained. "Such a cold day. And we needed a little pick-me-up."

179

The small group of family members smiled encouragingly at her as Shela took her vows and afterwards followed the newlyweds back to the neat house in Lovell Road, where Barry and Deborah waited for their mother and new step-father.

"I asked Christopher to be here, Mum," sighed Shela, when the cake was cut and Judith's husband proposed a toast to his new mother-in-law. "But I really didn't expect him to turn up today."

It was to be several more weeks before Shela's elder boy began to visit his family again, for Johnny had now moved to Finedon in Northamptonshire to start his own new life, after marrying again within six weeks of Shela's wedding.

"These Boots Are Made For Walking" warbled Nancy Sinatra on George's transistor radio. And Shela gazed around the furniture she had inherited from Olive, George's first wife. The strange feeling of not being alone in the house grew stronger as she stood beside the sink in the kitchen to listen to the news about the conviction of the Moors Murderers and then willed herself to go back into the living room to lay the table for lunch. There were no photographs of Olive displayed anywhere to remind her that another woman had been here before her. But Shela remembered the dark eyes of Johnny's young mother as they followed her around that other house where she was not welcome. And again she felt like an unwilling intruder into someone else's private grief.

"This is ridiculous," she said aloud as the last fork was placed carefully in position and she forced herself to return to the kitchen to turn on the gas ring under the vegetable saucepans. The growing feeling of not being alone, when George was at work and the children at school, made her nervy and over talkative when they all arrived home for the meal she cooked every day.

"It's so silly, Mum," she explained one day, when her mother and Beryl called in unexpectedly for tea. "I know perfectly well that there's no-one here. And I don't believe in ghosts!"

"You need to get a job, Shela," advised Beryl, just before she left the house. And when Mum was out of earshot, "It's not good to be here alone all day. And why don't you consider moving, now that you need another bedroom?"

What Beryl said was true, Shela reflected, as she watched her drive away. The Porters' name was already on the council transfer list but Shela suspected that George did not want to leave his carefully tended garden and well-maintained home where he had lived for the past twenty years. The opportunity for both changes came early the next year, when the family were offered the tenancy of a larger, three-bedroom house in Cardington Road, facing across Mill Meadows towards the river. A month later, Shela started work at The Gordon Fraser Gallery in Eastcotts Road, and the nerves she had suffered from so badly, and the feeling of stepping in to another woman's shoes, disappeared as she settled in to the new job and the family settled happily into the new home.

The old, brown leatherette, three-piece suite was sent to Peacock's sale-rooms in Newnham Street and new, modern furniture ordered from the Co-operative Furniture shop in Midland Road.

"You choose just what you like, my dear," smiled a cheerful George, and Shela looked carefully at a black, imitation leather suite with beige, furry cushion covers and then chose matching velveteen curtains and a patterned, blue carpet for the new sitting room of 225 Cardington Road. The Fenlake Anchor, just along the road from the new house, became George's new local and for the next few years he fluctuated between there and The Turnpike public house near to Shela's new office in Eastcotts Road. Often he would wait outside the office after she finished work at five-thirty, ready to take her to the pub for a drink on the way home. For a time, Shela went along with this habit, but she soon grew weary of arriving home after seven every evening to find the children waiting for their tea, with George anxious to eat his quickly, so that he could return to the pub until closing time.

"All You Need Is Love" sang the Beatles on the Dansette Record Player bought for the children at Christmas 1967, and Shela tried to agree with the sentiments of the song as she remonstrated with George over the hours and the money he spent at the pub.

"Why am I working full time if you give most of it to Charlie Wells?" she questioned in exasperation. Then watched in silence as George hung his head and apologised for the third time in a week for staying on until closing time and sometimes later.

182

The distressing cough that Christopher had so objected to when she first met George had gradually worsened and during the winter months it was sometimes so extreme that he was unable draw the next breath and dropped unconscious to the floor. In time, Shela learned to catch his head before it hit the ground, and then watch fearfully as his normally ruddy complexion turned a frightening putty shade, before the colour slowly returned and he struggled to his feet again. Then lit up another rolled cigarette from the gold and green Golden Virginia tobacco tin that he kept in his back trouser pocket.

"It helps to clear the old passages," he always explained with forced cheerfulness, although Shela could see that these episodes of violent coughing were getting progressively worse.

In later years, Deborah re-told the story many times of George's unexpected visit to her new secondary school, The Pilgrim School in Brickhill Drive, where he asked to see the headmistress to obtain permission to take his step-daughter out of school to buy her a new school mac.

"He had been at the club and was well sloshed," she recalled with a shudder. "And I was taken out of class and told to go to the head's study, where Dad was in the process of charming the old girl with his big, silly grin beneath that shabby, old trilby hat he always wore for work. As we left, he grabbed the head's hand and planted a sloppy kiss on it, leaving her very red in the face and me mortified with embarrassment. She was always very sweet to me after that incident."

"God knows how he drives the long distances he does," Shela confided to Judith one evening as they sat together in the lounge of The Black Hat pub in Wilstead, near to where George's daughter had now gone to live.

As a foreman electrician for M.P.B.W., George held a responsible and sometimes dangerous job, for it meant setting up and servicing heavy-duty electrical installations on R.A.F. airfields all over the country. Sometimes, he stayed away for a couple of nights, and, when he returned, brought his crew with him to the house to finish off the cans of beer they had bought en route.

"It was a crazy time," one of the lads admitted to Shela many years later. "We always tried to make sure that old George was fit enough to do his job and to drive. But there were many times when he wasn't well or wasn't sober. I don't know to this day how he got away with it for so long."

"The Mighty Quinn" sang Manfred Mann on the colour television set in the corner of the living room. And Barry, now a pupil at Silver Jubilee Secondary Modern School in Acacia Road, sorted out his new records to play on the Dansette for the friends coming to his fifteenth birthday party the next day. It was October 1968 and already this second son was talking of leaving school at the end of the year to start earning some real money.

"They pay me peanuts for those newspaper rounds," he complained bitterly to his mother every Friday. And then listened to George's tales of childhood hardship about working in the fields near Whittlesey where he was brought up.

"You don't know the meaning of work, son," George often told him. And Shela recalled her grandmother's tales of the heavy workload she had endured as a young nursery maid in a big house in Liverpool.

"But Dad!" insisted Barry, "this is 1968, not 1928!" And Shela was pleased to hear him call this man, who had many failings but was always protective of his wife and her children, by the name forfeited by the boy's natural father when he finally deserted them all.

All through the Christmas holidays, as her children enjoyed their new lives in a settled family unit and Christopher came to stay for a long weekend, Shela counted her blessings and succeeded in pushing the anxiety about her husband's failing health, firmly to the back of her mind.

"The careers teacher said I can leave school at Easter. I have an appointment with the General Post Office," stated Barry in late February 1969. "It's called work experience. And if it goes O.K.," he added with a grin, "I can apply for a job there."

The day after Easter Monday, Shela's son started work as a messenger boy at the big offices in Harpur Street. At nearly sixteen years old, his pay was eight pounds a week.

"Five of that goes to your mother," George informed him sternly. "The rest is yours. And that's being generous, my son."

185

"When I'm sixteen," the boy proclaimed proudly, "I can learn to drive a moped and be a telegram boy. And earn extra in tips!"

It was in July that year, as television showed grainy images of the U.S. astronauts, Aldrin and Armstrong, walking on the moon and four days later their miraculous and triumphant return to earth, that George suffered from the first of many prolonged chest infections that kept him off work for a month and the idea of early retirement was first suggested.

"But he's not yet fifty!" exclaimed Shela as Doctor Fitzmaurice followed her down the stairs with her stethoscope still hanging round her neck.

"But he has the lungs of a man of seventy," the older woman replied gently. "And a sick seventy-year-old at that." Then she added, when Shela looked at her in surprise, "Don't expect too much, my dear."

By the end of the summer, when the children seemed to do nothing else but talk about a new group called, "The Rolling Stones", whatever that might be, Shela wondered, she left her job at The Gordon Fraser Gallery to work part-time in the office at Kismet Manufacturing in Fenlake Road. Every day, she pedalled on her old, second hand bicycle past the Weaver Manufacturing and Engineering Works to her own office further along the narrow service road, and hoped that George would not be sent home from work yet again with the breathing difficulties that were especially bad on damp mornings. Her husband was a fiercely proud and independent man, used to earning a fair living for his family, and Shela knew that the thought of early retirement on sick benefit and a reduced pension went painfully against everything his hard, working class background had taught him.

At fifteen, the fair-haired, fresh complexioned boy had left his home at Whittlesey in Cambridgeshire to seek a new life as a boy entrant in the Royal Navy. At sixteen, he had travelled round the world to experience those new horizons that would never have been possible if he had followed his father into the brickfields for a living. The Royal Navy also taught George to drink. And drink hard. For, as he related many times over the years, the rum ration issued each day was saved for the weekend when he and the other young sailors could get drunk together before sleeping it off on Sunday mornings.

In 1939, at the start of the Second World War, Petty Officer George Stewart Porter, was stationed at Portsmouth. At nearly twenty, fit and well trained for his duties off the beaches of Dunkirk, on minesweepers in the Atlantic and in escort vessels for Russian convoys on their way to frozen Murmansk, he experienced much that became the stuff of a fine repertoire of stories of his service at sea. Sometimes, as the family gathered to listen to this old sailor as he stood with one foot perched on a chair, resting his elbow on his bent knee, with one hand holding a glass of beer, and the other a rolled cigarette, the medals would be taken out of the velvet-lined case and passed around yet again for the children to see and admire.

Behind the dramas, re-told with much humour and occasionally drink-fuelled embellishments, Shela detected the unspoken hardships of life in the war-time navy. And, as she listened, was constantly reminded of the outcome of her father's trench warfare earlier in the century; the disturbing nightmares that a lifetime habit of heavy drinking did nothing to alleviate. She also remembered her mother's outspoken view of her father's hard drinking days.

"Self first, self last and if there's anything left, self has it!"

When D-Day came, George was in Australia, while his young wife and baby daughter waited patiently for him at home in Beechdale Road, where they lived with Olive's father.

Their girl was just seventeen when her mother died, and George had once again lost the focus in life that had sustained him ever since leaving the navy and the terrible memories behind him.

On that February day in 1970, when he finally gave up work and the long years of illness and self-loathing began, Shela's husband was just fifty years old. He is only twelve years older than me, she thought, in an unexpected and unwelcome exasperation that took her by surprise. But the mounting sense of frustration that now sometimes threatened to overwhelm her, even as she tried daily to alleviate his distress and forgive his weaknesses, began slowly to turn to anger.

Nightly, as George lay sleeping noisily beside her, Shela asked herself the difficult questions she had put off for too long. Why was he wasting his life in this way? Why did he always expect forgiveness and understanding? And why, even as his health began to fail, would he not admit that the demons that plagued him were mostly of his own making?

Many times, after a particularly noisy evening at the club meant that George would not be home before midnight, Shela waited silently on her side of the big bed until he was safely in beside her. Then kept watch as his heavy sleep was disturbed by the frightening effects of sleep apnoea, made worse by heavy smoking and his overweight body. Always, on those lonely nights, curled tightly into a foetal position for comfort, with her body aching in frustration for the relief she knew George could never give, she cried deeply and silently for her loss. But the tears were also for the man who had failed them both. A bleak sense of betrayal began to pervade her waking moments, as Shela struggled to come to terms with both the state of her marriage and an increasingly ominous future for her husband and family.

The morning job at Kismet meant that Shela could be home when Deborah came in from school. Just as before, George sometimes met her outside the office to urge her to go for a quick drink with him in The Bricklayers Arms just down the road. Shela hated the place, for the small public bar reeked of draught beer and stale, yellow cigarette smoke that made her eyes and throat sore. And she silently resented the fact that the money she was earning was still going into the landlord's pocket every week. The need for a full-time job became apparent once more when, one day in late spring, the Telephone Engineers Department went on strike, and Barry was not paid for the time he was out with his work colleagues.

"Then you'd better find yourself another job," commented George shortly. "And be quick about it."

The job the boy found turned out to be a mixed blessing. Shela's nephew, her sister's boy, had told Barry of a vacancy for a trainee butcher at Safeways, the big, new supermarket in Greyfriars, Bedford. Within a week, he started on the new job with an enthusiasm that reminded his mother of herself when she started work for her father in the old café. At nearly seventeen, Barry was small for his age, but the harder, physical work required in the new job developed his physique and soon he was taller than his mother and almost as tall as George.

"We get cheap cut-offs, Mum," he explained gleefully, as he arrived home each day with a parcel of oddly shaped chops or the small end of a beef joint, which was enough for the family dinner on Sunday. "So can I pay for half my keep in meat and the rest in cash?"

Shela missed the money at first, for her housekeeping budget was drastically reduced when George was finally retired on health grounds, and the invalidity benefit and reduced pension did not make up for the loss of his good foreman's wages. She did not tell her husband of the new arrangement with her son, for she knew that it would hurt his pride and be a painful reminder of his own failing to earn sufficient money for the family.

"I have to get a full-time job, George," she stated calmly, soon after Barry left home to live in a bedsit in

Adelaide Square, nearer to his workplace. "We need the money and I want Deborah to stay on at school and go on to college."

The pale, thin girl who had come home to her family after five years in the hospital school, had benefited from the excellent education that she received there. Now doing well at Pilgrim School and restored to health again, although the asthma attacks still troubled her in the winter, Deborah was all set to excel academically. Shela secretly harboured ambitions for her daughter to become a teacher. The one career that she herself had been denied when she left school at fourteen all those years ago.

"She may decide to go into the theatre," she suggested to her mother one evening as they watched Deborah perform on the stage of the Civic Theatre in Horne Lane. The production that year was Jane Eyre and Shela's daughter, now thirteen years old and already bitten with the bug of amateur dramatics, was a keen member of The Bradgate Players, a local company well known in the area. There were good reviews of the production in *The Bedfordshire Times* and Deborah's performance of Adele was warmly praised, as was her portrayal of the blind, deaf girl, Helen Keller in "The Miracle Worker", the next year.

"If she is that keen, perhaps she could win a place at a stage school," smiled her grandmother as she recalled her own costume design connections with the young Flora Robson and that famous actress's humble beginnings in amateur theatricals.

"Just wishful thinking, Mum," sighed Shela as they watched the company line up to take their final curtain bows before an enthusiastic audience in the winter of 1969. "It all costs money, even with a scholarship, and we just couldn't afford it."

"I Heard It Through The Grapevine" chanted Marvin Gaye endlessly in the year that Shela found a new, full-time job that proved to be a mixed blessing. It meant working a five and a half day week, driving round Bedfordshire in one of the firm's vans and collecting money for goods obtained on credit from J. P. Simmons and Son, the big store on the corner of Queen Street and Tavistock Street. She did not like this job at all, for it reminded her of the days in Barton Road when she was forced to hide fearfully from the rent collector. Shela knew, without looking, that net curtains sometimes twitched when customers who could not pay looked out to see who was there before they would open the door to the caller. The job lasted for only a few months and then she took another in the office of an industrial cleaning company at Turvey, along the Northampton Road.

Sometimes, if George was well enough, he took her out to the firm and arranged to pick her up after work, only to arrive at lunch-time to take her for a drink or two at the Three Cranes, just along the road from Premier Cleaning Service in Bamfords Yard. On one memorable occasion, he arrived early, at twelve o'clock, and then sat in the boss's office regaling him with his sea stories until Shela was ready to leave at lunch time.

"That man of yours should not be driving in that state," commented the boss as the other girls in the office looked on in amusement and Shela flushed red with hot embarrassment.

At the end of the school year in 1970, when she was almost sixteen, Deborah suddenly announced that she did not want to stay on at school and that she certainly did not want to go on to college.

"I want to train as a hairdresser, like Aunty Beryl," she declared, but both her mother and George tried to persuade her otherwise. Shela looked in alarm at her clever and attractive daughter, when she stated defiantly "I've got a boyfriend now and he won't want me to be away from him at college."

A month later, Beryl told her sister that a hairdressing apprenticeship was vacant at Dusts Hairdressers in the Arcade on Bedford High Street and that Deborah would receive an excellent training there. "Then she can come to work for me," she added consolingly, for she could see that Shela was upset by the whole idea.

By the end of that summer, when Britain's voting age had been controversially lowered to eighteen, and Edward Heath voted in as the new Conservative leader, Rolf Harris sang "Two Little Boys" endlessly on "Top of the Pops", and the worry about her girl's future took second place in Shela's thoughts when George became seriously ill once more.

Every Saturday during those summers, Shela went down to Bedford market to buy shellfish for tea. When it was in season, she also bought a carton of marsh samphire, the nutritious seaweed that George remembered from his youth in the Cambridgeshire fens.

During the months since his enforced retirement from work, George had started making his own beer at home. And every Friday night, Shela opened the kitchen door to the overpowering smell of boiling hops as he strained the noxious liquid through a muslin cloth to mix it with cold water into two four gallon zinc buckets with Demerara sugar and malt, then left it to cool in the larder. Before he went to bed, two slices of toast, thickly coated with baker's yeast would be left floating on top of this brew. Five days later, he began to drink the raw beer, even before it had been bottled. Shela watched her husband slowly destroying himself, and once again slipped inside her bubble of self-preservation to observe, sometimes, it seemed, in slow motion, the final, dreadful act of the drama that had become her life.

Late one Saturday evening, when Deborah had gone out with her boyfriend, of whom George did not approve, Shela sat alone, scribbling in her old exercise books and waiting for her husband to come home from the Fenlake Anchor. The salad tea, now beginning to wilt in the warm, June air, was laid out ready for him on the table, and the dressed crab, that he always enjoyed so much, plated up in the small, built-in fridge in the kitchen.

George did not say a word as he opened the back door and came through to the dining table. And Shela thought it best to leave well alone as she poured out his tea, placed the shellfish in front of him and returned to

194

her writing in the living room. There was silence, broken only by his harsh breathing. Then a loud cry as he pushed the plate away and the knife and fork clattered onto the floor. When Shela reached him, the crab tea was spilled across the table, and she looked on helplessly at the man she had never seen crying, sitting with his head resting on folded arms, sobbing like a child.

"Get him into bed," Doctor Fitzmaurice instructed, when Shela made a frantic phone call to her house late that Saturday evening. "I'll come right away."

George stayed in bed for the next two weeks as the ravages of alcoholism and heavy smoking finally took their toll on his physical and mental health. The full horror of the severity of his condition became apparent in the weeks that followed. For he often awoke in the night, screaming about spiders crawling up the bedcover towards him and begging Shela to catch them before they could attack him. Several times during those first, desperate days, she found her pathetic, sick husband standing in the dark before an open wardrobe door, having mistaken it for the bathroom, and then led him like a child to the toilet, where he often fell asleep again on the seat. The doctor had known George since his demob from the navy, and had seen him and his family through the trauma of his young wife's illness and early death. And now she did her best to support the new wife trying desperately to cope with a situation that was beyond her control and which she found frightening in its implications.

"Here is the phone number of Alcoholics Anonymous, Mrs Porter," the doctor said, when Shela saw her to the door after her third visit that week. "You need some help, my dear," she added. "They can give it to you. But if you will take my advice, don't tell your husband that you have called them. He is still in denial, but I think he has taken my advice on board."

"The doctor told me that, if I don't stop drinking, I'll be dead in six months."

The shocking words from George, still weak from the frightening withdrawal symptoms and shaken by the doctor's diagnosis, echoed in Shela's mind as she gave in her notice at work and prepared to support the man who had supported her and her children so well when they were first married.

"I'm staying at home until you are better, George," she declared on his first day out of bed. "And that means no more beer. Homemade or otherwise."

A few days later, while The New Seekers cheerfully sang "I'd Like To Teach The World To Sing", she rang the A.A. number that the doctor had given her. That evening, two middle-aged men appeared at the front door to explain that they were members of the Alcoholics Anonymous family support group and asked if they could be of any help. To her great disappointment but no real surprise, George refused to talk to them.

"I'm going to bed. Let me know when they've gone," he stated belligerently, then stalked off upstairs and Shela heard the bedroom door slam behind him.

"That's not unusual," smiled one of the men. "He still thinks he can deal with this problem on his own. But at least he acknowledges that we can help you, or we would be back outside the door again by now."

Over the next hour, Shela learned that both these men were alcoholics, although neither had touched any form of it for more than ten years.

"Once an alcoholic, always an alcoholic," said the older of the two men quietly. "The only answer is to abstain absolutely. There are no half measures in this disease. For that is what it is. Not just a weakness or an indulgence, but an illness with only one treatment. Complete abstinence."

"We saw what it did to our own families. That is why we do this work now," volunteered the second man. "But I must warn you that the only person who can decide to give up drinking is the alcoholic himself. After that, medical help is available if he wants it."

Shela saw them out, listening to their reassurances of further advice if she needed it, and a card with the address and time of the next A.A. meeting, slipped quickly into her handbag. Shela suspected that George would not take kindly to the advice given so readily by the visitors. She was right, for the very next evening he left the house for the first time since his prolonged stay in bed and, with a cheery grin and a wave of the hand at the front gate, began the short walk down the road to his usual place at the bar in the Fenlake Anchor.

CHAPTER
FOURTEEN

Calmer Days

"It's alright. He's only drinking lemonade and orange juice."

Shela stood in the small space of the Jug and Bottle at ten that night, talking to Nen Shine, the landlord's wife at the pub, who came out to reassure her that George was still sober and advised her to get back home before he did. It was a very different man from the one who had left home earlier, who came quietly back in to the house to give his wife a big hug and tell her that his drinking days were over for good.

"I shall miss it," he said quietly, "and it won't be easy. But I've made up my mind. I promise that when I go down to the pub, it will only be for the company and I'll be home by nine at the latest."

George was as good as his word. Over the next few months, as Barry returned to live temporarily at home and later obtained a job at Safeways in Leicester, and Deborah continued with her hairdressing apprenticeship, Shela's mind was at rest. Perhaps now our lives will be on an even keel at last, she thought, and watched her husband struggle with his demons and tried not to condemn him for his past weaknesses.

George began to lose his beer belly and his mottled and puffy face regained some of its old freshness, as he began to eat sensibly and even talked of holidaying again at Yarmouth when the good weather returned.

It was then, as his health and temper improved, and a long overdue visit to the dentist resulted in the big smile that Shela was to remember with great fondness in later life, that George confessed his overwhelming regret that the intimate side of their marriage had been impossible from the start.

"I should have told you, my dear," he said sadly. "It wasn't fair on you."

Shela tried to comfort him and attempted to reassure her contrite husband and herself that there were other sides to marriage just as important as the physical aspects.

On the evening of April 14 that year, the whole world waited for news about the dangerously crippled space ship Apollo 13, and willed the American astronauts to land safely after their shocking transmission from space, "O.K. Houston. We have a problem."

George did not leave the house at all that night. Shela once again glimpsed the larger than life, cheerful character who had made her laugh when she had nothing in her life to laugh about. Who tried, in his own way, to give her the love and affection that was missing from her relationship with Johnny. But most of the old bombast was gone, and in its place she discovered the quieter, caring man who had been hidden away behind the false bravado of alcohol for so long.

Many times during the next year, Shela thought about finding another job, for, although the money situation had eased with George's hard-won sobriety, she found that simple housework did nothing to stretch her mind or her imagination as she worked on her pieces of writing or tried to invent dramatic lives for the characters in her short stories.

It was in the autumn of 1971, as she stood looking out at the now neglected back garden, for George was too short of breath to look after it properly, that a new idea began to nag away at her. Benny Hill sang, "Ernie, The Fastest Milkman In The West", with that cheeky grin on his face on "Saturday Night At The London Palladium", when Shela first broached the idea of exchanging the house for a flat to a very sceptical George when he returned from the pub.

"We don't need three bedrooms any more," she reasoned. "Barry is well settled in his new job and lodgings, and won't come home to live with us again. He's eighteen now and wants to live his own life. After all," she went on quickly, before George could interrupt her, "at that age you had already been in the navy for three years!"

The application for a transfer to a flat was being processed in the housing department, with a reassurance that the first available one would be offered to Mrs Porter, when, one cold day in October 1971, something completely unexpected happened. George's elderly parents had been living for some years in Teignmouth in Devon, with his older sister Julie, who ran a restaurant there with her husband. Shela was speaking on the phone to her sister-in-law, when George came back from the pub.

"It's your father, George," she said quietly. "He died early this afternoon."

So the plans for the move were temporarily abandoned. Arrangements were quickly made for Shela's mother-in-law to leave Teignmouth and move in with her son and his wife. After all, as George repeated, in an echo of Shela's own argument earlier, they still had three bedrooms and his sister had done her bit in looking after the old folk for the past few years. Grandma Porter was in her early eighties when she came to Bedford and settled in to the house in Cardington Road. Shela tried her best to make her welcome when the old lady took over Deborah's bedroom, with its two built in cupboard wardrobes, and the girl was moved into Barry's old, smaller room at the back of the house.

"It's not fair, Mum!" Deborah protested at the new situation, and Shela tried to placate her feisty daughter and told her that the new lodger would not be with them long, for she had put her name down for a small flat as near to her family as possible. Just over a month later, Grandma Porter was offered a small bedsit flat in Boswell Court on the other side of the town. The huge block of newly built flats now towered over the small houses in Queen Street, where Shela had first started out on married life all those years ago, and it was with mixed feelings that she first visited the old lady in the new flat and then called in on Granny Warner just across the road.

Grandpa Warner, who had tried to be kind to Johnny's wife in those early days, had died some three years previously and Shela was shocked to find that the condition of the house had deteriorated even further since her last visit. Granny Warner was now living in the tiny front room with only a one-bar electric fire for heating. And the squalid condition of the rest of the house resembled a slum. Shocked and angered that such things could happen in a supposed enlightened age of social welfare, Shela rang her ex-husband at his new taxi-office in Prebend Street to tell him of his grandmother's living conditions and her state of health.

"I couldn't wake her," she explained to George, when she returned to his mother's modern flat opposite. "I think she's in a coma."

"Get the doctor round there fast," she exploded as Johnny tried to explain that he had no time to visit his grandmother. "And then get in touch with the social workers. She needs help and she needs it now!"

The next day, Christopher rang his mother from Finedon to say that Granny Warner was in hospital, suffering from chronic diabetes and pneumonia and asking her to go with him to visit her that evening. Shela only visited Granny Warner in hospital once, but Christopher went several times before the old lady died. And the young nurses told how she repeatedly asked to see her grandson and her great-grandson towards the end. Her last wish was only half granted, for Johnny never saw his grandmother again.

CHAPTER
FIFTEEN

New Horizons

The feeling of restlessness and lack of purpose in her life was finally resolved when Shela found a temporary post as an assistant bursar at Hawnes School in the nearby village of Haynes.

"We need someone who can take on the responsibilities of the bursar when she is away and assist her during the school week," explained the headmistress, on the walk with Shela around the fine old building standing on a rise of ground just beyond the village.

All through that winter of 1970 to 1971, George kept his mother company and his word about not drinking and Shela enjoyed her work in the big boarding school and talked to the teachers in the school block who left work at three-thirty every day.

"I know one of them, George," she told her husband after the first week. "She was in my year at the Girls Modern School." Then she added wistfully, "She did what we both wanted to do with our lives when we were thirteen."

In the year when everyone struggled to cope with the new decimal currency, introduced gradually and almost imperceptibly to a less than enthusiastic British public, the seed of another idea began to take root in Shela's mind. In January of 1972, when newspapers and television news reports were full of "the troubles" in Northern Ireland and British troops were involved in the killing of protest marchers in Belfast on what became known as "Bloody Sunday", Shela talked to her mother about her new idea.

"It's my chance, Mum," she explained, with an enthusiasm that her mother had not seen for many years. "And I'm going to take it!"

All through the power cuts and seemingly endless cold days of the winter, when candles were in short supply and a Calor gas heater was installed in the living room, Shela had quietly noted the government's television appeals for more students to train as teachers.

"We particularly need mature students to train for posts in junior education," stated the smooth-voiced presenter. "Combine your family obligations with an interesting course of training and a successful career in a worthwhile, well paid occupation for life."

Shela was nearly forty years old, with more than twenty years of working life ahead, when she first enquired about the teacher-training course on offer for suitable applicants at Bedford Teacher Training College in Polhill Avenue.

"You have no formal educational qualifications?" queried the softly spoken man who interviewed her one afternoon in late spring. "But I see that you received a very good basic education at your secondary school."

He smiled encouragingly at the nervous but determined young woman sitting before him as he advised her that she would benefit from a year's pre-teacher training course at Mander College in Cauldwell Street.

"You need to learn how to study again," he said, before giving her all the details of the new course starting in September. "You will be among the first of our guinea pigs in this new venture! Good luck, Mrs Porter."

A letter from the college to the local education authority, confirming that Shela Porter had been accepted as a student from the following September, produced the promise of a generous student grant with the added confirmation of a top-up grant for her dependent husband.

"It adds up to almost the amount I am earning," she announced enthusiastically, after reading out the letter from County Hall to her sceptical husband.

George did not take kindly to the idea of his wife studying for the next four years and was even less enthusiastic about what would follow.

"You are too old to go into teaching," he stated repeatedly and at length. "Things have changed since you were at school. You'll never cope. Mark my words!"

In later years, Shela understood that these were the bitter views of a disillusioned man, unable to support his wife as he had promised when they first married. At the time, they caused an uneasy rift between them, which resulted in George spending more time than ever with his old mother, who had now moved again into a comfortable, ground-floor flat just around the corner in Lovell Road.

The year of study that followed opened Shela's mind once more to the great legacy of English literature that she had only just begun to grasp when she left school so suddenly at fourteen. And the patient coaching of the English tutor, Joe Grady, more than compensated for the hard slog of learning basic maths all over again. The history course, entered into with some trepidation, for it had been one of her weaker subjects at school, proved to be an enlightening and enjoyable romp through the last ten centuries.

The young woman who remembered old wartime history lessons as being inextricably linked with dear, old Miss Window and the unintelligible and unexplained poem beginning, "The Assyrians Came Down Like A Wolf On The Fold", began gradually to understand her place in the order of things and with the knowledge came a great yearning to learn more.

"Read, read, read," advised the head of department, and Shela took note and passed the written and oral examinations at the end of the course. "You have done well this year," he continued, then he shook her hand and wished her well on the teacher-training course the following September. "Good luck and remember my advice."

Earlier in that summer of 1972 and four months before she was due to start her training at the big college in Polhill Avenue, a housing transfer was offered to a top-floor flat in Dunham Close, near to George's mother, now well settled into her own small flat overlooking Silver Jubilee Park.

"If you can manage the stairs," she explained anxiously to her husband, when they went to view the small, two bedroom flat, "we can move in before I go back to college after half-term."

The move was made in early May and George appeared to be happy with their new home as he sat on the small balcony in the spring sunshine or watched the Munich Olympics and the gymnastic feats of a young Olga Korbut. Occasionally, he called in to the flat next door, where his first wife's sister and her husband had lived for some years. Shela's step-daughter and her husband often called in to see him when she was at college, and their two young children looked forward to visiting their granddad. But when his cough worsened, the visits became less frequent. And Judith explained, with much regret, that the sight of her father's purple face and bulging eyes, produced by his violent and sometimes prolonged coughing fits, had begun to frighten them.

Within six weeks of moving with her mother and step-father to the new flat, the beloved daughter who had spent so many years away from her home and family, began to talk of an early marriage to the boy she had been seeing for the past two years.

"We want to get married and find our own place to live," explained Deborah one evening. She and her prospective husband sat nervously on the sofa together, and George ignored the young man who wanted to take his step-daughter away from him.

"But you are only seventeen!" replied Shela in astonishment, glancing apprehensively at her husband as he took another long drag on his cigarette. "Much too young to think about marriage. And where will you live? And how will you manage with Ken only doing casual work?"

So the questions continued as George glowered away in his corner and the young couple argued resolutely that they would manage and that they had already found a small flat in Beverly Crescent.

"I need your consent, Mum," pleaded Deborah. Then, hesitantly, as the boy beside her nudged her arm, "I'm underage and, if you won't give it, I'll go to see my father."

Shela's heart sank as she looked at the young face before her, and old memories of her own hard years of early marriage and motherhood crowded into her mind. Then she slowly shook her head and took the girl's hand in hers as she told her that she would not give her consent and that she should wait for at least another year before thinking of marriage and all that it could bring.

Over the next few weeks, as she tried desperately to make her daughter change her mind and George resolutely refused to discuss the issue with either of them, Shela's only relief from the conflict in the home was to immerse herself in reading, and once again turn to writing as a way of escape from an increasingly worrying situation. At last, after many sleepless nights and mounting concern over George's reaction to Deborah's obstinacy, Shela gave in and reluctantly promised to sign the consent form for the marriage of her young daughter. Afterwards, she tried to come to terms with the idea, and admitted to herself that much of her decision had been influenced by her reluctance to encourage contact with Johnny again.

"She's not pregnant is she, Shela?" asked Joaney, who now had six children of her own and knew only too well the difficulties of early motherhood.

"No. Thank goodness," Shela replied. "And I'm thankful for that. But at seventeen!"

Deborah and Ken were married in the drab, old registry office in Brereton Road, where her mother had taken her own vows six years previously. There had been disagreement between the two families over the choice of church for the wedding ceremony. His were for a Catholic nuptial mass and hers for a Church of England service. Eventually, and after much ill feeling between the two sets of parents, the young couple opted for the registry office and a small reception in the Lewis family home in Luke Place, just off Mile Road in Bedford.

"I wish you both well," smiled Shela as she looked at her young daughter's happy face and shook the new father-in-law's hand before she said goodbye.

George did not attend either the ceremony or the reception afterwards. He stayed out until nearly eleven that night and afterwards slept for the rest of it in his old armchair.

Shela knew that he was hurt over her decision to give her consent to the marriage and that he was worried about how the young couple would manage. Deborah's apprentice-hairdresser pay was very low and Ken relied on sporadic painting and decorating contracts to meet the considerable rent of their flat in Beverly Crescent.

Four months later, after a week off work and morning sickness had taken its toll of her daughter's still fragile health, Shela learned that she was to become a grandmother in June the next year.

"We can't afford the rent for our flat when I leave work, Mum," the pale-faced girl explained as plans for the move to Plymouth, where Ken had obtained work in the docks, were discussed over tea one day in Dunham Close.

Later in that year of 1972, Shela's girl, already showing signs of early pregnancy and the digestive problems that would plague her for many years afterwards, moved away from Bedford and the anxious mother who had already missed so many years of her young life.

CHAPTER
SIXTEEN

Disillusion

The New Seekers sang "I'd Like To Teach The World To Sing" on the old transistor radio in the small kitchen as Shela prepared dinner and wondered why George was staying so late at his mother's flat. At seven-thirty, one cold evening in December 1972, and with the meal drying up in the oven, she closed the flat door behind her, ran swiftly down the two flights of stairs and walked quickly across the small green between the two blocks of flats.

There was laughter coming from the small, bed-sitting room as Shela opened Grandma Porter's front door and walked in unannounced. George and his old mother sat one on either side of the gas fire. On a low coffee table between them stood a half empty bottle and two full glasses of cheap, draught sherry.

"Hello, dear," smiled the old lady. "You are just in time. Get another glass from the kitchen and join us."

Shela looked at George's red face and the big, soppy grin he always wore when he knew she was angry with him.

"It's just sherry, woman," he protested. Shela turned and left the flat without a word, then ran all the way back to her own home. Later, she served the dried up meal in silence, and George tried to bluster his way out of the fact that he was drinking again.

"It won't do me any harm," he explained. "It's the first time I've had a drink in eighteen months. It's just a bottle of draught sherry from the pub. My old mum likes a drink now and again. And why shouldn't she have it at her age?"

The next day, Shela stood by the pump on the garage forecourt on the corner of Lovell Road and Cardington Road, filling up the tank of the second hand Ford Cortina that had been bought with the last of George's retirement lump sum. It was as she paid the bill that Malcolm, the garage manager, confirmed her worst fears.

"It started when his old mum moved here," the sympathetic man informed her quietly.

"And I knew that he'd been off the booze for over a year," he continued. Shela looked at him in disbelief. "So I was surprised to see him walking past every day with a bottle of that cheap, old draught sherry they sell at The Anchor. He always goes straight over to his mum's flat."

That evening, Shela sat at the small kitchen table and tried to concentrate on her written English assignment for the end of term. George sat in his armchair in the living room, defiantly drinking from another bottle of draught sherry and smoking one of the rolled up cigarettes, which stained his fingers and made him cough until his face was purple. The next day, he was back at his old place in the public bar of The Fenlake

Anchor, drinking pints of bitter laced with barley wine. And Shela knew that he had given up in the battle against alcohol.

"Please don't serve him, Mr Shine," she pleaded, when the landlord came to the door of the Jug and Bottle in answer to her desperate request to speak to him.

"My dear," the man replied gently, "if I do that, he will only go elsewhere for his drink. At least this pub is the nearest one to his home."

Money was once again so short in the Porter household, that Shela realised she must find another job to fit in with her college commitments.

"Shirley's father needs someone to work on Saturdays," suggested Joaney one afternoon in January as the two sisters enjoyed a cup of tea together in Shela's flat. "Why don't you try there?"

Shirley Carruthers was an old school friend of Joaney. Her family owned D. E. Carruthers and Co., a credit draper's business in St. Leonard's Avenue, near London Road Bridge.

"I need someone to work in the shop," smiled John, Shirley's brother. "All day Saturday with an hour for lunch. The pay will be three pounds."

The Saturday job was a godsend to Shela during the next two years, for the extra money meant that she could afford to buy the books she needed, instead of waiting for them to come in to the college library every week. It also meant that she could occasionally buy petrol for the car, which had not been used since George started going to the pub again.

"I can use my old bike to go to college," she confided in Norma, her next-door neighbour, who had become a good friend since she moved into the flats. "But I need the car to get out to village schools when I have teaching practice."

As in the old days in Queen Street, Shela had retreated into her own safe bubble of self-preservation as the end of the second year of the teacher-training course approached. She already knew that she would go on to complete it satisfactorily. Several of the mature students, who started the three year course with her, were told discreetly, at the end of the first year, that they could not go on to do the second, but that the option was there to try the first year again with the new intake.

"I think if that had happened to me, George," she said, "I would have given up!"

The only answer from her husband, who had been such a cheerful man and a perpetual optimist when she first knew him, was a muttered, "Pity it didn't, then."

Shela tried hard to ignore these comments. She realised that George resented her success at college and resented even more the fact that, within a year, his wife would be earning good money, while his contribution to the household barely paid the rent and rates.

John Denver sang "Annie's Song" and Harold Wilson became prime minister of a Labour/Liberal coalition government in 1974, when Shela's second son, Barry, decided to get married on his twenty-first birthday. This boy, who had lived away from home since he was sixteen, seemed to have grown up into manhood without her really noticing the change. And here he was, married to a pretty, friendly girl from Loughborough, and Shela was thankful that at last he had found the stability that had been missing from his childhood.

"Your father can't get to the wedding," Shela explained, as Barry arranged for Christopher to pick his mother up for the drive to Loughborough. "He's not well enough. He can barely walk to the pub now, let alone stand and talk all day to people he does not know."

Shela's sons visited regularly during those first years in the flat. She knew that both of them were impatient with George's lifestyle. Christopher condemned outright the heavy drinking and smoking. Barry tried his best to excuse it as he watched the man whom he had come to look on as a father bent on self-destruction and his mother trying to cope with an increasingly difficult situation.

At her mother's seventieth birthday party, in August of that year, held at St. Andrew's Church Hall in Kimbolton Road, Shela tried to appear unconcerned, while her husband drank his way through the evening and endeavoured to ignore concerned comments from her brothers and sisters about George's appearance. It was as her husband attempted to dance with her mother and had to stop half way around the room to regain his breath, that Shela's older brother told her quietly that she should try to get help for George.

"It's no good, John," she replied, as the tears came and she wiped them impatiently away before the others noticed. "He doesn't want to stop. He had the chance last year and managed it for a while. I've just given up on him."

The quick conversation with her brother, and the concern she saw on his face when he tried to offer advice, prompted Shela to make an appointment with the doctor who had monitored George's failing health since he retired from work.

"Is there any chance that he could have a liver transplant?" she implored. "I have been reading about successful ones recently." Then she listened apprehensively as Doctor Fitzmaurice shook her head and tried to explain the medical complexities of her old patient's condition.

"No chance at all, I'm afraid," the kind woman replied. "For a start, he has to lay off the alcohol for at least two years before being considered. Then there would be a long wait for a suitable donor. And lastly, but most importantly, his lungs would never stand up to the operation. He has advanced emphysema, my dear."

Shela sat and listened to all this in silence. Her mind told her that the doctor was right. But in her heart she longed to be able to do something, anything, to help the man who, even now, waited at home for her to bring him a fresh packet of Golden Virginia tobacco and the bottles of strong ale that would get him through the night.

Before Shela left the surgery, the doctor advised her to start making plans for her own life. "You must not expect too much future with George, I'm afraid," she added quietly. "His best years are behind him. Now you must start to think of yourself."

CHAPTER
SEVENTEEN

Hope and Despair

Life at college increasingly became an escape from the reality of what was happening at home. Morning lectures and afternoons spent in various schools in the town or in the surrounding villages meant that Shela had little time to think about that other life with George, which she entered every time she returned to the small flat on the top floor. As the months of 1975 went by, Deborah came to stay, bringing her dark-haired little girl, while her husband started a new life for them in the army. And Shela watched in quiet despair as George's health deteriorated even further. Old friends and relatives visited less and less as the dreadful coughing increased and her daughter, now pregnant again, sat with her dad as he slept in the big chair, while her child played around it as if everything was normal.

"I shouldn't have come here, Mum," she confessed one evening in October. The Bay City Rollers sang "Bye Bye Baby" on "Top Of The Pops" and the television news bulletins were full of the onset of deadly elm disease sweeping the country.

"You have your hands full," she said softly. Then carefully eased a lighted cigarette from her sleeping father's tobacco stained fingers. The arms of his chair were now covered with small burn holes where lighted ash had fallen as he slept, and Shela's greatest fear was that he would set fire to the chair and himself while he was alone during the day.

"Why don't you try to get him into a nursing home, Mum? You are wearing yourself out with all this. Just for a few weeks to give you a breather."

A week later, when Deborah had left to join her husband in married quarters at Catterick Garrison and both her sons had endorsed their sister's suggestion, George collapsed in Lovell Road outside the garage on his way to the Fenlake Anchor.

"He was unconscious, my dear," explained Malcolm on the phone. Then told Shela that he'd called an ambulance and she should come immediately.

A small crowd of people stood against the garage wall as Shela knelt beside her unconscious husband and took his head on her lap. And then retrieved his top denture that had skidded into the gutter as he fell.

"I'll follow the ambulance to the hospital," volunteered Norma from next door. "Do you want me to make any phone calls?"

But Shela's concerns on that cold morning were not with phone calls. Her fears were for the man in the ambulance as the paramedics gave George oxygen and resuscitated him twice on the short journey to Bedford General hospital.

"He's still with us," they reassured her. And Shela followed them into the same ward where, in the early days of her marriage to the man on the trolley, Granny

Warner had died from neglect and loneliness, calling out for her grandson as she went.

George was home in time for Christmas. Shela settled him comfortably in the old chair again, and noted, with silent thanks, the benefits that the short break from smoking and drinking had brought to him. The badly swollen and ulcerated legs, which gave him so much pain, were beginning to heal, but Shela watched anxiously as he lighted up another rolled cigarette on his first day back home.

"Let him have his tobacco," advised the doctor after an unexpected visit the next day. "He can't do any more damage to his lungs now." Then she added quietly, "If he wants a drink, let him have a shandy. Nothing stronger."

So Christmas 1975 passed quietly, with George wheezing away in his chair, where he now slept all night, for breathing difficulties meant that he could no longer lie flat in bed. Shela sat in the small kitchen and tried to concentrate on her final dissertation, "Charles Dickens on Childhood and Children", which was due to be handed in by the end of the Easter term. Bedtime reading was Malcolm Bradbury's new book, *The History Man*, and often she would read items from the newspaper to a strangely acquiescent George, watching his new fish in the big aquarium recently set up in the corner of the living room.

The first weeks back at college were hard ones for Shela, who was desperately torn between staying at home with her sick husband and the urgency of the training course requirements.

220

"I must admit," she laughed ruefully, "that I felt a bit out of place running round that hockey pitch at my age," she told her amused daughter, after relating the afternoon's activity on the college playing field. "It's thirty years since I picked up a hockey stick!"

Always, at the back of her mind as she attended lectures and wrote up reports on the week's teacher practice just completed with much enjoyment and a sense of real fulfilment, there remained the worry about the sick man waiting for her at home. In the week that the first supersonic aircraft, Concorde, made a record-breaking flight from London to Washington, and John Curry won a British gold medal for figure skating at Innsbruck, Shela called the doctor in again. Increasingly now, she could not fully wake George in the morning before she left the flat. It had become routine for her to rush home at lunch break, just to make sure he was still breathing. And every time she turned the key in the lock, she dreaded what she would find.

"What am I to do?" she implored the doctor, who was busy examining George's legs and feet, which were once again grossly swollen and breaking out into fresh ulcers.

"I'll arrange for the nurse to call in each day," Dr Fitzmaurice assured her. "Just leave a phone number to contact you if necessary."

As she left the flat, the kind doctor looked back at Shela and said, "You must finish the course, my dear. It is your future."

The six weeks block teaching practice that would confirm Shela's final grades began after the half-term holiday in mid February.

"You have been assigned to a teacher you already know," advised her personal tutor, handing out assignment notes and wishing his students good luck. "And it's a good school. They will look after you well."

He was right, for Shela was delighted to find herself assigned to Joe Grady's wife, Joyce, teaching at St. Joseph's R.C. Lower School in Chester Road, Queens Park, Bedford.

The short journey each morning, along Cardington Road to Cauldwell Street and then along Prebend Street to Queens Park Bridge and over into Ford End Road, took just a few minutes, and Shela used that short, precious time to both prepare herself for the day's work ahead and to calm her anxieties about George. Two weeks into the demanding but completely absorbing teaching practice, in which Shela so desperately wanted to do well, she found herself, once again, retreating back inside the bubble of self-preservation that had been her refuge in times of stress since childhood.

"A Schools Inspector is visiting today," announced the headmistress at assembly one morning. "He will make a brief visit to each classroom. So please be ready for him."

Shela had just started the Friday spelling test with her class of thirty children, when a middle-aged man opened the door and walked quietly to the back of the room. A few seconds later, the door opened again, to admit one of the young teaching nuns working in the school.

"The head asked me to bring you to her office," she whispered as the children waited for the next word on the list.

"Go ahead, Mrs Porter," said the inspector. "I'll finish this for you."

In the head's office, Shela sat trembling on the small chair by the desk and was gently told that her husband had collapsed again and that her next-door neighbour was with him.

"He's asking for you, my dear," continued the head. "You must go home immediately. Sister Benedict will go with you."

As Shela hastened to the staff room to pick up her coat, the head continued, "Don't worry about your work here. We will take care of that."

The young nun stayed with Shela while she telephoned from her neighbour's flat for an ambulance, for George was now unconscious and his breathing was so erratic that she feared every breath would be his last. For the rest of that day and into the night, she sat by the narrow hospital bed, where George lay unconscious. A drip lead had been inserted in his arm and a catheter tube protruded from beneath the bed cover. She sat there, observing, with a curious sense of detachment, that the bag hanging beside the bed was steadily filling with cloudy urine, and his round, white face, half-covered by a hard oxygen mask, looked like that of a stranger. Suddenly, incongruously, she wanted to laugh.

She felt that she was acting out a part in some bizarre dream sequence and that, if only she could laugh, it would end and George would sit up in bed to tell her it was all a big joke. Instead, she held the big hand lying across the stiff sheet, put her head down on it and wept.

CHAPTER
EIGHTEEN

An Ending and a New Beginning

"Go home, Mrs Porter," advised the ward sister when she made her round just after midnight. "Try to get some rest if you can. He doesn't know that you are here. We will call you if there is any change."

Shela was still trying to catch the sleep that had eluded her for the past two hours, when the doorbell rang at three in the morning. A young policeman stood on the landing, and with her dressing gown half pulled over her nightdress, Shela knew why he was there.

"Are you Mrs Porter?" he enquired, avoiding her eyes and looking down at his notepad. "We have received a call from the hospital requesting us to tell you that you should go there immediately. Is there anyone who can go with you?"

Shela looked past him across the small landing to where Norma, her next-door neighbour also stood, tying up her own dressing gown cord.

"I heard your doorbell, Shela," she explained as the policeman went back down the stairs. "I'll get dressed and take you in my car. You shouldn't drive there on your own."

An hour later, George's daughter, Judith, hastily brought from her home at Wilstead, sat on one side of the bed and Shela sat on the other and Norma kept the three of them supplied with vending machine coffee until just before dawn.

"Talk to him," advised the tired looking young doctor as he checked George's pulse and adjusted the drip before moving on down the ward to his other patients. "He probably can't hear you. But he just might."

A few minutes later, the doctor was back with the ward sister.

"I'm going to give your husband a heart stimulant," he explained quietly. "It will bring him round so that he can hear you and possibly speak to you."

Shela suddenly felt very sick and tried to quell the gall rising in her throat. Then watched hopefully as George regained consciousness. With a roar loud enough to wake all the other patients on the ward, he threw back the bedclothes and tried to sit up. The catheter bag hanging beside the bed swung violently and the drip stand crashed to the floor. The patient in the next bed joined in the shouting as the doctor and a nursing orderly rushed back down the ward. Shela stood back, horrified, as her naked husband swung his legs out of bed and tugged savagely at the catheter tube with one hand, while the other one tore the oxygen mask from his face.

The light above the bed shone directly down on the grossly swollen body below, and Shela saw, in shock and pity, that her husband's testicles were now the size of a large grapefruit. Then the three women were hastily ushered out, while George was once again settled down in his bed and order was restored on the ward. He was deeply unconscious again when they returned. Half an hour later, as his wife and daughter held his hands, he drew the last, long, shuddering breath that comes before death. He was fifty-five years old.

"He's gone, my dear," whispered the sister, pulling the curtains swiftly around the bed, and Shela bent to kiss the dear face for the last time.

"Do you think he knew we were here?" she asked anxiously, watching the two young nurses wheel the bed away into a side ward.

She was never to know the answer to that question but, as Judith observed later on the way home, "Well, Dad certainly went out in style. Just like his noisy, cheerful old self!"

And Shela felt an odd comfort, even as the pain and bewilderment of loss finally caught up with her and she grieved for the man George had been, but not for what he had become.

The next few days took on an increasingly dream-like quality. Family members and old work colleagues came and went. As each one offered their condolences, Shela longed to tell them that all she wanted was to be left alone. Alone to cope with the guilty feeling of overwhelming relief that the whole, dreadful business of watching her husband slowly dying was at last at an end.

On a cold morning in early March, she walked quietly past the flowers laid out on the landing outside the flat to climb into the first car following behind George's hearse, while family and friends gathered behind her. The deferential voices of the undertaker's men, ushering black-clad figures into other, long, sombre vehicles, failed to penetrate Shela's thoughts. She retreated to the back of her comforting bubble and observed, it seemed in slow motion, the hearse, with George's coffin now surrounded by the flowers from the landing, turning the wrong way out of Dunham Close into Lovell Road.

"Stop! Stop!"

Christopher's big hand closed quickly over her own cold one as he tapped on the interior window to tell the driver that Granny Porter was waiting by the window of her own flat further down Lovell Road to see her son's funeral go by.

"No problem, sir," the man assured him quickly and stopped the hearse outside the garage on the corner and then proceeded to do a U-turn past the petrol pumps, and Malcolm's astonished face, to rejoin the rest of the procession round the corner.

At the old, Victorian crematorium beside Bedford Park, Shela sat quiet and dry-eyed, watching a Salvation Army Major conducting the funeral service and saying good things about her husband.

"Write me as one who loves his fellow men," he quoted, from a poem about Abou Ben Adhem. And Shela nodded as she recognised, in that one line from an old poem that she remembered from her schooldays, the truth about George. He had not been, in any way, a religious person. But he was, the man in the pulpit assured them, a good man who would still be loved by his God.

There was strictly no alcohol at the funeral tea afterwards in the little flat. People began to drift away to the Fenlake Anchor at lunch-time, and the three women who had been part of his life stayed behind to talk over old memories of the man who had just left them.

"Dad had the last laugh," said Judith as she retold to her grandmother the hysterical moment when the hearse took the wrong turning. "He would have made the most of that at the club tonight!"

And Shela thought about the jolly, kind man she had known when they were first married and how he had done his best for the young mother left to bring up her children alone.

On a day in early summer, she packed George's clothes to take to the Salvation Army charity shop in Bedford High Street. And found a forgotten pair of his old shoes, tucked away beneath the wardrobe. For the rest of that beautiful day, she hugged the broken-seamed, misshapen shoes close, as the tears came and she cried at last for her old George.

Towards the end of that month of June 1976, during one of the hottest summers of the century, Shela stood on the lawn outside the college dining room after the valedictory dinner, to talk to her fellow students. Shela had made many good friends over the last four years and, as goodbyes and good wishes for the future were exchanged, she recollected the wise words of the college principal on that first, hesitant day in college.

"When you leave here, your lives will have changed for ever."

Shela's life had changed beyond all recognition. She had at last fulfilled her schoolgirl wish to become a teacher.

The other changes were harder to bear. But the same resolution that had sustained her so far, through the years that led up to this day, was now, more than ever, firmly in place.

PART FOUR

1976–1992

CHAPTER
NINETEEN

Making Changes

The air in the small flat at the top of the stairs, oppressive with heat and the odour of stale tobacco smoke, cooled and freshened as Shela opened the door and all the windows of her home one stifling day in July. All across the country, standpipes were being set up to supply water to a drought-stricken Britain and on the balcony George's geraniums wilted in the afternoon sun.

In the five months since his death and finishing college, Shela found herself leading an increasingly isolated life while others connected with George swung back, inevitably, into their own lives. Family, friends and neighbours, at first solicitous and kind in her bereavement, gradually retreated. Some simply did not know how to cope with the young widow, and several times, when she approached the checkout till in local shops, she was met with an embarrassed silence and a lowered head as she paid her bill.

"I really must get this place re-decorated and some new furniture in," she exclaimed to her step-daughter, Judith, who was looking at the yellowing paintwork and faded wallpaper. Then she gently touched the burn holes on the arms of George's old chair. "Everything in here smells of your dad's Golden Virginia roll-ups."

Since the funeral, Judith and her two children had become more regular visitors to the flat and Shela was thankful that some of the estrangement of the last few months before George died had now passed and she was able to renew the closeness she had always enjoyed with her step-daughter.

"There's a furniture sale on at Harrison Gibsons in the High Street," Judith volunteered when they said their goodbyes and promised to come again soon. "It's a good firm. Jim has done some electrical work there."

A week later, Shela stood before the big window of the old shop that had once been Wells Furniture Shop near Lloyds Bank opposite St. Paul's Square. The frontage had changed completely, she realised, and thought back to the time she and her friend Mabel regularly waited inside the shop arcade for two particular boys to walk past on their way to Paulo's Milk Bar further along High Street.

She smiled to herself at the memory of the name given to the Sunday afternoon walk up and down the main street of Bedford, with every girl looking out for her heartthrob. The "monkey parade" was a good place to find him. They had both married their sweethearts but Mabel's marriage was the one that lasted.

Shela spent the last of the money from George's small Life Insurance Policy on a smart, dralon-covered suite that brightened the newly decorated room and matched the new bronze-toned curtains. She was leaving the old, tired life with its worn furniture behind her and a new, fresh one was about to begin.

Now over eighty, George's mother relied on carers, meals-on-wheels and family members for support and looked forward to Shela's visits each afternoon. On Sundays, she enjoyed the roast dinner her daughter-in-law never failed to take across the small green between their flats. Each time she made the short journey, Shela remembered the day of the wine bottle on the table. The day when she realised that George was drinking again. The day of betrayal. She tried hard to forgive her mother-in-law for her unthinking part in that betrayal but it was to be many months before she looked at the old face and finally accepted, for her own peace of mind, that George's mother was not to blame.

Over those months, other more practical issues concerned her. The most important was the means of earning a living. When the student grant ended, her only income was the small M.O.D. widow's pension based on George's earnings in the last year of his working life and the even smaller unemployment benefit awarded by the Employment Exchange office in Allhallows, Bedford, the week after college finished.

As a newly qualified teacher, Shela's name was on the application list at the Local Education Authority in County Hall in Cauldwell Street. Every morning for the last two months she had rung the office on her newly installed telephone, enquiring about teaching vacancies advertised in the *Bedfordshire Times* and the *Times Education Supplement*. All to no avail and so dispiriting after the years of training and expectations for the future. After several hard-won interviews and disappointments, she knew she could no longer live in hope and must find work quickly.

"They spend all that money on my training and then there are no jobs available," she complained to Joycey, recently returned from Plymouth and now settled into her new home in Vicars Walk at Goldington.

"Joaney tells me that there is a vacancy for a receptionist at your doctor's practice in London Road," her sister volunteered. "Why don't you try there?"

"But you are too highly qualified for reception work, my dear," exclaimed the kind doctor who had visited George many times over the years. "You are worth more than this job," she continued. And Shela listened miserably at the end of the telephone line the next day, for she knew the doctor was right. "Think of all those years of training! You must not let them go to waste."

In September, as the hottest summer for many years turned slowly into a dry and dusty autumn and the newspapers were full of the outcome of the Entebbe hostage crisis, Shela answered a *Bedfordshire Times* advertisement for trainee social workers. A week later, she began work at the square office building in Kingsway, opposite Mander College, and was immediately caught up in the chaotic life of an underpaid and overworked social worker of the nineteen-seventies.

The heavy case loads and frustration with form filling and endless reports now made up her working days as Shela tried her best to make sense of the rituals of team meetings and seemingly meaningless assignments to deal with elderly, confused people who should have been in care, or truanting schoolchildren who laughed at her efforts to persuade them to go to school.

She knew that somewhere in the old files from the fifties were reports on her own young married life, when on one occasion her mother had contacted Social Services in alarm after her daughter was abandoned with three small children to support. In time, Shela found those old reports and was horrified to read that, in the opinion of her case worker, "The Winch sisters seem to have perfected an easy way to enlist state help for their young families."

"Cheeky devils!" exploded Joaney when told about the forgotten files. And then sighed as she recalled her own hard times when she and her six children had been dependent on state handouts after her marriage broke down.

All through Christmas, Shela tried to come to terms with the frustrations of her work and listened intently to the soothing voice of Johnny Mathis singing "When A Child Is Born". It was with great reluctance that she walked back into the big office in Kingsway to resume work after the holiday, for her heart was not in the job.

Three months later, Shela was asked to enrol on a two-year training course at Barnfield College in Luton. By then she had become familiar with the frustration of trying to sort out the tangled lives of young mothers with violent partners or trying to talk sense into disaffected runaways and youths bent on petty crime as a way of life. There had been experiences too of a more depressing or infuriating nature, usually involving dispossessed and lonely old men. They occurred when she was driving them to a hostel or cheap bed and breakfast accommodation. The journey on more than one occasion became quite tricky and Shela became adept at deflating the ego or thwarting the advances of an aged passenger who had assumed that a young social worker would offer something more than her best efforts to find him shelter.

Was this work satisfying enough, she asked herself, for her to dedicate her life to it? Flattering though it was to be thought worthy of training for the profession, Shela's experience so far was not particularly happy.

"I can't face another two years in college," she told Norma from next door, "and anyway, I need to earn more money now."

The humiliating, recent experience of being taken quietly on one side by the owner of the P and A shop in Goodmayes Close, just behind her flat, to be told that one of her cheques for groceries had bounced, still rankled in Shela's memory. The constant pen pushing and paper shifting of social work, however worthy an occupation, was neither lucrative nor satisfying, and she felt increasingly unfulfilled as the time drew nearer for her to make up her mind about the course on offer.

"That doctor was right," she said to her reflection in the driving mirror and listened to the breaking news of the death of Elvis Presley as she turned the car into Kingsway and St. John's Street on her way home after another weary day on the duty team in the big office. "I am worth more than this and I must be patient. No more college for me. I trained for teaching and that's what I must do." So the offer of social work training was declined and Shela once again began to scan the advertisements for likely positions in her chosen profession.

Over the years since her divorce from her first husband, Shela had always kept in touch with his younger brother's wife. Doris, now widowed, was only two or three years younger than Shela, and the two began to meet frequently for cinema visits and shopping trips. A package holiday in Tenerife, accompanied by Joycey, in the summer of 1977, cemented the old friendship even further.

"Why don't we book a course of dancing lessons?" queried Doris one Saturday afternoon on the way back from the cinema where the new scary film of *Jaws* was drawing full houses. Later, the two friends sat drinking tea in the comfortable lounge of her house in Cheviot Close. "How about it?"

"Well, I'm game if you are," replied Shela with a smile, while her mind went back to the dancing days of her youth when she would never miss the Thursday night hops at The Assembly Rooms in Grafton Road.

"It's called The Court School of Dancing," continued Doris, picking up the phone to dial the number advertised in *The Bedfordshire Times*. The following Thursday, she picked Shela up at her flat in Dunham Close, where her friend had been watching the Queen's Silver Jubilee celebrations all day. The two friends laughed and joked together as Doris's Mini threaded its way through traffic along Cardington Road, past Mill Meadows where Shela had gathered mushrooms with her young children, and her old school, Bedford Girls Modern, before turning right into St. Mary's Street and over the town bridge into St. Paul's Square. From there it was a short run round the old church into Harpur Street and then left into Midland Road at Marks and Spencer's corner.

"It's just like the old days," Doris laughed as they climbed the steep flight of stairs in the tall building in Grafton Road behind The Royal County Theatre in Midland Road.

It was in this grand old theatre that, as a child, Shela had watched with rapt attention the children's traditional patriotic play "Where The Rainbow Ends" and Christmas pantomimes, and in later years regularly applauded the local repertory company, The Ivy Players, as they produced their well-acted repertoire of plays. To many theatre-going Bedfordians, the actors had been a familiar sight as they queued for their sausages and pork pies at Saxby's in Silver Street or fresh butter deftly served up with butter pats, from Sainsbury's long, black and white tile-floored shop in Midland Road. Weyman Mackay, the leading man in the company, June Flavell, the leading lady and Iris Gilbert were all familiar names on the bills posted outside the old theatre in the nineteen fifties and sixties.

The Assembly Rooms had not changed at all, Shela observed, as they took their places on the same old chairs that both women remembered from their youth. But the men had. Some she recognised as self-assured and predatory married men. Others, obviously and painfully out of their depth, which showed itself in the

240

stumbling steps and awkward stance of middle age, tried to appear at ease as each one chose a lady partner for the first lesson.

Shela recognised the woman dance instructor as an old classmate from Goldington Road Junior School and later reminisced with her about their schooldays and Daphne's childhood home in Laundry Square opposite the school. Several times during that evening, Shela found herself targeted by a talkative, dark eyed man with a slight, foreign accent that she could not quite place, and who proved to be both an agile dancer and an equally accomplished flirt, who nevertheless made her laugh.

"I've joined the class for the exercise," he confided, while they carefully foxtrotted their way around the floor. "I had a heart attack three months ago and the doctor recommended ballroom dancing to get my weight down. It suits me," he added with a cheeky grin. "It's a good excuse to meet pretty ladies like yourself."

"You've got an admirer there," Doris laughed over their coffee during the break. And an eerie echo of the past came back to her friend as Shela remembered her first meeting with George at that long-ago wedding reception. The same man was there to partner her every week from then on and, when the course ended and he offered her a lift home, she finally gave in to his persuasive patter. Doris smiled knowingly and waved goodbye before driving away in her Mini and Shela climbed in beside Terance in his smart, black Volvo.

The next afternoon, a grinning young receptionist came up to the big, open office on the first floor of the

Social Services building, carrying a huge bunch of flowers addressed, somewhat flamboyantly, Shela thought, to "my Thursday evening lady", with a short note attached asking her out for a meal the next day.

"Be careful," advised a cautious Doris on the phone that evening, and Shela turned down the sound on the television news broadcast of the first supersonic aircraft flight. "You know nothing about him."

It was true that Shela knew next to nothing about the man who had partnered her so regularly over the last few weeks. But she knew that she enjoyed his company, and as a long buried yearning for something other than work and a lonely bed surfaced in her mind, she began, despite her initial misgivings, a new and very different relationship to any that she had known before.

In the same week that she discovered orgasms and a few days after her forty-sixth birthday, Shela met an old college friend in Woolworth's in Midland Road.

"I've had to pull out of my contract at a middle school in Luton," the younger woman explained over tea in the café at the back of the big shop. "It's in the English Department, Shela, and just right for you. If you apply tomorrow, there's a good chance that you'll be offered the vacancy. It's just for two terms, initially, to cover a maternity leave but it will be a start. And if the teacher does not come back to the school, you may get the position on a permanent basis."

Two days later, after a pleasant interview with the school head and an offer of the position with possible future prospects, Shela thankfully handed in her notice at the Social Services office. The twenty mile drive to the school on the outskirts of the town, not far from Luton and Dunstable hospital, meant that some of her much improved salary must be kept back for petrol costs, but, as she turned the old Ford Cortina out of Dunham Close each morning, Shela was happy at last. For now her life in the work she loved could really begin.

CHAPTER
TWENTY

Making Choices

Early in December 1977, Shela began making plans to stay with her daughter over the Christmas holiday. This third child, who started life with ill health always holding her back, was now well settled with her soldier husband and two small children in their married quarters on the big army base at Verden in West Germany. On Christmas Eve, the plane touched down at Hanover airport. Deborah's husband came to meet her at the barrier and Shela remembered all the upset over their wedding plans and silently thanked fate that her girl's marriage was so different from her own first attempt.

The week away from Bedford was spent in much careful thought about her future and, in particular, the role of Terance in her life. The new relationship, which had developed rapidly since Shela started her teaching career, now included weekends together in the little flat at the top of the stairs. Shela was aware that Terance was married when she first met him. But her initial unease with that situation was allayed by his swift assurances that he and his wife, although sharing the same house in Shortstown, opposite the camp at R.A.F. Cardington, also lived separate lives.

The old adage about a man's wife "not understanding him" came to mind as Shela began asking questions about his background and how he was able to live the life of a bachelor when his responsibilities lay less than a mile away from her flat. A part of her mind told her to back away from a situation that could once again destroy her hard-won independence. But the other part whispered insistently that she was entitled to some happiness after the long years of waiting for it to happen.

Her new partner was Anglo-Indian, with the deep brown eyes and lightly tanned skin that were inherited from his mixed race ancestors. After a chaotic, fatherless childhood in Bangalore and Madras, where he was placed in various Catholic children's homes run by the cruelly strict Christian Brothers, with their traditional tenet of rule by fear, Terance had left India in 1943 to serve with the British Army in Malaysia. There he married a Malaysian girl and they settled down in Kuala Lumpur after the war to raise their first three children. In the sixties, he came to Britain to study for an electrical engineering degree and, when this was accomplished, sent for his family to join him in Cyprus, where he then worked for the Ministry of Defence. Later, the family came back to Britain and his job at R.A.F. Henlow.

Several times during the weeks leading up to Christmas, Shela tried to persuade him to go back to try for a reconciliation with his wife and family. For, as the truth gradually came out, she was shocked to discover that he was the father of six children and that three of them still lived at home.

"When I get back from Germany I'll let you know if we have any future," she warned him, after tearful pleading from this disturbing but immature man who nevertheless fascinated her with his strange view of the world and her place in it.

"Kick him out," Norma from next door stated baldly. "He's a chancer if ever I saw one and you are a fool to encourage him. Whatever would George have thought of you?"

But George is dead, Shela thought bleakly. Then lay awake in the small hours wrestling with her conscience. The overwhelming passion she had first experienced with this fascinating man from a different country and culture, and her aching need for companionship and security, quickly dispelled any fleeting qualms she had about her new relationship. The new and exhilarating feeling of being wanted and loved, to the exclusion of all others, acted like a soothing balm on her fractured self-esteem. Now she had it all. A satisfying job and a man she could love.

The notion that her friend from across the landing was jealous of her grew in her mind when visits from next door became less and less and finally ceased altogether. When Norma began to ignore her as they passed on the stairs, Shela was upset but determined to live her life as she chose and not be ruled by others.

Within a week of her return from Germany, she gave Terance an ultimatum.

"You must either stay with your wife and family or leave them to move in here and live openly with me. I can't stand any more of this furtive coming and going and neighbours gossiping about us the way they do. The choice is yours," she stated firmly. "It's up to you."

Two days later, he stood on her doorstep with a large suitcase and several bundles of his belongings and told her that he'd spoken to his wife and a lawyer and there was to be a legal separation. And the reason he could not take Shela out socially was because he was always short of money. Now she remembered his meagre offer of ten pounds a week towards the housekeeping budget on his first day with her, and the meek way that she had accepted it without question when he explained that he must pay the majority of his salary to his wife in maintenance for her and their three dependent children.

A chance meeting with one of George's old work colleagues only added further to the confusion in her mind, when he revealed that Terance was not popular with either his neighbours or his workmates. "He's a dark horse, that one, Shela," the man repeated. "My advice is to steer clear of him. In my opinion, he's a womaniser and his wife has put up with a lot over the years that they have lived here."

"I don't want to lose you," he pleaded that evening, when Shela faced him with the accusations she had just heard. "And they don't like me because of the colour of my skin. It's colour prejudice. Can't you see that? It's the reason why I've not been promoted in my job and why the neighbours don't like me."

Shela listened in silence to the little boy lost in the big, wide world act, which she was to come to know so well. The pleading continued until well into the night, with the final promise that he would leave in the morning if that were her decision.

"But I'll have nowhere to go," he stated pathetically as Shela closed the bedroom door on him and he prepared to sleep in the spare room. There was to be no sleep for her that night as Shela once again wrestled with her conscience and finally lost. For the emotional manipulation that Terance applied with practiced ease began on that day and gradually increased in the coming months as he laid the blame for the break up of his marriage firmly at her door.

"I left my wife and children for you," he repeatedly reminded her every time Shela suggested that he go back to them. "And they don't want me back now."

Shela continued to visit her mother-in-law several times a week. She knew that the old lady sadly missed her son and that she did not take kindly to the idea of a new man in his widow's life. A painful visit from Judith, a few days after Terance was first introduced to George's mother, ended in a firm request for the return of her grandmother's front door key and the announcement that Shela was no longer welcome at the little flat across the green. So another connection with her old life was severed as she retreated further into her self-imposed isolation from all that had gone before.

The role of "the other woman" fitted uneasily into the persona that Shela had developed in her working life. For the anticipated renewal of the contract at the school in Luton did not materialise, and subsequent, intermittent supply teaching, although paid on a higher level than contract work, did little to fulfil her first, enthusiastic idealisms. Shela's next, unexpected but temporary appointment in the English department at St. Bede's Roman Catholic School in Bromham Road, Bedford, after a short refresher course on the subject, daily provoked a mild sense of hysteria at the anomaly of the situation as she taught her young charges the advantages of living up to the morals and standards which self-respect could bring. The self-respect that she secretly acknowledged, in painful guilt, she had lost when she started living with a married man with no hope of regularising that relationship through marriage.

"He is a Catholic," she explained to her bemused mother, who listened in non-judgemental silence to all the reasons why Shela was still "living in sin", as she put it. "His wife is even more devout in her religious views and will never agree to a divorce. I have changed my name to his through a deed poll," she continued quietly. "Life is much easier that way."

Since the arrival of Terance in her life, both of Shela's sons had stayed away and, as the months went by and they made every excuse not to visit her, she realised with growing sadness that this was their way of showing resentment at her new situation. It was to be nearly two years before she saw them again and, by that time and to Terance's great satisfaction, she and the source of their disapproval had left the flat in Dunham Close to live in a remote cottage on the outskirts of Willington, a few miles from Bedford.

CHAPTER
TWENTY-ONE

Another New Home

Shela had been working at Robert Peel Junior School in Sandy for several months when the decision was made to move. Part of the reason was that she could no longer afford to run her own car. The old Ford Cortina had seen better days. When she reluctantly offered it, for a few pounds, to the tenant in the flat below, the money rapidly became swallowed up in the expense of paying for two households. Shela felt that yet another part of her independence had disappeared. With the loss of her car came the loss of her job at Sandy and only after more frantic searching and hopeful applications was she able to secure a new position at Robert Bruce Middle School in Kempston.

Each morning, as she waited for the local bus to take her into the bus station in Greyfriars, she thought about Terance driving off in his Volvo to his office, and the first, uncomfortable pangs of resentment began to surface in her troubled mind. At the bus stop outside The Bedford Co-operative Society shop in Midland Road, where she had often queued with her mother for the annual dividend payout, she was joined by some of her own pupils as they all pushed noisily on to the

250

Kempston bound bus. And Shela thought longingly of her old car and the convenience of travel that she had given up so easily.

"I must have some wheels again," she protested in exasperation one evening after she had again missed the connecting bus from the town centre. "I'm often not home now until nearly six o'clock. It's ridiculous!" A few days later, Terance arrived home with a fold-up bicycle purchased from the NAAFI shop at Henlow.

"There you are," he announced proudly as he demonstrated the fold up mechanism to a dumbfounded Shela. "I've bought you some wheels. They are much healthier than driving a car everywhere. Now perhaps you will stop complaining."

The remaining justification for the move to the remote cottage in Willington was far more difficult to explain or accept. Since their first days together, her new partner never failed to attend the local Catholic Church every Sunday and it soon became clear to Shela that he expected her to accompany him.

"But I am not a Catholic," she protested as he began the usual persuasive tactics that invariably ended in her capitulation. "I have not been a churchgoer since I was a child."

Shela suspected that something other than money worries was troubling Terance and one night her suspicions were confirmed. The alarm clock by the bed read three-thirty when she was frantically shaken awake by the terrified man beside her.

"Listen," he whispered urgently in her ear as Shela tried to rouse herself from a deep sleep. "There it is again," he continued breathlessly. Both of them heard the sound of slow, dragging footsteps approaching the bedroom door, then stop and finally recede back along the hallway towards the front door of the flat.

"It's George," the terrified man gasped. "He's begun to haunt us. We have to get away from here!"

Then, to Shela's shocked consternation, he began to shout at the top of his voice.

"Leave us alone! You are not wanted here! You are dead!"

With all the lights on in the flat and after a short but chilly search around the landing outside, she climbed back into bed and told Terance that it must have been someone in one of the other flats on their landing.

"Sound travels very clearly at night," she stated calmly. "When you have been a flat-dweller as long as I have, you take no notice of odd sounds other tenants make. There are no ghosts here or anywhere else. It is only people moving around at all hours. Go to sleep."

But Terance was not convinced and every Sunday from then on he never missed going to confession, but would never tell Shela what was said in that mysterious cubicle at the back of the church. The footsteps were heard again several times after that first puzzling night and, although Shela eventually traced them to the old lady living in the flat below, Terance refused to accept that explanation and persisted in his assertion that the flat was haunted. His belief in the existence of ghosts was the precursor of many such convictions that revealed his innate immaturity. It was also the cause of much future heartache for Shela as she tried to come to terms with the fact that this middle-aged man was still influenced by his disturbed childhood background in India, with all its strange myths and a culture so different from that which he encountered when he came to live in England.

The semi-detached cottage at the end of Wood Lane, Willington, on land belonging to Hill Farm, was everything that Shela had hoped for when she first heard of its impending vacancy from one of her colleagues at the school.

"Forty pounds a month, with three months rent in advance," stated Gavin Wilson, whose family had worked the arable farm for several generations and whose son would eventually take it over when his father retired. Shela got on well with the hard-working farmer, and his wife Audrey, from the first day she met them. But she could sense, almost from the start, that the feeling was not reciprocated when it came to her partner.

"They are racially prejudiced," he repeated, the day after the first heated exchange of words with their landlord, concerning a car-port that Terance had built at the side of the cottage. "Just like the senior managers at work."

Shela had by now heard all this many times and had long ceased to believe that it was the reason that Terance was denied the promotion he should have been offered some years before. She knew that he was a clever mathematician, with all the qualifications required for his work in electronics. As time went by, she also realised that it was his complete lack of empathy with his work colleagues that inevitably resulted in his failure to advance up the promotional ladder.

Terance's attitude to women was a further source of distress. For the first few years they were together, he never failed to embarrass her in company, with the puerile and smutty remarks expected more of a schoolboy than a mature man in his fifties. Eventually she learned to ignore them, but as time went on she became more and more reluctant to socialise with friends and family when he was present.

Occasionally, when he was at work and she was at home during the school holidays, one of her sisters would arrive to take her to a girly lunch with the others. It was during one of these outings, which Shela enjoyed so much and which became, in time, a lifeline out of her isolation in the little cottage, that Terance turned up unexpectedly at The Kings Arms pub in Cardington. The humiliating scene that followed, while he raged about her deceit and the connivance of her sisters in persuading her to go out with them without his permission or informing him first, took them completely by surprise.

"There's something wrong with that man," advised one of the girls when she telephoned her sister the next morning. "And you are only making him worse, Shela. No man who is normal behaves like that in this day and age and, certainly, no self-respecting woman in her right mind would put up with it for long. He's nothing but a control freak."

254

Later that day, as she looked around her cosy home and wandered through the neat garden which Terance had worked hard to cultivate all through the summer, Shela tried to come to terms with her sister's comment. Yes, she acknowledged that she was uneasy about the behaviour of a man who was so jealously possessive of her that he regularly questioned her about male teaching colleagues or brief encounters with friends' husbands when they partnered her more than once at school dances or spoke to her in church. The way he expected her to dress so provocatively for those dances, in off the shoulder or low cleavage gowns which had been bought on his insistence and despite misgivings on her part, made Shela feel like a trophy that had to be shown off to all and sundry.

Sometimes, after these lengthy and prolonged inquisitions, Shela threatened to leave. But, she agonised, as Terance retreated into a sullen silence after each outburst, where to? This was the home she had helped to build with such high hopes for the future. And this was the man she had settled for, with all his faults and idiosyncrasies.

Shela had lived in the cottage at the end of the lane for nearly two years, when, to her enormous relief and in the same week that Prince Charles married Diana Spencer, her two sons started to visit once more and her daughter came to stay along with her three small children during the school summer holidays. Christopher's first short marriage had ended, after much heartbreak, in an acrimonious divorce, and, as she listened with compassion to her first child's anguished voice on the telephone, she longed to be able to put her arms around him and give him the motherly comfort he had not known since he left home at twelve years of age. A surprise visit from him, later that year of 1982, accompanied by a pretty, sensible girl who was later to become his second wife, gave his mother much pleasure as she watched her son getting on with his life, just like she herself had done after each trauma in her own.

On quiet summer evenings, when Terance was away on work assignments, Shela often walked alone in the woods high on the hill above the farm. And it was there, as an enormous harvest moon shone down through the trees, that the first idea for a children's book was triggered in her mind. The writing began and her ongoing and deep-seated unhappiness was pushed to the back of her mind as she lost herself once more in the magical world of her imagination.

CHAPTER
TWENTY-TWO

Consequences

The writing continued throughout that third summer and soon a second children's book manuscript was completed. But Shela began to suffer from agonising migraine headaches, which sometimes incapacitated her all day.

"You are going through the menopause," diagnosed the old doctor at the surgery in the next village. "I can prescribe painkillers, but what you really need is less stress in your life. As for the recurring bouts of cystitis," he continued gravely, "I think we both know what causes those. Tell that man of yours to leave you alone for a few weeks to give it a chance to clear up."

"Nonsense," was Terance's curt response to the doctor's advice. "It's good for you."

But for Shela, who was now in her fifties, the nightly onslaught of vigorous and sometimes bizarre sex which left her feeling dirty and used, and which Terance stated flatly that he could not sleep without, had slowly become a dreaded ordeal, to be borne in silence until it was over and blessed sleep took away the emotional and physical pain. When she at last refused him, he began to take more work away from home and the mysterious phone calls began. Terance denied any knowledge about the callers. Of course he would, for they were from angry women who wanted to inform Shela of their affairs with him. During one phone call, the woman poured out such vitriolic spleen about her short-lived liaison with Terance, that Shela, devastated by all she was forced to listen to, tried unsuccessfully to ring her back for more details with which to confront him. When she tried to dial out, the phone went dead.

"There's something wrong with it," she informed him calmly that evening as she served up the curry he loved so much. "I've been trying to ring Mum all day but it's not ringing through."

Two weeks later, and after several more accusatory phone calls that Terance curtly put down to work colleagues making mischief, Shela sought advice from her nephew who now worked for British Telecom. And she at last understood why the phone was not working properly. Terance had tampered, quite unlawfully, with the phone mechanism, making it impossible to make calls out but still allowing incoming ones. Another instance of his overpowering urge to control her life, she thought bleakly. Even down to phone calls that any normal person would not think twice about. Did he enjoy her humiliation, she wondered, or was it all part of his desperate need for her complete dependence on him?

Nobody in the family knew anything was wrong as Shela cycled daily down the lane to leave her bicycle at Bob Filby's motor repair shop at the end of it. With no car of her own, she now had to catch the local bus everywhere and she was working at Great Barford Lower School, when she came to the painful decision that she could no longer live in this way.

"Put the phone right or we're finished," she told Terance flatly. "And if you ever do anything like that again," she continued, looking closely at his guilty face, "I will inform the phone company and they will sue you for criminal damage to their equipment."

The next day, she was able to make the first phone call to her mother for many weeks and catch up with all the family news. Mum had been living at Speen, in Buckinghamshire, for the last few years in a small cottage near to Shela's older brother, John. And now she learned of the disturbing news that he would shortly be selling up and moving to America. Now a widower after the sad and early death of his wife, John wanted to live near his children, who had emigrated some years previously.

"I am coming back to Bedford," her mother stated cheerfully. "We have to start looking for a suitable place for me."

Shela's mother stayed with her for nearly three months during the summer of 1982, when the reporting of The Falklands War kept them all glued to the television set every evening. Mum's quiet presence in the little house seemed, to the distracted younger woman, to calm and soothe her tense relationship with Terance. She watched in astonishment as his behaviour moderated and he daily treated her mother with the same courtesy and care that she herself had known in their early days together.

When the family found a small cottage for their mother in the next village, Shela was glad for her. She was also secretly dismayed at the prospect of once more coping alone in her own isolated home with the mercurial man who shared her life and her bed. The regular visits to her mother in the small cottage on The Green at Cardington, when they shared old memories of the family and childhood and Shela was able to relax for a few precious hours, slowly became the highlight of her week.

When Mary's young husband, Roy, died so tragically at work, Shela was at the cottage and took Beryl's phone call asking her to tell their mother the bad news. At the funeral a few days later, when the Winch family gathered once again in support of one of their own, Shela looked around at her married sisters and brothers with their partners and grieved that she could not be like them. For Terance would not attend the ceremony.

"You can go," he had told her condescendingly. "I will not." And Shela was once again torn between family loyalty and the emotional manipulation of the man who was incapable of conforming to accepted custom and tradition. Even for a family funeral.

The regular visits to her mother became an increasing source of much resentment from Terance. After one particularly distressing outburst of jealousy, which Shela attributed to the fact that he no longer had any regular contact with his own siblings or his children, he stayed in bed the next day complaining of severe chest pains.

"I'm calling the doctor," she told him quietly. "You've already had one heart attack. This may well develop into another."

An hour later, he was in hospital in intensive care on a heart monitor, which eventually revealed that his heart was damaged and he must stay at home for the next few months to rest. At just sixty, Terance began to consider early retirement and urged Shela to do the same.

"What do you propose we should live on, then?" she asked quietly. "I've not had the chance to build up my own pension enough to think of retirement until I reach retirement age. And that is seven years away."

Shela had already talked to Terance's wife while he was in hospital, and soon afterwards, to her great relief, the two younger children began to visit their father weekly, while their mother assured her that she would light a candle for him next day in her Catholic Church of Christ The King, in London Road. When his eldest daughter at last came to visit, she confided to Shela that, when her father left the family home, her mother was very relieved.

"They were always like chalk and cheese," the young woman explained. "And my mother did not want any more babies. She'd had enough of that after six of them." Then she added, almost as an afterthought, "He always had a roving eye, Shela. I hope you realise that."

Terance's wife obviously didn't believe in birth control, thought Shela when she waved goodbye to his sensible daughter, who had two children of her own and, despite also being a devout Catholic, would make sure there were no more. The same daughter rang her father a few months later to impart the dreadful news that her mother was suffering from cancer and that she was already very ill and not expected to recover.

"You must go to see her," Shela urged an obviously very shocked man. "She is still your wife and the mother of your children. They would never forgive you if you didn't go."

Now began a strange time of frequent visits to his old home in Shortstown, coupled with episodes of tearful self-recrimination. And Shela watched with a new compassion as he turned to the church for comfort and guidance, for she realised that even at his age he was unable to cope with thoughts of death. When his wife died peacefully at home, later that year, Shela was thankful that Terance was there to say goodbye and able at last to try to assuage his conscience.

A few days after the funeral, they visited the place where she lay buried. The small mound of freshly dug earth in the corner of Cardington cemetery, still covered with wilting family flowers, seemed like a silent rebuke as Shela knelt to read the poignant messages with the ink already faded and brown in the hot August sunshine. Lying face down against the perimeter wall some distance away, she found the remains of the beautiful wreath that Terance had placed on the grave the day after the funeral. She guessed that it had been thrown aside by his family as an angry gesture against the father that they had never forgiven. The haunting memory of that broken wreath was never to leave her as she began to contemplate spending the rest of her life with the man who placed it there.

CHAPTER
TWENTY-THREE

Third Time Lucky?

"I have arranged for us to be married early next month," Terance stated one evening, barely a month after the funeral. "I explained to the receptionist that we had been together for eight years before my late wife died. You should have seen the look on her face when she read the date on the death certificate."

Shela stood speechless as she was handed the appointment card for the Registry Office ceremony some three weeks away. There had been no discussion and certainly no agreement that they should marry so soon after the funeral.

"Why can't we go on as we are?" she queried. Then hesitated, as the usual sullen look appeared again on his face and she knew he was about to start on the persuasive routine that had become so familiar to her over the years. An hour later, with the meal she had prepared going cold in the oven, and her protests about the unseemly haste to rush into marriage of no avail, Terance was once again complaining of chest pains, and Shela began, against her better judgement, to consider the possibility that within a month she would become a legal wife again.

264

"There's no need to tell anyone," she was told as she began to discuss plans for the wedding day. "We'll just go away and do it with no fuss. I've already arranged the witnesses."

Three weeks later, the quiet wedding, that Terance had planned at the same registry office in Brereton Road where Shela had married George some eighteen years before, had turned into a family celebration. All of her children were there and some of her brothers and sisters arrived unexpectedly, while Mum sat smiling in the front row next to Joycey. No one from the groom's family came to see their father marry the woman they blamed for taking him away from their home.

"That's understandable," sighed Shela, when the cake was cut and toasts drunk in the small dining room of the cottage at Willington. "But I wish at least one of them could have made the effort to be here." Outside, the roses were still in full bloom and the little garden gnome, that became a character in one of Shela's first books for children, smiled happily at the departing guests. And her new husband waited until the last one had gone before he confirmed what she had suspected had been on his mind for some time.

"I've decided to take early retirement. At sixty, my pension will still be quite substantial and there will be a reasonable gratuity. I'll be finished with the M.O.D. and Henlow by Christmas."

The next week, Shela gave in her notice to the head of Robert Bruce Middle School in Kempston, where she had again been working since the start of the new school year. She would be leaving two weeks before the end of the Christmas term.

She had been happy at this school, which was to be her final teaching post. And as the last day arrived, she thought back to all those other schools and the countless numbers of children she had taught over the years. Some stood out very clearly in her memory. They were the ones she had watched in anticipation as their understanding of good literature and the written word slowly deepened under her guidance. If for no other reason than this, Shela knew that the years of training and hard work in the classroom had been more than worthwhile. Her teaching had also become an important part of her own identity and had repaid her many times over in terms of personal fulfilment and the feelings of self-worth that had eluded her before she began to work with children.

"We are off to India," she explained to her teaching colleagues in the staff room the next day. "My husband wants to search out his roots."

"We shall be sorry to lose you," the head smiled as he wished her well in her new venture. "You may get to see the England cricket team in Bangalore on their Indian tour next year."

For many months, Terance had talked about returning to his birthplace in India to trace the old members of his family who had stayed on when independence and partition came in 1947. Soon after the news of the terrible bombing in the Brighton hotel where Tory ministers stayed during their annual party conference and which seemed to fill every evening news bulletin, travel plans were finalised and arrangements made to sell the contents of their home at Peacock's auction rooms near Shela's childhood home in Newnham Street in Bedford.

"I didn't want to marry again," she said as she hugged her mother goodbye at the gate of her small cottage on The Green at Cardington. "But I will certainly feel more secure as a wife on the other side of the world." Then she added softly, "Make sure that you are here when I get back, Mum."

"And where do you imagine I'll be?" laughed her mother, and Shela kissed the smiling face and prayed that she would soon see her old mum again.

"How long will you be away?" asked Deborah, when she was told of the plans for her mother and new step-father. She held tightly on to her mother's hand all the way back to her temporary home with her in-laws in Luke Place, just off Mile Road in Bedford. "You're not planning to live there permanently, are you?" she added anxiously.

Shela knew that this idea had been at the back of his mind when Terance wrote to his younger brother still living with his family in Coimbatore in southern India. But the notion of leaving England and all that was dear and familiar to her, to live in a strange place, was beyond her comprehension.

"We'll give it a year," she told him. "After that, I'm coming home. You must do what you want, but my place is here, near to my family."

The long flight to Bombay, with an overnight stop in Damascus, where armed police patrolled the airport and looked suspiciously at new arrivals, proved so exhausting that Shela was glad to sleep all the next day in the big airport hotel.

"Bread and jam for missee," smiled the young room service waiter as he placed a heavy tray on the bedside table. "Dorai (master) ordered an English tea for you."

Shela looked wearily at a plateful of thick, sweet bread and jam sandwiches already dry and curling in the heat, and decided that this was not her idea of an English tea. She was to learn very quickly over the next few weeks, that some remnants of the British Raj still survived, even in the big, bustling cities of that land on the other side of the world.

The small, internal Indian Airways plane, that took off three days later bound for Coimbatore in Tamil Nadu in the south of the country, seemed, in contrast to the huge passenger airliner they had boarded at Heathrow, to be overcrowded and inadequate for the number of passengers on board. The polite, young stewardesses did their best to make their English passengers comfortable, but the food offered was like no other that Shela had eaten before, and, when the small aircraft finally touched down on the dusty runway at Coimbatore International Airport, she was already ill with a tummy bug that would keep her in bed for the next week.

CHAPTER
TWENTY-FOUR

India

"It is so hot here. Does it never get any cooler than this?"

Shela sat weakly on the edge of the bed, while her sister-in-law bathed her patient's perspiring face and apologised once again for the local electricity shutdown that had put all the electric fans in the small house out of action yet again. Lou and her two daughters were kind and considerate towards their new English relation, and Shela gradually adjusted to the heat and the change of diet. By Christmas Day, she was able to accompany them to the old Roman Catholic Church in the town, where traditional hymns were sung in English but the mass was celebrated in Tamil.

Special prayers were offered on that day for the victims of the American Union Carbide chemical plant explosion at Bhopal in northern India. She listened in horror as graphic details of the disaster were read out from the pulpit. 2,000 killed and 200,000 others affected. And she tried to picture the reported "skies glowing red with funeral pyres" and wondered at the failure of the government to enforce stricter safety measures in a country where money talked louder than the casual wastage of human lives.

A week later, she danced in the new year at the Anglo-Indian Club, where a modern swing band played all the old dance tunes that Shela remembered from her youth and she wore a new low cut dress that Terance had chosen for her before leaving England.

"We'd better add a bit of lace to your dress, aunty," laughed one of her new nieces as they all prepared for the dance. "It won't do to display too much cleavage in front of the Indian servants at the club."

At midnight, as the church bells of the considerable Christian community in the town rang out and local Indian boys threw stones angrily at the windows of the club, Shela was forcibly reminded that the old divide of races and religions still existed in the country that had cut its ties with the British Empire nearly four decades previously.

Early in March of the next year, when they had been in India for just over two months and the hot season continued to sap relentlessly at her energy in dusty Coimbatore, plans were made to move on to the old hill station of Ootacamund, high in the Nilgiri Hills, north of the city.

"What you have heard is true."

The voice of the old Catholic priest droned on through the suffocating heat of a South India early evening.

"Yes," he answered Shela's query. "I was in England in the fifties visiting an old friend in Brighton. The Sussex Downs are truly just like the valley of

Ootacamund. Even the golf club is named after Hastings — though I think that refers to the old Viceroy and not your English town."

"One more day," Shela whispered tensely to herself as she tried to settle down under stifling mosquito nets for the last night in the hot and humid city. She couldn't wait to "make for the hills" like the Memsahibs of the old Raj days and, as she waited for sleep to come, marvelled once again at those women who found the strength and endurance to cope with the overpowering heat down on the plains. The next day, as the train, with an engine, she noted with surprise and some nostalgia, made in Derby, pulled slowly out of Mettupalayam Station at the foot of the Nilgiri Hills, Shela breathed a huge sigh of relief that at last the long, hot dusty days were nearly over.

All day, the little steam train puffed and whistled up impossibly steep gradients on the Blue Mountain Railway Line and the heat and humidity decreased with every mile until, at just over 8,000 feet, it pulled into Ooty Station and a climate like the Sussex Downs in high summer.

"That old priest was quite right," Terance observed as he tried to prevent an over-enthusiastic porter from making off with the luggage. There then followed a perplexing conversation in Tamil and broken English until he at last made the man understand that the luggage was not bound for the most expensive tourist hotel in the town, but a small bungalow in the compound of the Convent of St. Francis de Salles.

For the first few weeks, dinner was taken with the chaplain in the high, vaulted dining-room of the old convent but eventually Shela's English digestive system rebelled once again after too many masala dosays, pepper-water soup, better known as mulligatawny soup at home, and, worst of all, boiled milk in the tea. After the third bout of "funny-tummy" or "Ghandi's revenge" as the cheerful nuns called it, plans were made to look for alternative, self-catering accommodation. To this end, a visit was made to an elderly English lady in her eighties, one of a rapidly dwindling band of tea-planter's widows who had "stayed on" after independence.

"You must try the Canadian missionaries up on Missionary Hill," she advised as she poured scented Nilgiri tea into beautiful, fine china teacups and offered home made scones with honey.

Two weeks later, Shela gazed out on a lush, green lawn bordered by climbing bougainvillaea and decided that the small cottage, obtained on a short lease from the missionary society, was the next best thing to England. The tiny kitchen provided water for just three hours daily and the even smaller bathroom could only be described as primitive. But the sight of a western-style toilet, after months of coping with the usual Indian sanitary arrangements, more than compensated for the daily arrival of an ancient, insulated drum of hot water, complete with plastic jug, which was the shower system. The garden wallah charged only two cigarettes a day, and any left over food for his large family, for this invaluable service.

Since her arrival in India, Shela had been constantly shocked at the casual poverty she observed everywhere. The contrast between the rich and the poor was nowhere more marked than in the old hill station, where she now lived extremely well on an average English pension. The poor lifestyle of most of the townspeople was deeply disturbing, and Shela daily cooked extra food for them and gave away items of clothing and dispensed annas for the begging children who congregated at her door every morning to follow the white English "missee" along the road to market or to church.

"You must learn to ignore them," advised the old retired Scottish missionary living in the same compound. "Otherwise they will give you no peace."

Ooty Cathedral was not much bigger than a village church in England but it was truly beautiful. A whitewashed building with red roof tiles standing high on Cathedral Hill overlooking the little town. Every window, Shela noted, made of clear stained glass. No patterns or pictures of saints and apostles. But when the bright South India sun shone through those windows, it transformed the dim interior into a wondrous world of rainbow colours, matched only by the colourful saris of the Tamil ladies who sat cross-legged, but still graceful, in rows across the floor. Around the altar great bunches of wild, white arum lilies took on all the colours of the stained glass while the noonday sun moved across the valley.

At communion, the young Tamil priest changed from his native tongue to the familiar Corpus Christi when he came to the English lady at the rail. Sometimes he even recited The Lord's Prayer in very good English with a big smile which truly said "welcome". Always after mass, Shela liked to wander through the burial ground around the cathedral. The ancient tombstones, arranged in terraces like the Nilgiri tea plantations covering the surrounding hills, often told sad tales of early deaths from cholera or typhoid and on some, the heart-breaking inscriptions told of entire families of some nineteenth century servant of the Raj perishing in the fight against the relentless heat and overpowering epidemics which had raged at regular intervals in that far flung corner of the British Empire.

So the months in India passed and soon the monsoons came to the valley to make walking difficult on the steep roads, and drivers of bone shaking auto-rickshaws became reluctant to attempt the steep climb up Missionary Hill to the compound of Farley, the big house on Havelock Road. On long walks around the town, Shela noted, with pangs of homesickness, the familiar names on rows of decaying, late Victorian villas, each one probably named after the late owner's original home in England. There they stood, in the middle of India, a poignant reminder: The Hollies, The Laurels, Mon Repos, Bluebell Villa, Yew Tree House, Sunset House and The Lilacs. The street names were as familiar to Shela as they had become to the Indian townsfolk who took over the old houses after the British exit more than forty years before. Charing Cross became the main shopping street, while Kensington Gardens contained the only small park in the town.

Bloomsbury Road housed the local cinema, while Portland Place was the home of "The Snooty Ooty Snooker Club", or so Shela was told by a young back-packer she met one day on his travels through South India on the way to his destination of Goa.

Terance tried several times to gain admittance to this august institution, for he had heard that it was the birthplace of the ancient game of snooker. At length and only after an introductory letter from the Catholic priest in Coimbatore was proffered, were the visitors able to penetrate the outer doors of The Indian Ooty Snooker Club. Inside they found a smoking room barely touched since the days of the Raj. Hung around tobacco brown walls were sepia photographs of old members as far back as 1885. Best of all, Shela saw, were photographs of Ooty as it had been in the twenties and thirties. And there they were. The suburban roads and villas of England, the orderly crocodiles of English children on their way to school and the bands and flags of that little bit of England so far from home.

So the monsoon months passed and at last the sun came back in time for the second Christmas away from home. All over the small town, which had a very active Christian community, large star-shaped lanterns floated on long poles outside front doors. Coloured lights swung from the branches of fragrant eucalyptus trees and everywhere there was a feeling of expectancy. New Anglo-Indian friends from the Mission School further down the line in Coonor and a very modern boys school at Kotagiri, where Shela had been invited to help out with voluntary teaching when they first arrived in Ooty, met the newcomers at the old, grey church of St Mark's on the other side of the valley. This church had been used in several scenes for the film *Heat and Dust* and it was here that Shela found yet more weathered headstones bearing testament to the hard lives and early deaths of those empire builders of the past.

Inside the old, grey church, filled with the scent of lilies and incense, school choirs sang carols in Tamil and English, and Shela thought longingly of home when everyone greeted the Christ-child at midnight. Outside in the porch afterwards, amidst Christmas greetings of "namasti, namasti", with palms placed together and a small bow to everyone in earshot, sticky jilebis were passed around to those children still awake. High above the dark hills surrounding the jewel-lighted town, a huge, yellow moon looked down on the activities far below and Shela was comforted to know that it would also be observing midnight churchgoers in far-off England.

CHAPTER
TWENTY-FIVE

Returning Home

"When are we going home?" Shela asked wearily, one day in late February. "We agreed on a year and it's now well over that. I've had enough."

After several trips to Madras on the east coast, where most of his schooldays had been spent, Terance had still found no trace of the old aunts and middle-aged cousins who lived there when he left the city for active service in the British Army in 1943. Each of these trips took several days and Shela did not accompany him on any of them. "You would find it much too hot," he explained, each time he prepared to leave. And Shela was glad to be alone in the cottage on the hill, for his absence gave her time to think about the future.

Since their arrival in the country of his birth, the continual, intimate physical demands that Terance had made on his wife since their first days together, seemed to have lessened. Shela was thankful that nature had, at last stepped in to help. But the frequent visits to their home of an attractive, Anglo-Indian woman friend may have had something to do with that, she thought uneasily, as she began to pack their belongings ready for the long, return trip down to the hot plains. For she couldn't help but notice that Mavis never visited when Terance was away.

There was also the worrying matter of the recurring item on his bank statement. Since leaving the convent compound and settling in to their new home on the hill, her husband had begun to make weekly "charitable" visits to the home of a poor Indian family whose young daughter worked for the nuns. Queenie was a pretty twenty-year-old who would soon be married off to a local boy. She spoke no English, so Shela could not talk to her as she would to her own daughter, but Terance often brought the girl back for a meal and sometimes an overnight stay. He very often took her out shopping to the local market and then she would appear with another cheap bangle on her arm. Shela smiled and tried to look unconcerned at the childish giggles and whisperings between them in Tamil, that she did not understand and which sometimes went on for hours at a time.

Only when she discovered that Terance had arranged for a small monthly payment to be deposited in the girl's name in the local branch of the Bank of India, did she finally explode and ask him what exactly was going on.

"You are a silly woman," he laughed, when Shela faced him with the bank statement. "She's the same age as my daughter!"

The wife of the Canadian missionary took a different view, however. For she confided to Shela that the young Indian girl had visited the cottage while Shela was out and that people were gossiping behind her back.

278

"You must make sure that she does not come here again, my dear. Whatever that husband of yours tells you." Then she added gently, "We have to be careful with these poor people. It is so easy to be compromised and sometimes they are desperate."

Am I getting paranoid about all this? Shela thought to herself as the last few days dragged slowly on. Or is it just homesickness? But the monthly bank payments remained in place when they flew home and Terance refused to discuss the matter further, apart from a sharp, "That's my business." It was to be a full year before he cancelled the standing order, and, by that time, Shela and her husband had returned to England, with much rejoicing on her part and some reluctance on his. Later that year, when the missionaries wrote to say that Queenie had married and was the mother of a baby boy, Shela was living in Yorkshire, for Terance refused outright to go back to Bedford to live near either of their families again. And Shela recalled, with mounting apprehension, her husband's possessive and secretive behaviour in their early days together.

CHAPTER
TWENTY-SIX

Escape into Writing

For the first few months after their return to England, they lived on the top floor of a large Georgian mansion in West Yorkshire owned by Terance's niece.

"You and Uncle Terance can stay until your name comes up on the local housing list," smiled June. "I hope that is before the hall is sold. It's been on the market for some time now." The enterprising young woman, of whom Shela grew to be very fond, ran a business selling Italian furniture, with showrooms in Heath Hall at Heath Common on the outskirts of Wakefield. Shela loved the spacious rooms after the confines of the tiny bungalow in India, and when her daughter moved to Catterick Garrison in North Yorkshire with her soldier husband, she was much happier, for now she could begin to see something of her family again after the months away.

In time, her younger brother Robert, together with his new wife, Jacky, came to stay at the big house. Later still, Joycey made the long journey up the A1 with their mother to visit and exclaim over the beautiful furniture and the size of the rooms. During these visits, Shela and June watched with some amusement but not a little irritation as Terance assumed the role of lord of the manor. A painful reminder of his patronising attitude in India towards the garden mali and the old woman who had come daily to clean and wait for scraps of food left over from dinner the night before.

Four long months later, Wakefield Council offered the couple a two-bedroom bungalow in nearby Kirkthorpe, and Shela began once again to pack ready for the move. She had many misgivings during those months of waiting, for Terance continued to flirt outrageously, first with June's clearly embarrassed cleaning lady and then with a young Indian woman, the divorced mother of two young children who lived on the other side of the common. Shela knew that their neighbour had a drink problem and she suspected that Terance took advantage of this, explaining his many visits to her house with the excuse of helping with electrical work and odd jobs around the garden. She tried hard to ignore his faults, but often despised herself for making no objection when his blatant behaviour became too obvious. Shela desperately wanted this third marriage to succeed and so became adept at turning a deaf ear to whispered telephone conversations and ignored the broken toasters, steam irons and other old domestic appliances that regularly appeared in her kitchen, awaiting repair.

Television news on that December day in 1988 was full of the Lockerbie air disaster. Over 250 Americans flying home for Christmas were killed when their plane blew up over the small Scottish town and a further eleven people were killed as debris from the huge Pan

Am flight fell on them far below. In the neat bungalow, now surrounded by a carefully tended garden, Shela watched the horrific news unfold and decided that she must learn to count her blessings in the face of the human misery north of the border.

Early the next year, she became a member of the newly formed local branch of the Women's Institute and soon afterwards was voted in as secretary. Shela tried hard, in those first vaguely unhappy days in Yorkshire when life seemed pointless and she put on weight through comfort eating, to reach out to others who needed more in their lives than the boring round of housework, shopping, cooking and bed. To this end, she joined a Creative Writing course in the nearby town of Ossett and began to write regularly again for the first time since leaving Willington five years previously. The children's book, begun on the lawn of the lush, cottage garden in India, was now revised and completed. *High Summer Magic*, sent off hopefully to London, continued to do the rounds of publishers and agents, while Shela started another book, with the help and encouragement of the local writers' group.

She was not allowed to drive to those weekly meetings. She was not allowed to drive at all, for Terance had the sole use of the little Fiat car purchased on their return from India. "Your eyesight is not good enough," he stated flatly, in answer to Shela's mild protests. "You are not safe on the roads."

Her life, now ordered by the whims and preferences of her husband, took on a weird and dreamlike quality as the days passed into 1990 and she took refuge once more in her writing by completing yet another manuscript of a book for children.

A surprise holiday in Llandudno, arranged by her husband without her knowledge or agreement, resulted in a further retreat into the black hole of depression that daily threatened to overwhelm her and from which there seemed to be no escape. The only relief was in sleep and writing. On the day when Terance suggested that they should now live separate lives and he joined a local wine club, while urging his wife to sign up for another writing course, Shela weighed nearly three stones more than she had ever weighed before.

"Why don't you join Weight Watchers?" suggested a new friend from the W.I. Then she added gently, "A visit to the doctor might also be a good idea."

When family from Bedford visited, Shela made huge efforts to appear normal, for she knew how worried they would be if they realised what was going on in the small bungalow up there in Yorkshire and how miserable she really felt. But still she would not let go of this third marriage, for she could not admit, even to herself, that she had failed yet again.

Events came to a frightening climax on the day Shela tried to take an overdose of the sleeping pills prescribed by a sympathetic doctor. While Terance was out one evening, she found evidence of his current betrayal in the pocket of a forgotten jacket hanging behind the bedroom door. A woman's name, address and phone number had been hastily scrawled on a scrap of paper. The address was in Ossett, a few streets away from the education centre where she attended her writing classes. And now she remembered the face of the slim, fair-haired woman they had met on the coach to Llandudno and the barely audible phone conversations that she strained to hear as she lay on her bed every afternoon, trying to escape into blessed sleep.

When Terance broke the lock on the bedroom door and grabbed the small, brown bottle of pills from her hand, Shela vomited the rest of them all over the bedside rug and then lay exhausted as he phoned for the doctor.

"How many did you take?' the young Indian doctor enquired, looking carefully at his patient's white face and counting up the number of pills still left in the bottle. "I'll give you an injection to make you sleep now. I'll be back tomorrow. Don't leave her alone," he instructed when Terance saw him out.

Over the next few weeks, Shela was driven regularly to see a stress therapist at the local doctor's surgery and during that time lost weight so rapidly that the girl running the Weight Watchers class told her that she must now start eating normally again and to come back when she had stabilised. Gradually the depression of the last few years began to lift, but the weight stayed off and Shela found that she was unable to eat anything bulky at all. She now relied solely on tins of soup and creamed rice.

A few months after drawing her first state retirement pension from the sub post office in Wakefield, she came to the painful decision that her marriage was over. Terance continued to visit the house in Osset, and in the small bungalow in Kirkthorpe two people lived in awkward silence and slept in separate bedrooms while Shela began to make plans to return to Bedford.

Christopher held his mother's hand and urged her not to cry as his younger brother drove the hired van, filled with her belongings, back down the A1 towards Bedford. With each mile that passed, Shela thought of the neat home she had left behind that morning. She recalled bleakly all the hopes and effort she had put into it five years previously; the kindly neighbours who had supported her over the last awful months; the young Indian doctor who was so concerned for her mental health, and Margaret from the W.I. who had been a constant link with Bedford, for she had taught there at the same time as her friend.

In the small cottage on The Green at Cardington, Shela's mother and other Winch family members awaited the arrival of the prodigal daughter who had chosen, sometimes painfully against her will, to live apart from them for the last few years. How many weddings, baptisms and other family celebrations had she missed during her time with the flawed man who was dismally incapable of socialising with her family? And how often had she weakly given in to his controlling will in reproachful silence as each invitation was ignored? Only now, as her sons drove her away from her marriage and back to the family and place she loved, could Shela at last release the pent-up resentment and frustration of the lost traumatic years. And attempt once again to find peace in familiar places and family loyalties.

PART FIVE

1992–2006

CHAPTER
TWENTY-SEVEN

Moving On

The long, buff envelope containing the divorce petition lay on the bed beside her. In the two weeks since she returned to Bedford, Shela had spent many hours in her mother's spare bedroom looking out on the quiet green in front of the cottage, trying to make plans for the future. The shock arrival of the envelope in the morning's post jerked her out of her comforting bubble once more and made her face up to the reality that soon she would be a single woman again.

A visit to the grave of her husband's first wife in Cardington cemetery, close by the R101 Airship Memorial and communal grave of the survivors of that disaster, did nothing to relieve the turmoil in Shela's mind. The memory of the broken wreath, cast aside by Terance's children, haunted her waking hours in the little cottage on The Green. When sleep refused to come, the only respite was a sleeping pill prescribed by the doctor before she left Yorkshire. And in sleep, the restless dreams of repeated betrayal left her tired and depressed as Shela tried to make her peace with the woman lying in that quiet grave.

"Two weeks!" exclaimed Mum, when Shela slowly read out the words on the long form headed Wakefield Crown Court. "He certainly didn't waste much time."

Terance was petitioning for divorce on the grounds of desertion by his wife.

"Let it proceed," advised the young lady solicitor at the old offices in St. Paul's Square. "We could cross petition, but that would only delay matters. We will apply for maintenance and a share of his capital. In the meantime," she added, looking searchingly at the strained face of her new client, "take this letter to Social Security Services at Wyvern House in Bromham Road. You can't possibly live on twenty-nine pounds a week."

All of Shela's meagre savings had long since been used up in maintenance payments to her husband's first wife and later to his dependent children. For eight years she had been financially dependent on Terance, who controlled the household budget and every penny that came in through their joint pensions. Now Shela must rely on state handouts once again and was painfully reminded of the traumatic visit to the National Assistance office in Ashburnham Road on that long-ago day when her children were so young.

"You know that you can stay here as long as is necessary, my dear," comforted her mother when yet another application for a vacant flat in the town had fallen through. "The housing people will soon come up with something for you now that you've contacted the local councillor."

A month later, October chrysanthemums blazed in her mother's garden and Michaelmas daisies bloomed

290

by the front door, when Shela was offered the tenancy of a sheltered housing flat at Hanover Court in Bedford.

"I'll see to all the furnishings," volunteered Joycey as they looked round the spacious, second floor flat in the big block on the corner of Linden Road and Clapham Road. "Just go away with Beryl and forget everything. John will be pleased to see you after all this time."

A week after she signed the tenancy agreement, Shela boarded a hastily arranged and surprise Pan-Am flight to Chicago en route to Seattle to visit her older brother. Mum had left for the same destination the week before with her youngest son, Robert.

"Now don't fuss, Shela," stated Beryl when her sister started to worry about the cost involved and how she would ever be able to repay her. "I can afford it. You can't. End of story." And Shela was once again reminded of the past, when Beryl brought much-needed bags of coal and new bedding to the little house at Elliot Crescent while Deborah was so ill.

The long flight to Chicago and then onwards across to Seattle on the west coast, where John met them in his big people carrier, was an opportunity to re-kindle the closeness of the two Winch girls who had led such diverse lives. Shela never forgot the generosity of her practical sister who gave without sentimentality and expected nothing in return. Now joined by Beryl's husband, Geoff, the family spent the next few weeks touring, first southwards along The Big Sur and then inland to visit Reno, where Beryl financed Shela's small gambling ventures and the three men played on the roulette tables with some success.

After a tour of San Francisco, where John pointed out all the old haunts of the hippies and flower children of the sixties, they settled in for a week in log cabins in Yosemite National Park. Here Shela experienced a hair-raising and muscle crunching mule ride along a mountain track, where pebbles, dislodged by her mule, Chiquita, fell hundreds of feet to the winding streams far below. At the end of the ride, her legs were so stiff that she had to be lifted off her mount by the Indian guide, who laughed at the "dainty English lady" as he deposited her gently on a wooden bench beside the welcoming coffee shop at the top of the mountain.

Those weeks away, in the company of other beloved family members, were worth more to Shela than any amount of stress counselling or therapy. On that long trip, full of love and laughter, she learned to have fun again. She stopped looking over her shoulder in fear of what she might see and hear. And no longer did she habitually wait for the cutting remarks or, even worse, the sullen, secretive silences, which had pervaded and darkened the last few years of her life.

Too soon, it seemed, it was time to return to John's house near Mt. Vernon to begin preparations for the long flight home. All through the busy weeks in America, Shela's thoughts were often on what life would have to offer when she returned to England, for once she was installed in the new flat she would again be living alone.

"Close your eyes, Shela, and don't open them until I tell you," instructed Joycey. The two sisters and their mother stood at the door of the new flat and, although Shela was tired after the long leg of the flight from Chicago, she could not wait until the next day to see her new home. "Right! You can open them now," her sister laughed.

Shela gazed round at the freshly carpeted, curtained and furnished flat, looked at her mother's smiling face and promptly burst into tears.

"Well, I think this merits a nice cup of tea," observed her ever-practical mother as Joycey related how she and her husband had set about preparing Shela's new home from scratch. "We had a wonderful time," she said. "I never knew there were so many second-hand furniture shops in Bedford! In the end, we got almost everything from a big sale at Harrison Gibson's in the High Street. Bill Luff was the manager there and he helped us with everything. He remembered us all as children, when his sister Pauline took the babies out for walks on Saturday mornings. Do you remember? Most of us went to the Granada matinee, but you had to be different. You went to the library."

Shela sipped her tea and listened quietly as her sister recited the saga of the flat preparation and the rush to get everything done in time for her homecoming.

"I'm still different," she thought wistfully as the cups were washed up. Joycey led them down to her car parked behind the block of flats. "And all I've ever wanted to be is normal. Whatever that is."

CHAPTER
TWENTY-EIGHT

Old Memories

The first few weeks in the new flat were busy ones for Shela. She still had quite a few things to buy, for she had left most of the kitchen utensils and all of the bedding behind in Yorkshire. She could not countenance sleeping on the same sheets that she had shared with Terance, and the only piece of furniture from her old home was a small chest of drawers that she had taken from the cottage at Willington all those years previously.

With her state pension now registered at the sub post office in Roff Avenue and a small but regular maintenance order now settled through the solicitor, Shela managed to live on a limited income. One afternoon she quietly took her three redundant wedding rings into Geoff's shop in Church Square to be valued.

"They aren't of much value as wedding rings," smiled Geoff as he solemnly weighed the rings on a small jeweller's scales. "But if you want to sell them I'll give you the value of the gold content."

Shela was grateful for the two hundred pounds her softly spoken brother-in-law offered and it was not until years later that she realised he had paid her twice the real value of the gold. Another gesture of unspoken support for his troubled sister-in-law and one so typical of the quiet man she had come to respect over the years.

"Why don't you apply for Housing Benefit?" suggested Joaney just before Christmas. "I'm sure you will get something. And by the look of you," she added sternly, "I'm also sure that you are not eating properly."

It was true, for Shela's appetite was still very limited. She noticed, as the weeks went by, that an itchy rash kept appearing between her fingers, and no amount of antiseptic creams and washes would get rid of it.

"It will go when you are feeling better, my dear," advised the kind doctor at the big practice in Linden Road. "You are still under a lot of stress and your nerves are suffering as well as your body."

On Tuesday mornings, when her weekly state pension was due, Shela took a leisurely walk along Clapham Road towards the big, new roundabout at the junction of Union Street and Tavistock Street. A left turn into Roff Avenue, that had once been Park Road, took her along to the Post Office and General Stores, now run by a cheerful Indian shopkeeper. Sometimes she walked on as far as Queen Street and was at first amazed to see that all the old terraced houses had been pulled down and smart, new townhouses built in their place. Where small squares of garden had once fronted the tiny, nineteenth century houses, she saw that the new front doors opened directly on to the street. Behind her, as she stood before the place where number twenty-three had been, towering blocks of flats dominated the area, and Shela noticed that the small repair shop further down the street, whose owner had resisted right to the end of his lease, had at last given way to the modern estate all around it. She recalled, with amusement, that the local estate agents' advertisements now referred, somewhat coyly, to this area of the town as "the ministers" and wondered what Gladstone, Palmerston, Salisbury and Clarendon would have made of that.

The tiny corner shops and Win Hutchins' general stores opposite had disappeared, along with the narrow streets and small squares that had made up the Black Tom area of the town ever since she could remember. On the Tavistock Street corner of Queen Street, there now towered a multi-storeyed car park, and Shela remembered with nostalgia the off-licence on the opposite corner where she had bought Grandpa Warner's tobacco and sometimes lollipops for the children. On the opposite side of Tavistock Street, near the end of Bedford Prison wall, Tucker's fish shop, where the old man bought Friday fish and chip suppers, had gone. In its place, there now traded a double-fronted oriental restaurant, and, on her slow walk back to her flat, Shela realised, with regret, that many of the old, remembered shops in the road had become Indian or Chinese takeaways.

Occasionally, Shela varied her route into town to walk along wide roads, flanked by grand old houses, in the area known to all old Bedfordians as "poets' corner". Here, Shakespeare, Chaucer, Spencer, Sydney and Byron were commemorated in the names given to these old streets in the Victorian era as Bedford expanded to accommodate families anxious to educate their children at the excellent schools within the borough.

The walk along Lansdowne Road led her past the building that had been part of the old Bedford Teacher Training College campus.

Here she had dutifully sat through compulsory "psychology of education" lectures twenty years before. Looking back, Shela was still not quite sure what they were all about. But she admired the tenacity of the lecturer as he weekly faced a roomful of mainly mature students, who could have told him that child psychology was mostly all about applying common sense.

The way into town led her into Bromham Road, where she had once worked for her father in "Daphne's", his failed confectionery business. She noted, with amusement, that the sign above the green-tiled shop front now read "Mister Fish", and that the window displayed tanks full of tropical fish, instead of the sweet jars and dummy boxes of chocolate she had placed there so precisely when she was eighteen.

In St. Loyes Street, opposite the modern main entrance of Bedford Prison, she lingered beside the narrow fronted shop once owned by Ruth Browning, Ladies Hairdressers, where Beryl had completed her apprenticeship before setting up in business for herself. And further along the same street, she saw that an Estate Agent now occupied the premises that had been Barbara's Bun Shop, where, over fifty years ago, she sometimes met Johnny for tea and iced buns before dashing off to the last house at the Granada cinema in St. Peter's Street. On her way home, she glanced up at the high bay window of the shop in Harpur Street, which had once traded as D'arcy and Rosamunde, an exclusive fashion establishment offering designer ladies clothes at equally exclusive prices. Beryl occasionally splashed out to buy garments there and then thoughtfully passed them on to her sisters who were more familiar with Marks and Spencer's outfits.

The view from the balcony of the new flat was of the Bedford Modern School playing fields across the other side of a busy Clapham Road, and Shela often stood at her kitchen window looking out at the children, remembering her own days of playing hockey at the girls' school in Cardington Road.

Early one evening in late November, after a quiet day spent alone, and tired from the effects of a series of restless nights full of vivid dreams about the past, Shela was watching the boys playing football. On the television set in the corner of the lounge, shocking reports of the great fire at Windsor castle filled the six o'clock news bulletins. She was only half listening to it when a sudden, sharp pain in her chest, followed by a creeping numbness in her left arm, sent her reaching in panic for the alarm cord hanging beside her chair in the lounge. The next thing she remembered was Pat, the resident warden, kneeling beside her as she lay curled up in a tight ball on the floor beside the sofa. Suddenly, the room seemed to be full of tall men as first Robert, her brother, arrived and then the quietly efficient paramedics who gave her oxygen, before wheeling her quickly down to the ambulance waiting below in the car park.

Shela stayed in Bedford South Wing Hospital in Kempston Road for the next few days. First she was told that she had suffered a severe angina attack and then that there was some damage to her heart. That night, when the cannula attached to the back of her hand irritatingly impeded movement in the narrow bed, Shela put her head under the covers in silent rage at the diagnosis as she reluctantly accepted the truth. Her heart was physically damaged, but the emotional damage hurt the most.

"You must take things quietly," she was told while the young doctor measured her blood pressure yet again. "Take this letter to your G.P. He will prescribe medication which you must take from now on."

The first angina attack was followed at worryingly regular intervals by many more as Shela struggled to cope with her new situation. When the new medication began to produce results and outside the window box blazed with purple and white crocus and daffodils planted by a previous tenant, she hoped that the crisis had passed. Like the spring flowers, a new beginning had been made. With each day that passed, she grew stronger and the past began to recede to a comfortable distance. The woman who had made so many false starts in life, quietly began, yet again, to make plans for the future.

CHAPTER
TWENTY-NINE

Writing Again

Spread out on the drop leaf dining table before her lay the completed manuscript of *Phantom Island*. All day Shela had tried to ignore the carefully typed pages of the children's book she had re-written in the last few, unhappy months in Yorkshire. On a side table another completed manuscript lay untouched in its big buff envelope.

"Just get on with it," Mum had advised numerous times over the last few weeks. And today Shela was about to do just that.

Several days later, during which Joycey phoned anxiously asking why she had not been to the usual Sunday dinner at her house in Cople and was she alright up there in her flat, Shela typed up the last page of *High Summer Magic* and picked up the phone.

"Hullo, Doris," she said nervously, when her old dancing friend from pre-Terance days answered the phone from her home in Bure Close, North Brickhill. "I'm back in Bedford. Can I come to see you?"

Doris had met her second husband when she accepted Shela's invitation to a school dance at Abbey Middle School in Mowbray Road, Bedford. Dave had been Christopher's first father-in-law and, after the older man's divorce, it took some engineering on Shela's part to ensure that the two lonely people met on that summer's day when she still lived at Willington.

"I've got a publisher interested," Shela told her friend the next day. "But they want the work in manuscript and on disk. And I don't have a computer. Can you help?"

Over the next few weeks, the two old friends sat together at Doris's computer as Shela dictated the scripts and Doris, who was an expert typist, transposed the words onto the screen. With the typescript of *High Summer Magic* printed and on disk, Shela posted off the package to the publisher and waited hopefully for the reaction. Less than two weeks later, a contract for the book arrived, asking for her signature and also enquiring about any other material she may have to offer. *Phantom Island* soon followed the first manuscript out to Singapore. SNP Publishers, the only firm to have shown any interest in her work, despite Shela's trawl through *The Writers and Artists Year Book* for publishers or agents in the U.K., proved to be a polite and efficient organisation which kept in regular touch with its authors world wide.

Through all those summer weeks of 1992, when Shela began to write again and the divorce from Terance was finalised, she began slowly to emerge from her safe bubble to take notice of the world around her. She watched in horror as news bulletins gave details of a civil war breaking out in Bosnia. Later in the year she made friends with another tenant in the big block of flats that Shela secretly thought of as "Colditz". Ivy laughed when she heard this, and invited her for a meal. From then on, the friendship was cemented, and the two women, who had both been through their own various traumas, began to meet regularly for meals and trips into town.

Shela saw Christopher regularly in that year. Her eldest son now worked for Britannia Airlines and often called in to see his mother on his way home from Luton Airport. Sometimes, if she happened to be out when he called, she would find a small carrier bag, containing left over goodies from the airplane galley crew meals, hanging on her flat door handle. Always there was a cheerful note asking about her health and urging her to eat the contents of the little bag. Shela was very touched by these small offerings, although she could not always do as he asked, for her appetite was still not back to normal a full year after she returned to Bedford.

She sometimes visited her second son, Barry, who lived in Loughborough. Now with two children, he led a very active life working as manager of a butcher's shop in Loughborough Market Place. Always there were parcels of Walker's pork sausages and thick slices of ham to take home with her when she boarded the bus for the journey back to Bedford. And Shela would recall the anxious days when her young son joined Safeways in Greyfriars, Bedford, for his butchery training, and the subsequent payment of half his board in off-cuts of meat and leftovers from the shop counter. George never did find out about that small deception, she thought with a smile, as she put the meat into her small freezer.

Her youngest child, Deborah, now had three children and was currently stationed back in Germany with her soldier husband. She had left Catterick Garrison in North Yorkshire soon after her mother left Wakefield. And Shela thought often of the sickly child her daughter had been and how well she had coped with army life and all the moves between postings and married quarters. Almost as many moves as mine, she thought, whenever she posted the Forces Airmail letter at the General Post Office in Dane Street each month.

With her mind at rest about her children and with regular contact with them, Shela's health improved and, with Joycey making sure that she ate properly, especially on Sundays when she joined her sister's family for a big lunch in the bungalow at Cople, life began to settle into an ordered routine. The frayed nerves that had played up so traumatically since leaving Yorkshire were once more under control and she began to sleep more comfortably and put on some much needed weight.

Beryl also called in regularly and the two sisters often enjoyed a quick lunch of the healthy food she bought at Marks and Spencer's food counter. Now in business as a hairdresser and beautician at "Cameo", situated above her husband Geoffrey Millman's jewellery shop in Church Square, Beryl somehow always found time to visit her older sister in her flat at Hanover Court.

"What are you doing tomorrow morning?" Beryl asked one day as Shela put the kettle on to boil to make the green tea that her sister liked so much. "I've got something to show you. Better still, come in to the shop for a hairdo in the morning and we'll go together."

She would say no more and Shela spent half the night wondering what it could possibly be to make her usually outspoken sister so mysterious.

The small, red Fiat Uno car stood waiting in bright sunshine on Henman's Garage forecourt in Clapham High Street.

"There you are, Shela," announced Beryl. "That's just right for your needs. And going at a reasonable price."

"Which I don't have," Shela replied slowly. The little vehicle, more like a toy than a real motor car, gleamed in the sunshine. Beryl persuaded her sister to get behind a driving wheel for the first time in ten years and to give it a trial run. By the time they returned to the garage, Shela had fallen in love with the gutsy little car but knew she could never afford to buy it outright.

"I'll take care of that," insisted Beryl and ignored Shela's protests, until the car, which was quickly christened Miss Fifi, was safely parked behind her flat. "You can pay me back when and if possible. Until then, don't worry about it. Just enjoy."

The ongoing angina condition, which often left her breathless and exhausted after just a short walk, was eased in the next few weeks when she was awarded a state Disability Living Allowance. From then on, Shela carefully saved a few pounds each month to begin to pay her sister back for her generosity. She had not worked out how long this process must continue before the full amount was repaid, but at least, she thought, every time she handed the money over, Beryl will know I'm not taking all this for granted. With her new transport, Shela was able to visit her children regularly and on several Friday evenings drove over to Mary's house in Stanhope Road, where she had been invited to stay for a long weekend. This younger sister, widowed, like herself, in her mid forties, had made a new life in a more challenging job and was involved constantly with her children and young grandchildren. But Shela suspected that she was often lonely and knew only too well the feeling of shutting out the world when she closed the front door of an empty house behind her each evening.

"You are still young, Mary," she encouraged, when the two of them talked over their joint circumstances. "You will meet someone else," she predicted with a smile. "Roy would have wanted that, I'm sure."

Shela had been living at Hanover Court for nearly two years when she decided to move yet again, to a flat nearer the town centre. The opportunity came when she met up again with her old friend from her office job at Sanger's.

"There's a vacant flat in the complex where I live," Peggy announced one day early in the summer of 1994. "It's right in the town centre and very convenient for the shops."

Within a month, the new tenancy agreement was signed and Shela once again prepared to move. "This place was a good beginning," she confided to Ivy, when she gave her surprised friend the news of her departure.

"But I've never really settled here. Probably because it is too near to Queen Street and all the bad memories the area holds for me."

The new flat in St. Cuthbert's Court was just a short distance away from Shela's childhood home at 14 Newnham Street, just round the corner from St. Cuthbert's Street. It was also a convenient stopping place for various members of her family when they came into town, and Shela had plenty of company as she settled into her new life. Her cosy, new home looked directly out onto the narrow street. Almost directly opposite, The Old Castle pub lights shone out nightly whenever she closed the curtains and re-membered how her father was a regular customer there when she was a small child. Along the road, W.H. Peacock's auction rooms and sale yards attracted customers for viewing day on Thursdays and the auction on Saturdays. On these days, the familiar street was lined with customers' cars as they queued to get into the sale-room car park. Shela watched all this activity as the busy life of the street continued and she felt part of that life as she daily watched the heads passing by her small bay window.

The old church of St.Cuthbert, where the first six Winch children were baptised, was now, she saw with surprise, a Polish Catholic Church. And the local sweet shop, that also sold paraffin in those long ago days of her childhood, had been taken over and developed into Pizzeria Santaniello, a smart, Italian restaurant, where once a month Shela and Peggy enjoyed a good meal together. They also often shared a fish and chip supper bought at the smart fish shop near Peacock's sale yard. Next door to the fish shop, Shela called in regularly for good fresh coffee at The Cappuccino Bar, where the tiled floor and small, wrought-iron tables reminded her of those few days in Paris with her mother all those years before. On the corner of St. Cuthbert's Street and Mill Street, she paid weekly for her newspapers in the shop that had once been Bank's the greengrocers but was now a general store and newsagents run by another cheerful Indian shopkeeper. Further along St. Cuthbert's Street, she noted on her slow walks around the familiar old streets, a shoe repair shop still traded under the familiar name of Odell's Boot Repairs. Across the road, on the opposite corner, facing the church, the butcher's shop, still known as Linger's, provided Shela's small weekly chops or portions of chicken. Above the shop door, there now towered a gigantic replica of an old-fashioned butcher, complete with striped apron and straw boater. At Christmas he was dressed as Santa Claus when customers came in to buy their fresh turkeys and chipolata sausages for Christmas dinner. Shela noted, however, that the floor was no longer strewn with sawdust to catch any blood drippings as it had been when she was a child and that everything about the modern interior was now bright and clinically clean.

The old fire brigade station in Mill Street retained its original façade, she noticed with quiet satisfaction on her morning walk into town. The building now housed a mobile phone shop, but on the pavement outside the proprietors had placed a larger than life figure of an old

307

time fireman, complete with helmet and fire-axe, tethered to the nearest lamppost, as a nod of deference to the building's past history. At the top end of St. Cuthbert's Street, where she had once danced on the sprung floor in The Crofton Rooms, Shela saw that the building was now a furniture store and smiled as she remembered the square dances she had enjoyed there in the late forties. The house on the corner of Grove Place, where her parents lived when she was born, had long since lost its high brick wall surrounding the lawn with the shady tree in the centre. In its place was a car park beside the old house now converted into high class watch and jewellery premises. Whatever would her father have made of that? Across the junction of St. Peter's Street and Goldington Road, she saw that the site of the old American Red Cross Officers Club, where Mum had worked so hard during the war years, was now yet another council car park. The dark antiques shop in St. Peter's Street, where she had once bought a small wooden back scratcher as a wedding present because it was all she could afford at the time, was now a Greek restaurant. As her thoughts wandered back to those days of her young married life, she giggled to herself and wondered what had become of that backscratcher.

On her daily walk along Mill Street, Shela passed the three steep steps leading up into the building that had housed The British Restaurant in 1945. And she remembered, with great fondness, those bland but nutritious meals carried five high, each plate divided by an aluminium ring, as the volunteer waitresses tried to serve the packed rooms for six days every week. Across the road from that building, later to become The Citizens Advice Bureau before it moved again to premises in the old town hall, the Bunyan Meeting Church advertised daily coffee mornings and afternoon teas and Shela often stopped there on her way home from shopping or from the library, which she had rejoined as soon as she came back to her home town.

The debilitating illness and stress of those first months after her divorce had now almost left her, but there were still days when she felt unwell and really rather sorry for herself. As the summer wore on, she sometimes sat on a bench along The Embankment beside the slowly flowing river, or climbed the shallow steps up to Castle Mound, where she had taken her young children and now occasionally her grandchildren to tell them the story of the Great Siege of Bedford Castle. Those quiet days spent wandering around the familiar and comforting streets of her childhood were like a soothing balm to her troubled mind and Shela at last began to feel optimism overcoming the black beast of depression that she had fought for so long.

The publication, in late summer, of her two children's books completed the therapy her mind and body craved. When she was asked to sign the books at WHSmith's bookshop in Midland Road and later at County Town Books in the High Street, Shela knew that she was almost fit again and could look forward with confidence to the future.

CHAPTER
THIRTY

Meeting the Future

Preparations for Mum's ninetieth birthday party were well under way in the first week of August 1994. For many weeks, the Winch family met secretly and regularly at each other's homes to discuss arrangements for the big event, which was to take place at Haynes Village Hall, the village where Beryl's younger daughter, Debbie, now lived.

"Don't worry, aunties," she said cheerfully when the idea was first mooted in early spring. "I'll book the hall and make all the arrangements. You just concentrate on the catering."

On the evening of the ninth of August, the whole Winch clan waited in silence as John opened the door to usher their beloved Mum and Gang-Gang into the hall. Then they erupted into a chorus of "Happy Birthday" as she was led up to the top table where all her children sat waiting for her. It was a moment that Shela would never forget. They were all there. Children, grandchildren, great-grandchildren and a few great-great-grandchildren. Well over a hundred people celebrated that special day with the old lady who had been the lynch pin of the family for so long. And Shela looked at that old face smiling happily at all she had started in 1927, and silently prayed that Mum would have a few more years with them all.

The visits to Joycey's bungalow for Sunday lunch had become a regular feature of Shela's week. Now she was able to collect her mother as she left church in Cardington and drive together down the road to Cople, where Joyce's large family came and went throughout the day and Shela was made to feel that she was now a part of it.

The leaves on the trees surrounding the playing field behind the bungalow were slowly turning to a russet gold. The last cricket match of the season was in full swing on the day that Shela walked slowly past the beautifully tended lawn of a back garden further along the field. A tall, white-haired man, solemnly mowing the grass, raised his head for an instant and nodded a reply as Shela wished him, "Good afternoon."

"That poor chap lost his wife a few months ago," explained Joycey later over tea. "He seems to spend hours on that lawn. He must be so lonely."

Over the next few Sundays, Shela's nodding acquaintance with the neighbour developed slowly into quiet conversations over the fence as she learned more about the tragic circumstances of his wife's death. Freda had just taken up her position as President of Bedfordshire County Women's Bowling Association, when the illness she had been battling for all of the previous year finally overcame her and she died at the age of sixty-four.

"She achieved what she wanted more than anything," he explained. "But before she died, she made me promise to get on with my life and live it to the best of my ability." Then he added, so quietly, that Shela had to lean forward to hear the words clearly, "She told me not to go on alone. To look for happiness after she was gone."

A few days later, Shela invited Bill for tea in her flat. There they sat comfortably together and talked all through the afternoon and late into the evening. She sensed the sadness in the softly spoken man beside her. But there was something else. A quiet resolve that at first unnerved her and later prompted her to try to back away from the growing affection she felt for this gentle man. The months leading up to Christmas 1994, when Bill came to dinner and stayed overnight, were full of a lifetime's doubts, for Shela could not entirely shake off the ghosts of the past.

"What are you thinking of, Mum?" demanded her son, Christopher. And when Bill was introduced to the other son, Barry, in the bar of The Old Castle pub across the road from the flat, his reaction was entirely predictable.

"If you mess my mother about, you will have me to deal with," he stated shortly. And Shela left the two men to talk and went back alone to her flat, close to tears.

It took many weeks of quiet reassurance from Bill before Shela at last allowed herself to begin to trust him, for she was constantly looking for the male flaws she had encountered in the past. Over those weeks,

Shela opened her heart to the kind man, who listened patiently to her tales of woe and then comforted her endlessly with undemanding hugs and gestures of gentle understanding. Slowly, but sometimes painfully, her inner world began to steady itself and she allowed herself to think that her life could at last get back on an even keel.

CHAPTER
THIRTY-ONE

Another Try

"We have decided to get married in August, Mum."

The pair of them sat close together in her mother's small living room in the cottage at Cardington and Shela suddenly felt like a young girl again as she displayed the diamond engagement ring placed on her finger by Bill only the day before. He had wanted them to get engaged at Christmas but Shela insisted on waiting until a year had gone by since Freda's death. Now it was Easter 1995 and after regular weekends away and a few weeks spent at his timeshare in Tenerife had brought them closer together, her frequent tears of apprehension slowly grew less as she began to prepare for the wedding, planned for a few days after her sixty-fourth birthday.

All through the summer she walked with Bill around her home-town and showed him the dear, remembered places of her childhood. Not the brash, modernised face of Bedford, but the buildings behind new shop-facades and the familiar streets where she grew up. The old school, now known as Castle Lower, with its back entrance gate still in York Street, had lost the small field where she played before the war. A tasteful close of new town houses now stood in its place at the Rosamond Road end of Pembroke Street. Most of the shops had changed hands over the years between, but in her mind's eye Shela thought of them still as they had been before she left Castle Road. The circle of trees and shrubs at the junction of Rothsay Road had been pruned back and the high fir tree that had dominated the centre bed was gone. In its place now stood a contemporary lamppost, shedding light on the four benches where Shela and many others had conducted their courting in the shadows of "The Ring", as it was known locally. The old pavilion at Russell Park Bowls Club in Bushmead Avenue, near the Embankment, where Bill was a member, had not changed since Shela's childhood and only the graffiti on the football pavilion further into the familiar park served as a shock reminder that the year was 1994 and not 1934 after all. The green tiled roof of Mr Elphick the vet's house on the corner of Rothsay Road, where the Winch children had climbed on the wall to look into the sunken garden, still remained as a fond memory of those days of innocence when it seemed that life would go on forever in the family home at number fourteen Newnham Street.

Most of the High Street shops and banks had also changed hands, she noted, as they walked companionably through the town to the market, now moved temporarily from its traditional St. Paul's Square site to the old cattle market site in Commercial Road. By the Corn Exchange, they stopped to look at the new commemorative bust of Major Glenn Miller, the great

American orchestra leader from the forties who had played his "Glenn Miller sound" to delighted dancers in that building many times during his days in the USAAF. And there he was, looking down on all the grandparents who had thrilled to his distinctive music in their youth. She was pleased to see that Goldings, the ironmongers at the St. Peter's Street end of the High Street, still offered its friendly, old-fashioned service to the many customers who had shopped there since long before she was born. The old Dujon ballroom above Dudeney and Johnson's grocery emporium, where, before the war, her father called as a commercial traveller for The Shredded Wheat Company, was still there, forlornly silent and empty. Shela wondered, in a fanciful moment, if the mirrored glitter ball, suspended from the ceiling, still rotated hopefully on Saturday nights to reflect on the ghostly dancers of the past who foxtrotted or quickstepped around the big pillar in the centre of the floor. Below it now flourished a branch of Lloyds Bank and Shela pointed out the site of the old Dujon coffee shop at the top of the stairs beside the big shop with a view out on to the High Street.

Opposite, the golden bull clock of John Bull, the jewellers, still stood proud above noisy High Street traffic, although the business had recently moved to a new shop in St. Peter's Street. The old shop, where her father had bought some of the family silver with the profits from the café business, now displayed trendy spectacles in the windows instead of the expensive jewellery she remembered. Close by, she noted that the old plough, sited on the roof over the old Bacchus shop premises and so familiar to older Bedfordians, had disappeared, together with its owners. A new, long-fronted shop selling everything from garden to kitchen equipment now traded in its place. Nearer to the river, Paulo's Milk Bar, the favourite surveillance place for teenagers in the fifties, had also disappeared, and Shela remembered with nostalgia, the summer afternoons that she and Mabel had spent there, sipping endless cups of Espresso coffee while they waited for their boyfriends to saunter by. On the corner of Mill Street and the High Street, where once her friend Edie had worked in the photographic department of Taylor, Brawn and Flood, the big chemist's shop, the windows now exhibited pictures of houses and businesses, offered for sale by Beard's, the estate agents, later to change again to become an employment agency.

On the other corner of Mill Street, a modern shop façade had replaced the old green and gold Edwardian shop front of Grimbly, Hughes and Sons, the grocers where Dad had taken regular orders for Shredded Wheat in the thirties. Further along the High Street, a charity shop now traded on the site of the old Home and Colonial Stores, also one of Dad's best customers in his commercial traveller days.

On the opposite corner, Debenham's smart shop windows, full of impossibly thin mannequins wearing equally impossibly short and revealing clothing, could not completely erase the memory of its predecessor. E. P. Rose and Son was the Mecca of fashion for Shela's generation in the forties and fifties. Its tasteful arcade of windows provided a convenient vantage point on Sunday afternoons to meet boyfriends, and try to dodge the ever-vigilant police Sgt. Kirby, methodically moving on the groups of youngsters all down the road.

Further still along the High Street, Shela and Bill looked through the new, modern windows of the shop on the corner of The Arcade that had once been The Cadena Café, where Mum and Joycey often parked their prams safely outside while they enjoyed coffee and cream cakes on Saturday morning shopping trips. And in The Broadway, they visited the premises that had been The Broadway Milk Bar, where both Shela and Joycey had once worked the evening shift when their children were small and they needed the extra money. Castle Hill Café, she noted, on a walk back to her flat through John Bull Passage into Ram Yard, was now a Chinese Restaurant, not particularly imaginatively named Chef Beijing. Shela wondered what the proprietors would say if she asked to go up into the old kitchen where her mother had worked such long hours during the family's time in the catering trade. Filby's garage and repair shop still flourished in extended premises behind the café. She often called in to chat about the old days with Alan Filby who now ran the business. Across the space in front of the café, George Ford, the mattress maker and upholsterer's premises had long since been pulled down to give reluctant way to council car parking. And on the corner of Castle Lane, in the building that had once housed H. H. Bennett, the ladies' clothing manufacturers and The Consumer's Tea Company, The Bedford Gallery and The Bedford Museum now invited visitors in to view local, historic artefacts and a model of Bedford Castle as it had been in the thirteenth century.

So the long summer of reminiscing drew to a close. On a warm August morning, Shela and Bill were quietly married in Hitchin Registry Office. Not in the old premises in Bancroft where Shela's parents had married in 1927, but a tasteful, modern building so different from the dark, cramped rooms in Bedford where she had twice started out so hopefully on a new life. Both of their daughters and their husbands were there and some of Bill's grandchildren, happy to see their father and grandfather, who had painfully lost two wives to cancer, settle down once again with a loving companion. In the afternoon, the whole family met at All Saints Church just along the road from the bungalow in Cople and watched as the vicar welcomed the newlyweds and blessed their marriage vows.

"He did everything but actually marry you," laughed Deborah later. Then stood beside her mother as the house filled with people and Bill kept disappearing into the kitchen to do yet more washing up. "If the bishop had allowed it, I think he would have married you two properly in church."

Shela thought back to her first wedding at the "tin tabernacle" in Denmark Street and recalled the fleeting happiness she had known as she walked back down the aisle with her first husband. And in that moment of quiet reflection, as their families gathered to celebrate with her and Bill, forgave the father of her children for all that came after.

In the small, spare bedroom, Shela's wedding present from her new husband sat invitingly on the desk. Microsoft Windows 95, just launched by Bill Gates and Paul Allen, blinked enticingly at her from the new computer. She was anxious to begin work on it, for over the last few years she had built up a huge folder of handwritten manuscripts. There were articles, essays, poems, children's book manuscripts and, at the back of her mind, a new idea for a book already beginning to take shape.

CHAPTER
THIRTY-TWO

Coming Home

The first few months in her new home were a time of increasing happiness for Shela. They were also a necessary time of adjustment. She was initially nervous about being left alone in the building that, not long before, had been another woman's home. Constant reassurances from Bill that his late wife would have approved and the discreet replacement of most of Freda's pictures with their own wedding photographs, did not fully compensate for the odd feeling that she was not alone as she moved around the bungalow when he was out. Memories of the first few weeks of her marriage to George made the situation even worse as the same sense of being watched began to take over and her dreams were constantly full of disturbing images from the past.

"Pull yourself together!" she kept telling herself sternly. But the recurring angina attacks and the nervous condition that she thought was a thing of the past returned to disturb her days and necessitated regular night time trips to the A and E department at South Wing Hospital.

"Would you like to see a therapist, Mrs Baines?"

The concerned voice of Doctor Crawford at the surgery in Great Barford broke into her thoughts as Shela held tight to Bill's hand and tried to stop the foolish tears that came unbidden and always, it seemed, at the most awkward of moments.

A month later, the fortnightly visits to a psychotherapist began. And although at first Shela could not tell her anything, the patient prompting of the skilful young woman eventually opened the floodgates and it all poured out in one huge deluge. Many times during those visits to the clinic at Biggleswade, Shela tried to hold back the most traumatic events from the therapist. But by the end she had told it all. It was like shifting a heavy load from her shoulders. The relief was unbelievable. Shela had recovered.

"Come back if you need to talk again," advised the therapist. "But for now, get on with your life and be happy."

With the angina now under control and restful sleep returning rapidly with the occasional help of sleeping pills, Shela began to write again. It was the best medicine possible, for she was able to forget herself in writing and by the end of the year had produced two more children's book manuscripts.

"Come down to the club with me, Shela," urged Bill one day, late in the bowling season. "If you don't mind wearing Freda's old bowling shoes and using her woods temporarily, we can have a roll-up. You might enjoy it."

The following April, Shela joined the ladies section of Russell Park Bowls Club in Bushmead Avenue near The Embankment. The lady members, who had known

Bill's late wife, took her under their wing and taught her the rudiments of the game as she began to enjoy the sunshine on the immaculately tended green and the friendship they offered so unconditionally.

In that first year of marriage to Bill, he also encouraged Shela to join the students at the Retirement Education Centre in Rothsay Gardens, Bedford, where she joyfully began to open her mind once again to the excellent teaching of Christine Taylor and later, Sue Panter in "Exploring Literature" classes and the Creative Writing courses run by a succession of tutors who plainly loved the art of writing and were keen to share their knowledge with their elderly but enthusiastic students. During that year, Shela also completed a Creative Writing course at Sharnbrook Upper School where she met the woman who would play a significant role in her future writing career. Dawn Wells became a friend as well as a mentor and it was her wise guidance in matters of the half-forgotten rules of syntax and punctuation that helped to produce the manuscripts which followed. Membership of The Bedford Writers' Circle followed later that year and Shela, at first inhibited in her writing and nervous about reading her work aloud, soon began to enjoy and value the company of a small group of friendly and talented people.

One hot Sunday afternoon in June, when Bill's garden was looking its best and the lawns were as good as any on the county bowling greens, Shela and her mother sat together on the patio after lunch watching the fish coming to the surface of the small pond for food. The insistent ringing of the telephone in the house behind them disturbed their quiet conversation as Bill came to the door to call his wife in. His face was grave as he gently told her that her younger brother, George, was on the line with some bad news.

"I've just heard from John's girl in the States," the quiet voice of her brother stated calmly. "Her father died suddenly this morning. Can you break the news to Mum, Shela? I'm leaving home now. I'll be with you in an hour."

"Get Joycey along here, Bill," she called back urgently over her shoulder as she went out to bring her mother inside, and the familiar pain in her chest started up again as she took the small hand in her own to break her mother's heart with her next few sad words. The following hours, full of ringing telephones and doorbells and constant cups of tea, merged slowly into evening. Joycey took Mum back with her for the night and Bill and Shela talked into the small hours about the brother who had now so unexpectedly left the family circle and the mother who had outlived her eldest son.

The memorial service for John took place in the church of St. Mary's, Cardington, the following month, when the Winch family once again gathered around their mother and Gang-Gang to support her and remember the son and brother who would never join them again for family celebrations. From her own seat next to Bill, Shela watched anxiously as her mother walked bravely and calmly down the aisle to the front pew. In that old, white head, she thought, is a lifetime of stories, and I am the one to write them down. At that moment, in the quiet church, where the small urn containing her brother's ashes rested quietly beneath the altar, the idea for a book came suddenly into full focus.

Several times a week over the next few months, she visited Mum at her little cottage on The Green in the next village, to talk and make notes about the past and all the half-forgotten memories the old lady had stored away in her head over her long and eventful life. When the year was ended, Shela's notebook was full and she began to write her mother's life story, just as she had heard it throughout her own childhood and through all the years since. Photographs of familiar places in Hitchin and Bedford were gradually gathered together as Bill took her on guided walks around his home town of Hitchin, to point out all the place names that Mum had talked about in those months of memory-gathering in her little cottage. A year later, Shela delivered the finished manuscript to the potential publisher.

A few anxious weeks later, when she had almost given up hope of ever hearing from him again and she was enjoying an afternoon snooze, Paul Bowes from The Book Castle at Dunstable telephoned to say that he was interested, but why had she not used the correct family names?

"If you can persuade the family, and especially your mother, to allow you to do that, we can use family photographs," he suggested. "Talk to them and let me know as soon as possible."

That night, Shela put the new idea to her mother.

"Well, dear," Mum laughed, as Shela voiced her concerns about using real names. "They are all real people after all. As for me," she continued, "I am too old to bother about what people think of me. Don't worry. I'll have a word with the others."

When the telephone rang at midnight, with Mum calling to say she'd talked to them all and the family had agreed, with one or two doubters, that it was the right thing to do, Shela went to bed and slept peacefully through the rest of the night. The next morning the fun began, as old family photograph albums and long forgotten packs of black and white negatives were unearthed and at last Shela had everything she needed to complete her book in time for the new millennium.

The look on her mother's face, when the first copy off the press of *Threads of Time* was presented to her, was worth all the effort and hours spent in first writing and then endless editing of what Shela thought fondly of as "living history".

"Wow! Fame at last!" exclaimed Mum, as her daughter signed the book and she looked closely at the old prints of Ted as he had been in his youth. "Your father would have been proud of you today."

Less frequently now and only in good weather, Shela walks slowly along Bedford Embankment. She is glad to leave The Town Bridge, noisy with traffic, behind her to make her way past the site of the old Plaza cinema where she once queued hopefully to see "Snow White and the Seven Dwarfs". The Bridge Hotel, she observes, has morphed into a much bigger building and taken over all the ground beside it for use as a car park. The Bedford Castle Mound, where her children played and watched medieval pageants over the years, now stands denuded of most of its trees and shrubs, with an observation pagoda looming above it like a lone tooth in an enormous jaw.

The Embankment gardens, bright with summer flowers, lead her along to the old Suspension Bridge, now lit at night, she observes with dismay, by violent purple floodlights. On the area of grass beyond the far bank of the river, Shela remembers the steam-powered miniature train from pre-war days, as it puffed its way around the short, narrow gauge track between the Suspension Bridge and the green, engineer's bridge. She sits quietly for a few minutes on the bench placed there by the Winch family as a memorial to their beloved mother, the year after she died, at the grand old age of ninety-seven. The new, graceful butterfly bridge to the left and the old, familiar Suspension Bridge to the right, somehow seem to frame the years of her own life. The waters of the Great Ouse, flowing gently beneath, remind her of a verse from a seventeenth century hymn by Isaac Watts. The words, barely remembered from childhood, now come clearly to her. She sings them quietly under her breath, and smiles at the memory of a long-ago Sunday School in the thirties.

> Time like an ever-rolling stream
> Bears all its sons away

> They fly forgotten as a dream
> Dies at the opening day.

So many of those sons have been borne away in her lifetime. Most recently came the news that Johnny had died and she mourned quietly for the lost love of her youth and then sent her condolences to his widow. A few months earlier she had read, in the obituaries column of *The Beds on Sunday* newspaper, of the death of Judith's hard working husband, Jim, and tentatively contacted her step-daughter again for the first time in many years. Then she heard of the sad loss of Mabel's husband, Ben, her old friend's lifetime love and companion. Only the year before, her younger sister Beryl's softly-spoken husband Geoff Millman had died, and Shela remembered his many kindnesses over the years when she needed them most. The most painful loss of all came with the recent shocking and tragic death of a beloved grandson, whose adult life had only just begun.

Recently, her daughter's marriage had failed after twenty-seven years of life in the army when the subsequent difficulty of settling down in civvy street once again had strained the relationship to breaking point. She was now, Shela reflected thankfully, happily remarried to a hard working, affectionate man and living near to her own children and grandchildren in Kettering, where her older brother had been settled for some years.

Shela sighs at the memories and takes comfort from the familiar scene before her. She looks across the

Embankment towards Russell Park, where the old café has been modernised and extended and now sports trendy outdoor tables beneath colourful sunshades, all bordered by stylish, cast iron fencing. Bland blocks of modern flats replace some of the grand, old houses, once standing proudly beside the carefully tended Embankment Gardens. Further down the river an innocuous, but far more sensible, concrete structure has long since ousted the old, wooden Newnham Bridge, and a cinema and nightclub complex now covers the area once occupied by the old Newnham Swimming Baths of her youth. The children's playground in Russell Park, once situated beside sombre air-raid shelters at the Denmark Street entrance has been moved, quite unnecessarily, she thinks, to the site of the old park valley of distant, disturbing memory.

Shela often calls in for a good cup of coffee at a small, side-street bistro, just off Castle Road. The Jaffa Orchard in Pembroke Street, on the site of the old Ruff's Bakery, where hot cross buns were bought by her mother every Good Friday morning of her childhood, is now a successful community café, offering home cooked meals, computer lessons and goods sold for charity. Across the road, she discovers with some sadness that Woodward's, the Post Office where Mum collected her army wives' allowance during the war years, has now closed, like so many other branches across the town. Just another step towards the destruction of the friendly local community she once knew and loved.

The slow walk through her memories leads eventually to the old family home in Castle Road, much changed but as dear to her now as it was before she left to begin on the great adventure of life.

She knows that Bill is waiting for her in the comfortable bungalow in Cople. And it is here, as they sit companionably together to nightly view the ongoing madness of the world outside which seems to race past them at an ever-increasing pace, that Shela is at last at peace.

She has come home.

EPILOGUE

March 2006
Mother's Day

Daffodils are blooming again in St. Mary's churchyard in Cardington. The church clock behind me reads almost three o'clock as I walk slowly towards the small clump planted in Mum's memory.

"I've finished it, Mum," I murmur softly. Then smile as I remember how this all started. "I've been getting on with it for the past year."

It's not been easy. Some parts were hard to write down. Others were a joy to remember. Several times I nearly gave up. But then I thought of my old mother, who never gave up on anything in her long life.

There were agonising times of grief and other times of great happiness in both our lives, when the support and loyalty of the family were constant. No doubt there will be more of the same to come for me. And now I can cope. The catharsis is complete and I am "getting on with it", just as she had done.

The clock strikes three as I close the gate of the churchyard and leave my memories behind in that peaceful place.

Also available in ISIS Large Print:

Kept in Czech

Margaret Austin

"Once in the dance hall for the second Saturday running I scanned the crowd in search of the Little Czech, as I had heard him referred to by another student who was also obviously quite smitten with him."

Margaret had just arrived in Leicester to begin her English course at the University College (as it then was), when she saw Fred and thought, "You look as though you're used to getting your own way, but you're not going to get me!" How wrong she was! Three weeks later they were firmly involved with each other and have remained so for 61 years (so far!). Almost immediately, Fred was totally accepted into Margaret's family and her home became his home.

ISBN 978-0-7531-9564-2 (hb)
ISBN 978-0-7531-9565-9 (pb)

Poppies in the Corn

Fay Garrison

"My Father rented for us a rather run-down bungalow in the tiny Hamphire village of Redenham, a few miles from Andover. My mother, a city girl all her life, was horrified. Anything rural was anathema to her, from the dark country roads to the watchful cows in the fields."

When the Second World War broke out, Fay Garrison with her mother and sister moved from their native Birmingham. Her idyllic existence was then shattered by the news of her father's capture at Dunkirk.

Later in the war she returned to Birmingham, to a very different school system with new friends and teachers who shaped her future. A heroic aunt, captured by the Nazis who escaped to fight with the Resistance became a strong influence in her life. Eventually qualifying as a teacher she settled down in Solihull and married a journalist with whom she shared a love of music.

ISBN 978-0-7531-9576-5 (hb)
ISBN 978-0-7531-9577-2 (pb)